Experimental Film
and Video

'Nothing that has ever happened should be regarded as lost for history ... To articulate the past historically ... means to seize hold of a memory as it flashes up at a moment of danger. Only that historian will have the gift of fanning the spark of hope in the past who is firmly convinced that *even the dead* will not be safe from the enemy if he wins.'
Walter Benjamin
'Theses on the Philosophy of History', page 247
Illuminations, (London: Pimlico, 1999)

Arts & Humanities
Research Council

university college
for the creative arts
at canterbury, epsom, farnham
maidstone and rochester

Experimental Film and Video

Blackburn
College

Library
01254 292120

British Library Cataloguing in Publication Data

Experimental Film and Video: An Anthology

A catalogue entry for this book is available from the British Library

ISBN: 0 86196 664 3 (Paperback)

Published by
John Libbey Publishing, Box 276, Eastleigh SO50 5YS, UK
e-mail: libbeyj@asianet.co.th; web site: www.johnlibbey.com

Orders: **Book Representation & Distribution Ltd**. info@bookreps.com

Distributed in North America by **Indiana University Press**, 601 North Morton St, Bloomington, IN 47404, USA. www.iupress.indiana.edu

Distributed in Australasia by **Elsevier Australia**, 30–52 Smidmore Street, Marrickville NSW 2204, Australia. www.elsevier.com.au

Distributed in Japan by **United Publishers Services Ltd**, 1-32-5 Higashi-shinagawa, Shinagawa-ku, Tokyo 140-0002, Japan. info@ups.co.jp

Printed in Malaysia by Vivar Printing Sdn. Bhd., 48000 Rawang, Selangor Darul Ehsan.

Contents

Forewords

Foreword by Sean Cubitt

There have been honourable exceptions like Mike O'Pray and Stephen Heath, but few of the leading film critics and theorists of the last forty years have spent much time with artists' video and film. Though film-maker Laura Mulvey's essay on visual pleasure remains one of the most cited in the humanities, her films are more and more rarely screened in graduate classes. The demands of genre study, narratology and industrial analysis of national cinemas have led media scholars away from their interests in the avant-garde; while the avant-garde, especially in the United Kingdom, have been driven further away from media-based funding towards the gallery world or the digital underground.

Political radicalism is not the cause of this: radicals like Ken Loach can still make feature films. But it may be a result of marginalisation by the film business and increasingly by funding agencies whose brief must stretch from popular entertainment to documentary intervention and grassroots training. Everybody has a reason to step aside.

Yet there is a powerful tradition of artists' writings on vanguard media practice in the UK. The writings of Peter Gidal and Stuart Marshall informed many young artists' projects throughout the 1970s and 1980s, sometimes as inspiration, sometimes in reaction, a constant articulation with emerging practices in film and video arts. The fabled inarticulateness of the creator was never much prized among film and video makers: talk was always integral to the art where making relied so heavily on other people's help. I remember a New York based avant-garde filmmaker amazed that his London crew on a jobbing music video were all reading Kafka and going off to Fassbinder screenings. The art school tradition of demanding a written dissertation as part of the degree still impacts on the distinctive willingness of the UK artist to engage in ideas, and to generate them.

For lack of a continuous tradition of critical writing – despite the efforts of *Undercut* over the years – this collection is likely to prove a treasure trove for new readers. Piled up in one-off little magazines and catalogues, mimeographed sheets and letraset layouts are the fragments of a thriving culture swept under the carpet of history by a sad confusion of missed opportunities, crossed wires, confused responsibilities and overcrowded archives. Given the technological savvy of its practitioners, film and video art in the UK has been for the most part an oral culture, and every time one of its old guard dies, like the African adage about fathers, it is like a library has burnt down.

These were not theories in the sense of coherent discourses grounded in axioms and built brick by brick as theorems and theses. They were assertions, political manifestos, memos from cutting rooms and gallery floors. They spoke from the delirium of greeting a new machine – the Film Coop's legendary optical printer, LVA's first non-linear suite. Some come from the lost ages of 16mm film and monochrome television. Whole aesthetics have evaporated since video migrated from open reels to cassettes, as they did when television and shortly thereafter video migrated to colour. The possibilities for invention were no less then, though the palette was perhaps more limited – just as Dürer's prints are scarcely poor compared to his oils.

Despite everything, the discourse is still in hock to the gods of time: progress and fashion still rule the ways younger artists approach older art. The voices seem faded and stilted perhaps, the concerns remote and old hat. Most of all, of course, there is scarcely anything available to them or their teachers of the roar and shove of the Coop and LVA, or the irrational passions that drove regional initiatives in the South West, the East Midlands, Hull and Liverpool. Startling loyalties and antagonisms between film and video folk, strange destinies each pursued often separate from the other. Odd allies that emerged from the British Council and Canada House when the national collections found it impossible to buy or archive the culture of artists working in the moving image.

This Anthology, *Experimental Film and Video*, is one of a number of moves to reinstate a lost history. It does so not only to secure a pension for unjustly neglected artists, not only to fill a blank in the annals of the culture; nor even to bring an era of extraordinary achievement in the arts back into public view. Most of all, the *Anthology* exists in a broader action to bring to the emergent artists of the 21st century some flavour of the pioneers of the 20th. Great as they were, Picasso, Duchamp and Pollock are poor masters for artists whose media move in time, make noises, connect to networks. In some ways the only genuinely native avant-garde movement of the 20th century in the UK, the film and media avant-gardes of the 1960s, 70s and 80s set the groundwork for the emergent digital arts. These stories are alive and infectious.

Sean Cubitt
March 2005

Foreword by A.L. Rees

This collection of new critical writing by film, video and electronic media artists is exceptionally timely. Digital technologies have revolutionised the artists' cinema, to push towards the *'polyexpressiveness'* proclaimed by the Futurists ninety years ago in their 'Film Manifesto' of 1916 ('synthetic, dynamic, free-wording... immensely vaster and lighter than all the existing arts'). At the same time, the incorporation of classic avant-garde techniques into standard digital software, but stripped of context and offered as a tool-kit of effects, challenges artists to re-appropriate the medium and its language for time-based and screen-based experiment.

This gives bite and focus to the essays and statements by the three generations of time-based artists represented here, all of whom have lived and worked in, or have originated from, the UK. The artists' narratives are various, as this collection represents a wide body of working processes. Among the topics of debate are questions about the materiality of film and video art in the digital age; the photographic trace and its digital simulation; linear and non-linear time and sequence; story-telling and abstraction; single-screen and multi-projection; the gallery, cinema and television intervention. The three sections are organised to draw out the strands of argument, as well as to reflect different individual opinions and insights. This Anthology, *Experimental Film and Video*, articulates some of the complex philosophies stemming from artists' practice, and the aspiration towards a critical artists' cinema is explored from the inside out, from the artist's intention and perspective to the projected image in frame and on screen.

The texts newly commissioned for this book are part of a long tradition of critical writing by artists in experimental cinema. It begins with the manifestos and avant-garde journals of the period 1916 to 1935, the era of the abstract, cubist and surrealist film, when international modernism greeted the brand-new artists' cinema in euphoric and visionary terms, much as digital media were hailed in the post-modernist 1990s. As early as 1919 the pioneer abstract filmmaker Walter Ruttmann said that the 'acceleration of information', and 'the increased speed with which individual data are reeled off', both 'floods' the individual and 'defies traditional treatment.' He foresees a 'wholly new type of artist', the filmmaker, 'who stands roughly in the centre between painting and music.'

The vivid texts of the early period were often as experimental with typeface, layout and picture montage as they were in style and content. In seeking to theorise their work, artists themselves constructed a discourse and dialogue that parallels and counterpoints the first studies of 'Film Art' by cultural critics. This was taken up and massively amplified by the international explosion of avant-garde film and video in the second half of the twentieth century. A fusion of personal, exploratory writing along with analysis or theory runs through a period that includes *Film Culture*, *X-Screen*, *Studio International*, the *Structural Film Anthology* and many other contemporary journals and books. Digital web sites devoted to film and experimental media continue to enlarge the field of discourse and debate. Paradoxically, the spread and diffusion of media technologies may underpin a recent revived interest in structural and minimalist film and video among younger artists looking for clarity in the digital era of 'non-material materialism', El Lissitzky's term for the expanded media arts such as VR and holography that he predicted in 1925.

A particularly strong vein of critical reflection and polemic ran through much UK film and video making in and around the London Film Makers' Co-operative and London Video Arts during the late sixties and seventies. This collection features new writing or interviews by some of the pioneers of film and video who (now as then) have very divergent views about the past and future of film, time-based art and electronic imaging. The focus throughout, across the generations represented here, is however on the contemporary scene. Some contributors discuss their own trajectories, to give unique insight into their practice, methods and ideas. Others retrace lost or ignored histories that need to be told and researched, or insist on the role of subjectivity and personal voice as a measure of meaning in the arts of 'mechanical reproduction'. As a whole, the *Anthology* illuminates an often under-exposed but vibrant aspect of international experimental cinema, a beat or pulse often drowned out by more spectacular or commercialised manifestations, but one that this collection uniquely allows us to hear.

AL Rees
March 2005

Introduction

Jackie Hatfield

For artists working with moving image in the early twenty first century, the past forty years of technological innovation has revolutionised the possibilities for experiment and exhibition. Not since the invention of film has there been such a critical period of major change in the imaging technologies accessible to artists. Bringing together key artists in film, video and digital moving-image this Anthology, *Experimental Film and Video*, revisits some of the resonant philosophical and critical discourses of the 1960s and 70s and re-positions them relative to contemporary practices and debates. It is a document of current practice led theoretical dialogue alongside historical review, with writing by notable artists whose working processes have traversed broad technological and critical histories. Artists reflect on their work considering how emerging technologies and new imaging materials have shifted the theoretical and philosophical agendas.

To highlight key philosophies and discourses there is a structure and narrative to this collection of writing. Concerns around mate-riality are woven throughout the essays, and film video and digital moving-image are placed in sequential order, each representing part of a whole picture of experiment and process. The selection of artists reflects the abundance of experiment and the multiple dia-logues, and places electronic and digital moving-image debates relative to the critical histories of the film avant-garde.

Importantly, the *Anthology* is not meant as a definitive collection of artists, but a snapshot and précis, an analysis of experimental film and video at this moment – dialogue by some. To clarify the logic behind the editorial decisions for selection, as well embodying in their practice and writing the shifts in technologies, the invited artists fulfilled one or more of the following criteria: is actively making work, and where possible will have practiced over a signifi-cant period; has written; having published texts; books; articles; and/or contributed to practice led dialogue through critical writing or publication; works, or has worked within the academy, Art School or University and is committed to the culture of moving-image, practice led research. Additionally for inclusion in the illustrated colour section of the book artists will have been mentioned within the texts.

Philosophies and Critical Histories of Avant-garde Film and Current Practice

Since the 1960s, there has been diversity of debate led by practice, although particular philosophical agendas have sometimes been taken as orthodoxies; or as blueprints for definitions, or for the categorising, grouping and positioning of works within an avant-garde canon. The confident international dialogue that evolved around film during the 1960s and 1970s was highly influential and although the technological and material conditions have changed; the theoretical debates and philosophies of this period still resonate. When artists' led the discourse, it was a characteristic of practical process and by no means intended as definitive, and giving textual shape to film's nascent languages has provided a foundation to advance them. Grahame Weinbren has worked in film and video since the early 1970s and is a pioneer of video and digital computer augmented expanded and participatory cinema. He has published widely, and since 1986 has been a member of the editorial board of the New York based *Millennium Film Journal*. In 'Post Future Past Perfect' he discusses the very nature of writing the matter, form, and substance of practice into history, and describes a metaphor for transposing the 'language' and thought processes of cinema into text. Weinbren challenges prevailing canons of the experimental film avant-garde and argues for multifarious readings of practice that reflect the complexities of ideas and processes in any one work. Peter Gidal is a leading exponent of British Structural/Materialist film, an influential filmmaker and theorist (*Structural Film Anthology* (1976); *Materialist Film*, (1988)). 'Matter's Time Time for Material' is the transcription of Gidal's talk for the *X-Screen Symposium* at MuMok in Vienna 2004, and includes his analysis of *Upside Down Feature* (1972) and review of related aesthetics. Disentangling practice, its processes, and Structural/Materialist theory, Gidal makes the point that at the London Filmmakers Coop the practice always came before the theory; and that philosophical debate was triggered by collective passion for the practice. The artist Chris Welsby has been making and exhibiting his films, and film/video installations since 1969. With 'Film and Installations – A Systems View of Nature', Welsby discusses structure and structuring, and considers structural film in relation to *structures* determined by the systems within landscape and the interconnectedness of landscape, filmmaking material and process. Nicky Hamlyn is a filmmaker and writer (*Film Art Phenomena*, (2003)) and was a founder of *Undercut*. With 'A Line Through My Work' Hamlyn analyses in detail some of the recurring themes of his work since 1974, and traces retrospectively, emerging patterns and materiality. In 'A Few Notes on Filmmaking' the filmmaker Jayne Parker describes her reasons for using film; the material, the grain, the physicality of the projected image, and considers how she uses film language to express things that words cannot express. In 'Film Noise Aesthetics' the filmmaker/artist Rob Gawthrop discusses the context and history of sound in experimental film; and introduces the radical use of noise as an under-explored area. Lastly in this section, the renowned filmmaker Anthony McCall discusses his sculptural 'solid light film' (McCall) *Line Describing a Cone* and raises some timely questions around the relationships between artwork and audience, the environment of exhibition and the experience of viewing.

Languages of representation in Film and Video: Thresholds of Materiality

There is a wealth of artists who have discussed their work in political terms, and defined the philosophical, theoretical and historical arenas of their practice outside any prevailing ideologies. Technological innovation post-film, has enabled experiment with languages of representation, notation and forms, and initiated a need to interrogate gaps in historical knowledge; and challenge canons of thought. Acclaimed artist Lis Rhodes has been key to theoretical dialogue around the formal conventions of film and the viewing experience; feminist theory around the politics of filmmaking; and was a founder of Circles, Women in Distribution. 'Trilogical Distractions' is playful and polemical, prose, an artwork in itself, and a labyrinth of words. Rhodes uses wordplay to weave us in and out of an apparently illusory space, and gives cryptic clues as to our whereabouts whilst using the language as a net. In 'The 'auto-ethnographic' in Chantal Akerman's *News from Home*, and An Analysis of *Almost Out* and *Stages of Mourning*' the filmmaker Sarah Pucill re-examines the Structural Materialist debates of Peter Gidal with reference to Catherine Russell's study *Experimental Ethnography*, and offers an analysis of Chantal Akerman's *News From Home*, Jayne Parker's *Almost Out*, and her own recent film *Stages of Mourning*. The filmmaker Nina Danino has written extensively around experimental filmmaking, and was co-editor of *Undercut* from 1986–1990. In 'The Film, The Body, The Fold' she talks with Susanna Poole about her film *Now I Am Yours* and the feminine articulated through the languages of representation; the image and voice as presence. She discusses her collaboration with the singer Shelley Hirsch. With '*Attitudes 1-8*' the artist Katherine Meynell, whose work has crossed between performance and installation video, describes the processes and historical context of *Attitudes 1-8*. She provides an insight into how this video artwork was conceived, produced and exhibited in the gallery. David Critchley has worked with film, video, performance and installation, more recently collaborating with Susie Freeman and Liz Lee. With 'Video Works 1973-1983' Critchley gives insight into the context of his early video works and the spontaneous qualities of the then 'new' technology. In 'Early Video Tapes: 1978-1987', Chris Meigh-Andrews, describes how he explored the plasticity of video and electronic imaging, with the pioneering synthesising device, the Videokalos; processing and assembling image streams to create video 'languages'. The artist Andrew Kötting with Gareth Evans leads us through an artists' alphabet in 'What he does, how he does it and the context which it has been done: the Alphabetarium of Kötting'. From E for Experimental, to D for Digression, Kötting describes a place of practice, weaving sensation through history, theory, context and process. With 'Ardent for Some Desperate Glory: Revisiting *Smothering Dreams*' the artist Daniel Reeves who has made notable single screen and installation video artworks, gives voice to the personal history underlying *Smothering Dreams* (1981). His written account is an emotionally charged and powerful document of the trauma of war and the reality underlying the image. Videomaker, curator and writer Cate Elwes (*Video Art: A Guided Tour* (2004)), focuses on the artistic and personal motivations behind her recent documentary and biographical artworks around military conflict '*War Stories*, or why I make videos about old soldiers'. Filmmaker Vicky Smith tells a personal history of the London Filmmakers Coop in 'Moving Parts, The Divergence of Practice' and feminises the mechanical and technological processes of printing and animation.

Philosophies and Critical Histories of Video Art to Cinema

This section concentrates on video and digital forms, the conceptual and philosophical debates around the languages of emergent technologies; the opportunities for exhibition, and the material transformations brought about by digitality. Karen Mirza and Brad Butler have worked collaboratively since 1997 with their film installations, and have recently set up No.w.here, a London based workshop facility for production and debate around the moving image. With 'Mutation on a Form' they question their use of the 'old' technology of film, and posit arguments for its relevance in an era of digital media and emergent moving-image technologies. Since the 1970s the artist Stephen Partridge has made a number of important video works for both the gallery and broadcast. He has played a key role in the promotion of video and electronic art within the academy, and in the 1980s broke new ground by setting up high-end technological facilities for use by artists at Duncan of Jordanstone College of Art in Dundee, which through residency programmes enabled the production of many key works. In 'Video: incorporeal, incorporated' Partridge reviews the material debates of the 1970s, studying the changing form of video as it is incorporated in the digital domain relative to the material of film and, he argues, its simulation. In 'Tamara Krikorian – Defending the Frontier', Cate Elwes reviews and analyses the important early video artworks of Tamara Krikorian. Krikorian was a contemporary of luminary Video Artist David Hall, and played an important part in promoting video as a gallery art form outside the broadcast context. Based on a recent interview for the *Anthology*, Elwes acknowledges Krikorian's important contribution to early Video Art and discusses some of her artworks, which were often installation, multi-image video and lyrical image landscapes. Sculptor, filmmaker, and video artist David Hall is a pioneer of television intervention i.e. broadcast television as a context for radical conceptual art works. Based on an interview with the artist, in 'Another Place, David Hall', I consider Hall's interventionist art works, and his political actions of intervening in the broadcast flow. I debate the conundrum of writing work into history that is by its nature transient and non-object based, and the problem with historicizing and therefore de-contextualising an artwork with context at its conceptual centre. In 'Alchemy and the Digital Imaginary' the artist David Larcher talks with Stephen Littman about the materials and processes of his multi-layered and vertically edited artworks. Larcher describes the material transitions from film to high-end digital compositing systems, which within the studio environment enable him to compose image labyrinths, tones and cadences and to intuitively produce imaginary structures possible only in electronic space. As well as being a prolific artist and filmmaker, experimenting with film, video and computer imaging technologies, Malcolm Le Grice has played a key role in the institutional promotion of avant-garde moving-image, and has authored many key texts (e.g. *Abstract Film and Beyond* (1977); *Experimental Cinema in the Digital Age* (2001)). In 'Reflections on my practice and Media Specificity' Le Grice describes the media transitions he has embraced since the late 1960s, and discusses the processes of his practice and philosophical concerns, from filmmaking, through to video, computers and digital forms. 'Expanded Cinema, Proto, Post Photo' stems from my own cinematic practice and research into electronic forms of moving-image, new forms of experimental cinema and emergent philosophies, concepts and related intertextual languages. Here I discuss expanded cinema, concentrating on the *video* history of participatory expanded (post-photo) cinema. Since the 1960s Mike Leggett has made key works across film, performance, video and digital media, and has practiced as a curator, writer, director, producer, photographer and computer consultant. In *Image Con Text* (1978–2003) Film/Performance/Video/Digital, he discusses the shifts in technology from the analogue to digital (film, video, digital and computer) traversed through the series of artworks, the *Image Con Text* project. Leggett contextualises the complex processes of his work alongside the relative critical and philosophical debates, from the analogue technologies of film and video to interactive computer augmented multimedia.

Section I

Philosophies and Critical Histories of Avant-Garde Film and Current Practice

Grahame Weinbren
Post Future Past Perfect

Peter Gidal
Matter's Time Time For Material

Chris Welsby
Films and Installations – A Systems View of Nature

Nicky Hamlyn
A Line Through My Work

Jayne Parker
A Few Notes on Filmmaking

Rob Gawthrop
Film Noise Aesthetics

Anthony McCall
Line Describing a Cone and Related Films

Chapter one

Post Future Past Perfect

Grahame Weinbren

In a historic passage Mallarmé describes the terror, the sense of sterility, that the poet experiences when he sits down to his desk, confronts the sheet of paper before him on which his poem is supposed to be composed, and no words come to him. But we might ask, Why could not Mallarmé, after an interval of time, have simply got up from his desk and produced the blank sheet of paper as the poem that he sat down to write? Indeed, in support of this, could one imagine anything that was more expressive of, or would be held to exhibit more precisely, the poet's feelings of inner devastation than the virginal paper?
Richard Wollheim[1]

The contemporary equivalent of Mallarmé's blank sheet is the infinite plain of a blank word processor window, so effortlessly populated with trivia or outright nonsense that one might easily find typing the first character a formidable obstacle. My issue with creativity is the opposite of this, however. I am cursed with a kind of coagulation or infrangibility. An idea comes to me clear and sharp. However it appears as a single unit, like a mass of hair, straw and scraps of fabric, stuck together with mud, gum and all kinds of gook. The main characteristics of this ball of matter are its density and its indivisibility. It is so heavy, so densely packed that one can't identify a single piece of material as central or binding. At the same time the ideas that form this fecal mass are tightly interwoven, so much so that it appears, to me at least, to comprise one single idea, which ought to be speakable in a single sentence. But it never is. Even though the individual elements when finally broken apart are as often salacious, scatological or feculent as logical, aesthetic, or theoretical, each one is necessary. There is no excess, nothing superfluous or extra, and perhaps the metaphor is not quite accurate for this very reason. To omit one sticky shred would result in incoherence, a failure to lay out a clear line of meaning after the processes of decomposition and reassembly are completed. To turn this superhairball from thought to writing involves unraveling the

fibers, piece by piece, and laying them out one behind the next. Often one bit emerges still entangled with others, and what looks like an individual idea or a unitary stream is really itself a complex of thoughts and ideas that themselves cannot be easily individuated. Another problem is that what seems to be a unique element repeats itself again and again like a DNA sequence, but each time in a different context within the mass and therefore with a different meaning.

A picture not unlike my problem with writing is drawn by Freud in his descriptions of the struggle for an analysis of a dream – especially in his case history of the Wolf Man, where the dreamer's most emotionally charged memories, his deepest fears, and his darkest obsessional images are displaced and condensed into the opaque and highly symbolic image of white furry-tailed wolves, sitting on the branches of a walnut tree, staring, staring at the terrified dreamer. Freud admits that there is no logical or correct sequence for the dream components to appear during the processes of psychoanalysis, and that the written sequence of the case history can hardly capture the non-linear, repetitive, emotion-charged process of discovery/invention that the patient has gone through. Now whether this is myth or scientific fact, whether the process of psychoanalysis has any validity as treatment of mental disease, or as depiction of the human mind, is irrelevant. The point is that Freud's description of untangling a highly compressed image into its logical or emotional strands describes, as closely as anything else

I've seen, my difficulties with writing. My original concept always seems lucid to me. However, it is a single entity. Taking it apart, disentangling it into its elements and laying them out in a sequence that makes sense, i.e. putting it into words, is the whole process, the whole problem of writing.

With this epistemology as my basic psychological condition, one might wonder why I choose the cinema as my medium of expression. Sculpture or installation may seem to correspond more closely to the inner architecture I have described. However, though the initial image or idea can be best imagined as a spatial form, it is incoherent and incommunicable in this state. The mass must be deconstructed to be comprehended. I am interested in communicating my ideas, not just expressing them. So it is natural that the elements be disengaged from one another and recoded into a form that is characterized by duration. This is the process by which I make my works, and I've tried, in different ways, to capture this process in my films and cinematic installations over the last 30 years, looking always for cinema structures and forms that, paradoxically, can be multi-streamed while unfolding in time. The linearity of the filmstrip doesn't easily adapt to these concepts, so I've repeatedly looked for ways both to undermine and to expand it without rejecting it.

The hair/mud-ball I have in mind for this essay can be partially decomposed into the story of the power of a particular book. The book is elegant, carefully written, and precise, by a man who obviously cared sincerely for his subject. It does not claim to be the last word, and in the preface it announces its shortcomings. Published 30 years ago, the book's influence still hangs over the field of avant-garde, experimental, independent, personal, call-it-what-you-will cinema (each adjective implies a contested aesthetic position). It changed the notion of independent filmmaking, erecting fences between filmmakers who belong in the same yard, and herding together some who ought to be kept fields apart. It is a coherent book. But its very coherency is its wrong-headedness. It ignores, in its analyses though not in its descriptions, the most important thing about cinema – duration – and as a consequence the book's underlying presuppositions and explicit conclusions about the nature of art and art-making belong more to the 19th century than the 20th. Because of these fundamental misunder-standings, combined with its substantial influence, it has left a swathe of destruction in its wake. The shortcomings of this book and its consequences deserve a full-length study. However, this is not the context for it, and I am probably not the person to do it.

1974 was a turning point, not only for me personally as a film-maker, but for avant-garde cinema in the United States. I had lived in the USA for a year or two and had made a couple of films that fell somewhere between documentary, poetry, music, and concep-tual art. In 1974 the borders separating documentary and experi-mental film were open. There were extreme cases of 'cinema verité' on one side (for example *Salesman* (1967), by David and Albert Maysles and Charlotte Zwerin and *Don't Look Back* (1967) by D. A. Pennebaker), and the semi-abstract, dance-like films of Marie Menken, Scott Bartlett, Stan Vanderbeek, and Pat O'Neill on the other, but most independently made works fell somewhere be-tween the exploration of the cinematic image in and of itself, an expression of the idiosyncratic nature of individual vision, and an investigation of some aspect of reality. Fiction film, on the other hand, was another nation. Still the most popular form of cinema, narrative film was the mesmerizing monster that we all had to contend with. And almost all experimental filmmakers acknow-ledged in their work the magnetism of narrative transposed to film. Indeed the most notorious 'structural' film, Michael Snow's *Wave-length* (1967), has Hollywood's primal scene at its focal point: i.e. a mysterious unexplained death, the dead man played by filmmaker Hollis Frampton, his body discovered by actress and writer Amy Taubin.

1974 was the publication year of the first edition of P. Adams Sitney's *Visionary Film*.[2] It is a study of about thirty filmmakers, with precise descriptions of many of their films. The book was read carefully by filmmakers, programmers, and, most significantly, in the backwaters of the academic world of the liberal arts. At that time these swamps were populated by mostly young, 'hip', professors in the English Departments of distinguished major universities. Sitney's book was respectable in a way that the films and filmmakers were not, and therefore filled the gap between the increasing isolation of the university from the culture at large and the recent (but getting more distant) memory of the university's power and influence, its *threat* in the late 1960s. With Sitney's book as a guide to the films, college classes could stay in touch with underground culture without the danger of interference by racial or economic – i.e. class – difference.

Visionary Film is reactionary. Backed up by a monolithic pre-Foucault view of history as causal and linear, its theoretical approach is based on the literary analytic techniques of Paul de Man and Harold Bloom. Because of these very qualities, it was well understood by the young English professors. They were trained in reading and analyzing poetry, and de Man and Bloom were the intellectual heroes of their party. Sitney's techniques of literary analysis domesticated the raucous films that were its subject, making them appropriate study materials of middle-class higher education, even if (or especially because) there were occasional glimpses of pubic hair. Based on its credentials, combined with its readability and teachability, the book had wide general appeal to the academic world. *Visionary Film* became the defining voice of the avant-garde cinema, canonizing certain filmmakers, validating certain tendencies, and at the same time, needless to say, excluding other filmmakers and invalidating other approaches.

Sitney's descriptions of films are, as I mentioned earlier, articulate, thorough, and sensitive. His analyses, however, are more problematic. They eschew the time-based aspects of the films in favor of poetics and (in the case of Brakhage) comparison with painting. The painting references are largely to Abstract Expressionism. But the book was written in the early 1970s. Abstract Expressionism is a movement associated with the 1950s, hardly an issue of import to practitioners in the 1960s or 70s. The current art world was dominated by Minimalism, Conceptualism, and the still-vigorously-kicking Pop, with parallels in the world of music of minimalism, free jazz, and indeterminacy. There is no question that such filmmakers as Paul Sharits, Hollis Frampton and Michael Snow were at least aware of, and, more likely, embedded in these very movements. However, in his analysis of their films, Professor Sitney either ignored, or was ignorant of, the concepts and practices that animated the arts of that time. Perhaps an even more troubling problem with Sitney's position was that he had a tendency to view works as monolithic, driven by a single idea or motive. For Sitney,

grasping this single idea constituted understanding the film. So Structural Film, most reprehensibly, 'insists on its shape.' This is as vague as defining narrative film as 'telling a story'. The label was rejected by most of the filmmakers that Sitney included in the category, and criticisms of his definition have been repeatedly rehearsed, for example by George Maciunas, who points out, among other things, that his field of view is restricted to a certain clique of filmmakers. It not worth repeating yet again the short-comings of the definition.

My point is at an angle to the critique of *Visionary Film*: it is about the *effects* of the book. Despite its limitations, the notion of struc-tural film spread like a forest fire among young filmmakers, some of who began to make films using Sitney's description as a formula. These may have been the only actual structural films ever made, and they were disastrous – films inspired by *Visionary Film* were, in a word, thin, and, in another, academic; and finally insignificant.[3] The second effect was that it effectively defined a canon based on aesthetic criteria. It was odd timing – during this period the very notion of the canon was under attack on the grounds that it was, in principle, symptomatic of cultural, gender and racial biases, nevertheless, after *Visionary Film* it was almost as if experimental film was over and done – here is the list of filmmakers, here is the list of relevant issues, and the shop is now closed. No later book had the impact or influence of *Visionary Film*. It defined the subject, the objects of study, the relevant figures and the approach to the whole ball of wax. Not only were we younger generation of filmmakers shut out, but we remained shut out, as a lost generation of filmmakers whose work was ignored or reviled.

It is difficult to find in *Visionary Film* any reference to the elementary notion that the understanding of cinema depends on the fact that the film image undergoes constant transformation. This is a more serious shortcoming than the book's narrowness of vision. To experience cinema is to rely on memory and re-evaluation of what one has seen, on anticipation of what is to come, on milestones and signposts, on repetition and variation. Furthermore, films that attempt to do what is, to my mind, most appropriate to the cinema, that is perform multiple functions simultaneously, were either considered unworthy of consideration, or their multi-facetedness was ignored. Sitney's underlying critical philosophy was: one concept per film. It is this sense of unity that allowed his definition to become a formula, and differentiated those films that are thought of as the core avant-garde film canon from those that followed. One must keep in mind, however, that the most interesting films, not only of the 1960s and 70s, but throughout the hundred year history of cinema, have been those that keep many balls, many kinds of ball, in the air at once.

Of course Sitney was not the only critic active during this period, but his influence can be clearly felt in the work of others. My examples are Fred Camper and Paul Arthur, both highly respected, astute, and prolific observers of avant-garde film for over 25 years. In essays published in 1986, each expressed his own disappointments with the direction avant-garde film had taken since 1972, though Arthur is much more positive than Camper. I joined the three-person editorial board of the *Millennium Film Journal* for the '20th Anniversary Special Edition' published late in 1986, for which Camper, Arthur, and Amy Taubin had been invited to contribute reviews of the current independent film scene.[4] Taubin wrote a short piece insisting that video was, though underrated, an essential component of the independent cinema. Arthur's article 'The Last of the Last Machine? Avant-Garde Film Since 1986' compared structural film and the 'new narrative' that had emerged in the later 70s and early 80s, and Camper's article 'The End of Avant-Garde Film' was an expression of regret at what he saw as the demise of creative filmmaking. Both Arthur and Camper are in general agreement with Sitney – Camper's A-list of filmmakers is coincident with Sitney's, and Arthur explicitly embraces the concept of Structural Film, refining and sharpening the definition but applying it to the same group of films originally identified by Sitney. He even goes so far as to explicitly describe these films as 'the Structural Canon'.[5]

9

But first we must, reluctantly, turn to Fred Camper's ugly attack on the work of several filmmakers of the 1970s and early 80s. My focus is Alan Berliner, from whose work I derive great pleasure and with whom I felt an affinity, though his work was quite unlike my own. Camper devotes three paragraphs to dismissing Berliner's films, comparing them unfavorably to the work of Peter Kubelka and Bruce Conner. Kubelka is invoked because Berliner, like him, makes sync events out of images and unrelated sounds, and Conner because Berliner also works with found footage. In reference to Kubelka's *Unsere Afrikareise* (1961-66), Camper finds in a picture and sound moment that 'one feels that the filmmaker has combined two elements [...] into a new entity.' Berliner, in contrast, 'tends to produce an undisturbing smoothness of texture and tone'.[6] Camper misses not only the point, but the poignancy of Berliner's work. His *Myth and the Electric Age* is a compendium of images drawn from the filmmaker's collection of found footage. The images cover a vast array of subjects, and Berliner links each shot to the next by precise editing based on movement, color, composition, and occasionally subject-matter, or by continuing the sound from one shot to the next in a magical sync, though images and sounds are almost

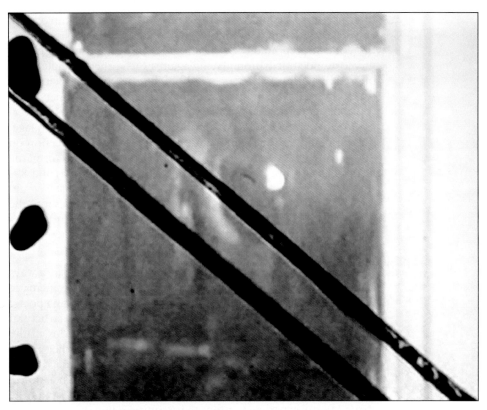

always from quite different sources. There is a special pleasure for the viewer in this 'smooth texture' (to quote Camper), especially when one realizes that the film is rapidly traversing a universe of places, materials, things, and people. One of the operations of the film is a negotiation between continuity and discontinuity, which is pointed out by – of all people – Marshall McLuhan, in an unexpected voice-over commentary. McLuhan's surprisingly modest voice is heard several times, in a commentary that is apparently about the structure and subjects of Berliner's film, e.g. how 'the electric age' collapses discontinuities and compounds continuities. Berliner exploits unintended ambiguities in McLuhan's words, playfully setting them against literal visual realizations of the metaphors he uses. Thus in the film the conceptual is weighed against the sensual, the sudden pleasure of a sync moment offset by the delicate transformation of, for example, the release of a satellite from a space station match-cutting into a man's dive from the top of a cliff into the blue ocean and then to the shimmer of a turtle far beneath the surface elegantly continuing the diver's arc though the air. Berliner is a gifted montagist, and the viewer delights in his virtuosity. It is a wonder that material drawn from such a diversity of sources can present so smooth a texture. Themes are introduced and developed (liquid, light. fire, smoke, steam, wind, space, circus, fireworks...), repeated with variations, eliciting a musical response, memory and anticipation playing against each other. The pleasures offered by Berliner's film are manifold, but they do not include the self-conscious existential dilemmas that enchanted Camper in the tortuous work of Markopoulos and Brakhage. There is no tormented reading required, no decoding of densely built up collage, no grappling with the filmmaker's sexual identity or reflection on one's own. These are, for Camper, the virtues of the avant-garde films of the 1960s. But for the filmmakers of the late 70s and 80s these virtues have become the vices of arrogance, mastery, and self-indulgence. Berliner does not ask us to insert ourselves into the psyche of the filmmaker, but rather to navigate through the meticulous, multiple pleasures of the cinematic, to share these pleasures with him. Times had changed.

Paul Arthur argues that the Structural Film is reductivist, always centered on a metaphoric reference to the materiality of cinematic construction 'in the hope of blunting if not totally expunging poetic association from film's semiotic array'.[7] Understanding a structural film requires not a 'reading' of layerings and disjunctions in the film's images, as was the mode of interpretation for earlier avant-garde films, but a comprehension of the film as a whole, 'clearly Bazinian in its insistence on univocal (even seamless) enunciation'.[8] This is an echo of Sitney's notion of the film that 'insists on its shape.' In my experience, a film that requires a univocal view of its entirety, and nothing else, is agony to sit through. In contrast, many of the films that Arthur and Sitney refer to as central to the Structural Film enterprise are replete with small pleasures as they unfold in time. In these films there is usually a governing materialist metaphor, and it is this spinal structure that differentiates them from the work of the following generation of filmmakers. However, to ignore their cinematic detail is to render an interpretive disservice to the films. To amplify this point, I would like to reconsider the film that is perhaps the paradigm of Structural Film, *Zorns Lemma*.

Hollis Frampton's *Zorns Lemma* (1970) is the last work discussed in the 1974 edition of *Visionary Film*. It is a film that is centered on the notion of ordering inherent to the Latin alphabet, and each of the three parts uses words as its organizing principle. The central section consists of one second scenes of words, mostly images of public signs in New York City, arranged in alphabetic order. The alphabet is navigated many times through, and one by one images replace the words. Over the forty-five minute course, all words are eventually eliminated and a regulated montage of 24 frame shots remains. The notion of an ordered set dominates the film, and endorses the authority of the filmmaker's intelligence, his ability to master his materials. However, subsidiary to the front-line metaphors of order and authority, the film offers multiple pleasures and themes to engage the viewer as it progresses. Occasionally supervening alphabetized words reveal little phrases – 'lady madonna', 'limp member' – encouraging the viewer to watch out for secret messages. And thematically there is much to occupy the mind as the film unwinds. *Zorns Lemma* references *minimalism* in its undifferentiated, regulated time structure (cf. Carl Andre's sculptural work of the time), *pop* in its celebration of the anonymous visual artist (i.e. the designers of the many public signs and letters), *narrative* in its small segmented stories that replace some of the letters, *memory* and *anticipation* in its multiple forward and backward indicators, a contrast and interplay between *nature* and *culture*, minor moment-to-moment pleasures and puzzles, *indeterminacy* (in John Cage's sense), and the indefinability of time's passage. These different themes and experiences do not support each other or build on each other; on the contrary one often undercuts or obscures the next. The viewer must navigate between them, though the sense of playfulness is always restrained by the fact that the single alphabetic organizing principle holds the film together from beginning to end. For me it is the multiplicity of themes that makes the film watchable. Filmmakers who emerged in the early to middle 1970s tended to reject the strategy of centering their work on a single idea and forcing other ideas into subsidiary relationships. Rather, as I have suggested for the work of Alan Berliner, they liberate many ideas to float together simultaneously, supporting or contradicting each other in a fabric composed of multiple weights and weaves. It is for the viewer, not the authoritative filmmaker, to navigate the tapestry, to break the conglomerate into its individual strands.

I'll conclude by describing a film I made with Roberta Friedman in 1978 called *Future Perfect*. It was filmed and finished in the illegal loft we were living in at the time, above an Irish bar on the corner of Wall Street and Water Street in New York City, a couple of blocks from the financial heartbeat of Western Capitalism. The back room of the loft was dark and unfinished, its one window looking out onto another building that cut out any daylight. We had our lights, our tools, our rewinds and viewer set up there, as well as a 16mm Moviola, and when friends visited they would sleep on a trundle bed in that gloomy studio.

A friend of ours was an architecture student and we asked him to draw a plan view of the studio, which was more or less in the ratio of a wide-screen cinema frame. We thought about the possible ways

13

geometric marks could be made on this film frame – a rectangle around the edges, a diagonal line from one corner to the other and back, dots down one edge, a line that would cut the bottom edge and re-emerge at the top edge if it traversed the horizontal frame line, arcs in upper and lower quadrants. We planned to move in these patterns through the room and record our path on 16mm film. The cinematographer Anthony Forma agreed to help us. We recognized that a primary experience of the photographic cinema is indexical – the viewer looks through the frame like a time-space window into the period and place when the image was produced. However, against this depictive aspect of the cinematic we wanted to play the fact that the film image is materially a small flat transparent surface the function of which is to transform the light that passes through it. We wanted to make a film that highlighted the materialistic and illusionistic aspects of cinema while keeping both of the aspects floating in parallel. We were also interested at the time in the fact that the labor that it takes to make a film is not inscribed in the finished work; rather in most cases it is deliberately obscured, and we wanted the labor involved in the construction of the film to be part of its content. The general idea, in other words, was to expose everything. So after we plotted our camera paths through the room, forming these geometric figures, we placed stenciled signs at the end points of intended camera moves. These signs indicated our intentions for finishing the film. We would stop the camera in front of each of the signs. The plan was to draw on the exposed and developed film the same geometric shapes that we had plotted with the camera movements to create the photographic images. Only after these figures had been drawn directly on the surface of the emulsion would the film be finished. We used a calculator to figure out a series of decreasing numerical series, which would determine the intervals between the marks that we would place on the film. Thus the stenciled signs were, for example:

A RECTANGLE WILL HAVE BEEN DRAWN
AROUND SOME FRAMES. THE NUMBER OF
FRAMES BETWEEN DRAWINGS DECREASES
ACCORDING TO A FIBONACCI SERIES

The photographed texts in the film, in other words, state the formulae that generate the images, which eventually dominate the film. The shooting plan features the stenciled texts which function both as milestones and signposts, as targets aimed for in the erratic camera movements so that the camera pauses when it finds them, as descriptions of visual composition of the final film, as well as plans for the filmmakers to follow. The connection is obvious with a conceptual artist like Sol LeWitt, whose work at that time consisted of plans as to how a painting or drawing was to be realized.

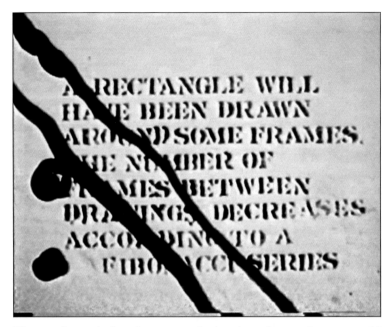

The mathematical series were calculated so that each one would yield values of less than one frame (if it was an asymptotic series) or would end, at about eight minutes from the beginning. Thus *Future Perfect* gradually builds in density and rhythm according to mathematical principles, until at about eight minutes there is a copious display of drawn figures and an emergent music (since each drawing was to be accompanied by a sound produced by bowing a kitchen utensil) which transmutes into a continuous discordant metallic humming as the space between drawings and sounds becomes less than a single frame and in effect continuous. *Future Perfect* was both how we thought of the completion of the film, plus of course the grammatical tense in which the sentences about intentions were stenciled on the walls of the studio. We printed out lists of the frames numbers that were to receive marks, set the exposed and developed reversal film on a rewind bench in the studio, and began to mark the appropriate film frames with special transparent inks intended for overhead transparencies and slides. In contrast to the shooting, which lasted an agonizing but delimited 33 minutes (running the 16mm Arriflex at eight frames per second), the marking of the frames took months, but we kept the perfect future in mind, the deferred time when the film would have been fully marked up and complete.

Viewers are thrown back in time by the tense of the texts, looking forward through the film from the time of production to the time when the various marks will have been made, which is of course the time of the continuous present when the film is finished and finally shown. So the film invites its viewers to see their way through and around multiple temporalities, while it is also a nostalgic record of the dark loft in the financial district where we lived as young filmmakers, and a record of the different kinds of work it takes to make a film, with the aid of mechanical equipment, light sensitive materials and chemistry, in contrast to the more traditional way of making art by marking materials, and the way the two types of labor play against each other parallel to the inexorable relationship of technology to natural law, and all of this is realized in more or less a single gesture unwound into an eleven minute strand of time, which does its best to break out beyond its own temporal frame by referring clearly to its own future and its own past. There was something very compelling in the idea that an entire film could be contained in six statements of mathematical formulae. I hope that readers can see how *Future Perfect* is generated by a compressed set of interlocked ideas, like the dense hairball with which I began this essay. The film's apparent complexity is largely a result of the way it must be described, since English is much less efficient than mathematics.

In a subtle argument based on distinctions made by Peirce, Wollheim argues that the blank sheet of paper proposed in the epigraph to this essay cannot possibly express the poet's terror of the void that swallows and demolishes creativity. A poem, Wollheim points out, is not an object like a sheet of paper, but rather a type of which its individual instantiations are tokens, but a poem nonetheless. The identity of a poem is presupposed by its non-materiality: it remains the same poem throughout its re-printings and dissemination. We need a parallel ontological distinction between the semantics, the mechanics of meaning, of those works that are characterized by duration and those that are not. Though comparison with painting and poetry may be useful as starting point, finally it will be music, storytelling and theatre, dynamic media, that will serve as models for the understanding of cinematic works.

The most gifted theorists of art undertake the analysis of a work because it has moved them. There must be a powerful first read, an appeal, a rush of unanalyzed impression that attacks the mind or emotions and motivates the critic to devote the hours and days required for a comprehensive analysis of how a work *works*. It is the complex first 'thin slice'[9] sensation that I attempted to depict in the description of the superhairball with which I opened this essay. I am sure that the three critics to whom I have referred, write in order to comprehend and communicate their genuinely felt immediate responses to works. My disagreement is never with an initial response, only with how it is theorized and how that theory affects later evaluations and responses to other works. When a text like Sitney's happens to emerge at the right historical and cultural moment, it can become more than one writer's individual response and analysis. Seized by institutions, it can itself become an institution, a standard against which later work is judged, ignoring the fact that standards need to be adjusted to fit changing cultures. An authoritative book, *Visionary Film* celebrated films that accepted as given the authority of the filmmaker. Adopting this view of the artist makes it difficult to comprehend works, which undermine his or her dominion.

And this leads to my own dominion over the ideas expressed here. I cannot capture in an essay, one letter after another, one word after another, one paragraph after another, the sense of compressed cogency that characterizes the works that move me and that I aim for in my own work. One can only ask for the reader's indulgence, for him, for her, to ride along and to attempt to see things, for an instant, through my eyes.

Notes

1. Richard Wollheim, 'Minimal Art', ed. Gregory Battcock, *Minimal Art: A Critical Anthology* (New York: E.P. Dutton and Company, 1968), p. 388.

2. P. Adams Sitney, *Visionary Film: The American Avant-Garde 1943-1978* (New York: Oxford University Press, 1974).

3. They are better left un-referenced and un-described, though if desired, one can refer to Fred Camper's acerbic article 'The End of Avant-Garde Film', *Millennium Film Journal* Nos. 16/17/18, Fall/Winter 1986–87, pp. 99–126, in which he describes, with some relish, films he disapproves of. I am in fundamental disagreement with much of this article, though I believe that the view he expresses is sincerely and deeply felt.

4. *Millennium Film Journal*, Nos. 16/17/18, '20th Anniversary Special Edition' (Millennium Film Workshop, New York, 1986).

5. Paul Arthur, 'The Last of the Last Machine? Avant-Garde Film Since 1986', *Millennium Film Journal*, Nos. 16/17/18, '20th Anniversary Special Edition' (Millennium Film Workshop, New York, 1986), p. 77.

6. Fred Camper, 'The End of Avant-Garde Film', *Millennium Film Journal*, Nos. 16/17/18, '20th Anniversary Special Edition' (Millennium Film Workshop, New York, 1986), p. 118.

7. Paul Arthur, 'The Last of the Last Machine? Avant-Garde Film Since 1986', *Millennium Film Journal*, Nos. 16/17/18, '20th Anniversary Special Edition' (Millennium Film Workshop, New York, 1986), p, 77.

8. Ibid., p. 78.

9. The term is Malcolm Gladwell's, from his book *Blink: The Power of Thinking Without Thinking* (New York and Boston: Little Brown and Co., 2005).

Chapter two

Matter's Time Time for Material

[Zeit der Materie (bzw.) Zeit für Material]

Peter Gidal

Translated from a talk given at the X-Screen Symposium: 28 February 2004, Museum Moderner Kunst (MuMok) Vienna

I have seen this excellent exhibition for the first time today even though I already saw the catalogue[1] which reached me at Christmas and which is also brilliant. The exhibition is impressive, precise and correct. For instance, setting up the lights in such a manner that they can't flood into a room when someone enters a space, rebuilding the walls on two floors so that sound is isolated from each screening, setting up double-screen projections on endless loops of 16mm film instead of going to video or digital, etc. Architectonically brilliant. And it should be mentioned that since I am not included in this exhibition I can say this all the more easily. Especially as I make single screen work – thus: *films*! (laughter), or: pictures, as Germans sometimes say (*bilder*), which I find a bit confusing actually. As this will not be about me, I still want to introduce myself. I have been making films since 1967, working with the London Film Co-op since 1968. Even though they were individual artworks, films made at the Co-op involved everyone, and we were always a collective because no one was able to produce a film totally on their own. We tended to be reliant on each other, whether sharing theoretical or political notions within the collective or not, so that at the Co-op it was inevitable that we should work together, and out of this practical co-operation came all those films. Single-screen film modes of production shared the aesthetics and theoretical ideas that underpinned the multiple-screen films and

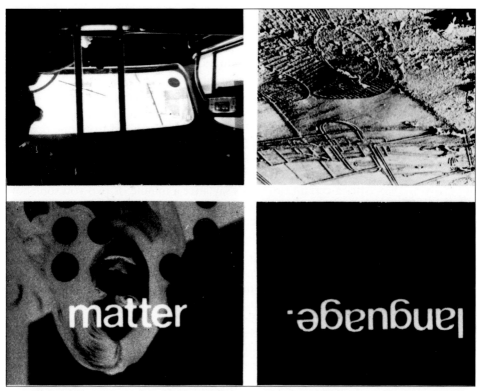

installations (or vice versa), which resulted in the emergence of a collective philosophy. Though we were never a homogenous group, never a group even of common – or commonly held – notions, and there were always stark contrasts, every day, in every attitude, in every production of a film and in every manner of working. The most important thing was that people's work – processes and ideas for their films – was distinct. My first point here is that in England, theory always came *after* practice. Whilst we didn't decide this consciously, it automatically resulted from our working methods, whereas more usually aesthetic and philosophic works start with a premise and then you work everything out until everything fits – more or less. And if things don't fit into the premise you just change the premise a little, ideally with nobody noticing that you've done so, and then you still go ahead with it. In our case it was the opposite. To exemplify what I mean I am going to tell you how we worked in an ideal case. Ideal not as normative but as exemplary. I will take my own case as ideal because I am standing here. Someone else could take his or her own case as ideal case. I hope that if I will talk about my own films this will hopefully have implications on aesthetics and theory. But I will begin simply historically. (I should add that in correcting this

Upside Down Feature, 16mm film, 1972.

19

translated version of my German talk it sounds as if I learnt halting English rather recently. This is not the case. But it means even now rewriting this I have a strange, and estranged relation to the text, as if it were a marionette that operates with some difficulty).

In 1972 I began the film *Upside Down Feature*. I began shooting this film in 1967 but 1972 was the beginning of the end so to speak. This film consisted of words, and sentences of text deriving from Beckett's 1931 essay about Proust, every word from one page on time and death filmed for approximately a third of a second. Right from the beginning of the film you see these words flashing on screen each back to front so quickly that you hardly recognise them. After a certain time, let's say after a minute or two you somehow acclimatise to the speed and the left/right switch (i.e. reading backwards) and suddenly you are able to read the words, word for word. Still backwards.

After three minutes it switches to 'normal' left to right, front to back, everything is re-reverted. Now the spectator again needs time, at least half a minute to assimilate, to take on a normal, ideological and narrative position and to continue reading – but everything is simultaneously extremely difficult to grasp, you can't grasp the image. You can indeed see it, there is perception, there is cognition, but in my film there is no *recognition*. One knows that there is something deriving from the true world so to speak. This issue has always been very important to me – that there is no assimilation of the world through film. I could never explain to myself philosophically why one makes a film at all if one would be able to recognize what pre-exists the process of representation. The whole process would be useless. I don't state that as a polemic now, in that whether this is true or not isn't the point of this example, I just say that this has been – and still is – my aesthetic political position.

My plan was to realise the same thing with a text in the one described segment of this film (the film is 76 minutes long, the segment discussed is perhaps 7 minutes). This seeing and not seeing, this knowing but not knowing. But what do you do after one minute when it becomes readable? There the problem began. In my perception it took about one minute until Beckett's text became readable, became *apparently* natural to read. This explanation for such a small part is going to be a bit long but bear with me. After 60 seconds when the reading appeared left to right, i.e. natural, again, and the reading became narrative, literary, I decided that now it should switch to the filmic visual again. But that this shouldn't be done in a clear, transparent and quasi-naturalistic manner. So it should be not only *difficult* to read, but unreadable. Something had to be changed. The text was there, so what could be changed? The image should become dark red. The film had been black and white – the whole experience was of black and white and when the colour came through now in some parts it changed the whole film. I added the colour on the film through printing via a red filter, which had the necessary effect that the already barely readable words, though no longer reversed now, became again less self evident. The film became red for some time to de-clarify the clarity. Then when the text segment ended it went again to the 'outside' world; the next shot was in the streets.

The point of all this is that I was not able to do all this technically at the Co-op with the printer and I needed whoever was able to put the red onto the words segments via the printer. In this case it was Malcolm Le Grice who could help me. So we went to the printer room and printed it together. Together means: I didn't do anything, stood in the corner or pushed right up against the printer staring into the flickering 16mm frames flashing by, requesting this and that be done as he printed it. Saying 'darker' or 'if possible not so dark that you can't see anything' or 'please make sure the red comes in right near the end of the sequence and covers also the beginning of naturalistic imagery ... by darkening it obliterating some of the difference between image of text and the next filmed sequence ...' Much of the time silence, then sudden bursts of the above. Malcolm worked highly concentratedly and ignored me also some of the time; in a nice way, whilst listening to me also reply to the requests he made, questions he brought up instantaneously, importantly, whilst he was continuing with the ongoing process of printing. Remember what was being printed was in fact a new original, nothing 'pre-existing' that anymore, making what was to now be the present-original *Upside Down Feature*, made at that moment (editing to follow).

Half an hour later we watched it with a few people, and talked about the segment. We talked for instance about the meaning of red, what is the semiotics of red? Is it an allusion to Godard? To Wittgenstein? Is it colour as end in itself? Is it 'pure' colour? Does such exist? Question of transparency. Relation to painting, etc. For a quarter of an hour we sat there, five or six Co-op filmmakers, talking, and without having a theory seminar, we talked about colour, words, narrativity, temporality, words versus colour or image versus thought. We also thought about the spectator, thought about how one could *mis*-define ... well maybe not mis-define, though I would have said that at that time. The word mis-define is actually a bit pedantic.

This was a small example, maybe a little bit too long, to show the path from practice to theory. In the midst of this came thinking about what kind of position the spectator could inhabit. What are the ramifications when the spectator suddenly says: red is a pure colour. Does that then go along with the film or would it become contrary? Being right or not is a totally different thing. We knew that already, knew at that time that 'right' or 'wrong' wouldn't be the limit of any definition. Yet it was our belief that all this was a collective process automatically. In a sense what this does theorize is how perception leads to thought, so that the two are never completely separate.

For the first time in twenty years I looked at an issue of *Artforum* recently, published in September 1971, the 'Structural Film Issue'. And there you find the fact that the Americans have always been, the critics as well as the films, consciously or sub-consciously, rigorously formalist, and that for them, Structural Film was a formalist theory. This next point is about Structural/Materialist film versus Materialist film, working itself into a theory and definition of Structural-Materialist film. Most though not all of the Americans were savagely anti-materialist. For example P. Adams Sitney has always happily admitted that for them 'the shape is more important than the content.' For us in England the shape was not the main interest because if you can interpret/decipher/disentangle a composition and if you can have a clear idea about it and have an insight into it, then at least for me it is the same as clear narrativity. And that is exactly the reason why we argued that there must be something other than the apparently pure in fact naive, empirical, descriptively formalistic American Structural Film. The latter reliant upon conventional apprehensions, however 'poetic' or 'visionary' would rigorously disallow radical political and ideological positions for the viewer, for viewing, to be inscribed in the work (let alone in the theory), positions that might disallow secure self-identity (or even self-identities, plural). An avant-garde that reproduces dominant political and ideological positions of viewing, or representation, of meaning, of even truth, beauty, pleasure, is useless. Anyway out of all this emerged a theory of structural materialist film in 1974, – although retrospectively I realized that this idea was not a theory. Of course there were others at the Co-op who didn't write such polemical pieces. Even some of my friends were, additionally, anti-theoretical.

The next point is about a fact that is generally known and self-evident: that the *process* is most important, and not the object, not an ostensible object I should say. I will explain what process can mean in filmmaking. We soon realized that if the process while making a film and during watching of a film is the main function of vision for the spectator then it is thankfully impossible to create coherence out of the encounter. Whether a film is one hour long or ten minutes or two minutes doesn't matter. It is impossible to create coherence because the process always intervenes; it is evident, therefore it is problematic. This problem can deal with the fact that if you are suddenly able to see how a film has been brought together you may see the *relations* of how it has been brought together. You suddenly see both what is, what makes up the image, and viewing itself as problematising. Such (apperception) is then an experience of moment-to-moment filmic *perception*. All this means is that there is something that at least in this moment you don't know. And know you don't know. This leads the audience back into the process. If this actually happens, no matter whether that's for a minute or an hour, once it becomes evident, it won't be possible to form an *object* from or of this experience. What is evident then is that as long as the subject (in this case: the audience) does not establish an object (in other words, a pretext), it can't establish a self-identity and therefore can't endlessly rely on such. If a process is continuous, in time, then watching it *can* only be 'watching it', as you can never make of the self ... a self-identity. A subject becomes completely impossible, its other can't be 'the other' either. Therefore we can say that here and there through this working and thinking mode the whole issue became political.

If this is a different way of 'watching' and a different way of creating coherence, then this isn't only about the object 'film', which can't be an object any longer, but also about narrativity, its ideology in film and in life.

What some didn't understand was that once a film is a formalistic object that can be defined and experienced as a closed object, that then also the viewer is defined as a whole closed object. Through this different position (QED) you have a completely different politics because you are not able to describe 'the other' as the *other*. It is quite obvious that this circumstance would imply a radically different set of ideological and political consequences. I don't have to give examples why *the other* is already questionable in terms of political ideology. We simply didn't really understand why art should repeat exactly the things we thought to be most politically negative in our culture. Coherence and identity. And I don't mean by that, that film did or did not mirror culture but I mean simply that process, the politics of representation, the always existent political, intervened.

The next problem was within experimental film itself, the growing fetishising of process. One can see how this happens. As process became fetishized, it became just an image, an image of process. And then we have the same problem paradoxically of a coherent experience, or an audience with a coherent self-identity versus the other.

Even after thirty years of work there's still the same problem; whilst you approach it from different angles it never changes in itself, there is no 'in itself' nor 'in history' – it *is* history. In retrospect I think we all found an almost aesthetic philosophy within our work. For instance at the 'Live in your Head' exhibition at the Whitechapel Art Gallery in 2000, Gill Eatherley showed the three screen work *Aperture Sweep* (1973–1974), where she performed with a broom sweeping the screen. Suddenly you see the same woman performing this piece about twenty-five years later, it appears to be completely different, which means that it poses totally different questions in relation to perception and memory. Exactly this happens with other films as well. I have always liked [William] Raban's installations a lot and at the Whitechapel show I saw a double screen film, *Surface Tension* (1974) which is a wonderful film, astonishing physical double screen black and white film, making and unmaking simultaneously, process and film at once, sound versus image whilst moment to moment materiality, physical and metaphysical, yet endlessly self obliterating of metaphysics and of material without a moment of reductiveness to either. A real film! And astonishing not to have taken in that film of someone who is sitting in the same room at the Co-op twenty five years ago, showing that 'same' film. That can happen too. It just escaped me then, it's there now. Historical in that sense of the present moment to moment real in time.

And this is the next point that I would like to underline right now: that we were not a coherent group in terms of that we knew what everyone else was making or thinking, or that we went home and thought about everything, then somehow theorised everything. In fact it was far more anarchistic, and may probably be the reason why so many people from the journal *Screen* thought of the Co-op as a film practice somehow intuitive, artisanal, romantic. As if that were the only imaginable opposite of their reified academicism. Some of our work was in fact theorized by us to show them that we were actually better than them at materialist theory, at aesthetic politics, and this turned out to be right in the end. For me, this was the perfect proof concerning the difference between the Co-op and academic institutions. And god, we had fights! I'm quite happy though that *Screen* existed. It was one of the necessary contexts for theoretical polemics. This is also the point: defensive polemics as those *Screen* provoked in some of us, especially within me I must say, could be very productive. Later the process shifted from defensive polemics to theory, but the outcome of all this was that some really tried hard to be a little more specific in our writing, make theory and not just consume it. None of this was as one-dimensional as this makes it sound.

Now comes the true last point of this talk, together with the very first point, namely that theory came out of practice. The work of everyone at the Co-op had always been reflected upon by one another, not necessarily the morning after it was made but over a period of say a year or two. This was often the starting point for the next work. And I think that this was a wonderful way of working because on the one hand it was not really personal and on the other hand it was quite personal – because you love it, because you make it. So it was not only the film process as such that was important, in fact it was equally the social process of the making of the films.

Initially the subject that I wanted to talk about the whole hour this afternoon was time. The main experience of experimental film. I have completely forgotten that. No matter which experimental film; it is, if process is present, material time; the viewer viewing is a continuous intervention. The temporality of a projected film is maintained, so is continuous intervention in – and as – the process of spectating, immeasurable possibility, endless. Then it is impossible to repress the time experience whether it be someone's 2 minute or (interrupted-or not) 20 minute or 60 minute film. However seemingly at first incomprehensible, perception maintains. That is what finally brings us all together in this exhibition.

Note

1.   Ed. Matthias Michalka, *X-Screen: Film Installations and Actions in the 1960s and 1970s*, Museum Moderner Kunst Stiftung Ludwig Wein, 13 December 2003 – 29 February 2004, (Koln: Verlagder Buchhandlung Walther Konig, 2004).

Initially transcribed and translated by Claudia Müller Herman.

Chapter three

Films and Installations –
A Systems View of Nature

Chris Welsby

Colour Separation,
16mm film, 1975.

During the 1960s American physicist Edward Lorenz turned his attention to the seemingly mundane field of weather prediction. Devising a mathematical formula known as the Lorenz Attractor, he mapped the course of chaos itself. The study of complex systems such as the weather has since been seen to have applications in all fields of the life sciences and humanities. Systems theory, a science that looks at process and change in response to input from

the environment, sees living systems and social systems in terms of the dynamic relation between the parts and the whole.

Wind Vane, 16mm film, sound, colour, 1972.

Some of the most interesting applications of Systems thought took place in the field of microbiology where a new definition of life found expression in the Santiago theory:

> At all levels of life, beginning with the simplest cell, mind and matter, process and structure, are inseparably connected ... The Santiago Theory (Humberto Mantura and Francisco Varla) proposes a concept of cognition in which the mind as a separate 'thinking thing' is abandoned in favor of a model in which mind is not separate but part of a process, the process of cognition which characterizes the existence of life ... Cog-

27

nition as understood in the Santiago Theory is associated with all levels of life … and … consciousness is a special kind of cognitive process, which emerges when cognition reaches a certain level of complexity … . The relationship between mind and brain, therefore, is one between process and structure.[1]

In this worldview the phenomenon of consciousness is not separate from nature, as it is in Cartesian scientific thought, but is instead an essential part of all biological processes. This new understanding of nature focuses on the relationship between the parts and the dynamic processes where the flow of energy gives rise to new forms, placing human beings and human consciousness back within the complex fabric of nature and not on the outside like some disembodied brain looking in.

Around the same time that complex systems theory was transforming the sciences, a transformation was also taking place in the arts, where the relatively new fields of film and video were beginning to gain ground as radical alternatives to the traditional disciplines of painting and sculpture. In North America the focus of experimental filmmaking appeared to be shifting way from the Surrealist and Romantic traditions of the early European avant-garde. In an attempt to categorize the work of filmmakers such as Michael Snow, George Landow, and Paul Sharits, the American film historian P. Adams Sitney formulated the following definition, which would characterize an entirely new direction in the history of film:

> The structural film insists on its shape, and what content it has is minimal and subsidiary to the outline. Four characteristics of the structural film are its fixed camera position (fixed from the viewer's perspective), the flicker effect, loop printing and re-photography off the screen.[2]

In the UK, where the availability of printing and processing equipment at the London Filmmakers Coop further facilitated this materials based practice, both single screen and multi-screen Expanded Cinema works of Malcolm Le Grice, Annabel Nicolson and William Raban, heralded an entirely new approach to nearly every aspect of film making, film exhibition and film viewing. In the UK structural filmmakers rejected the expressionistic or transcendental elements, still evident in the films of their American colleagues, in favor of a more politicized model rooted in the Kino Eye Manifesto of the early Soviet filmmakers. Inspired by the political upheavals of the 1920s, the Kino Eye filmmakers had rejected the theatrical illusions of the cinema, condemned the passive consumption of filmic illusion, and called for a materialist practice that would inspire a conscious and critically aware audience.

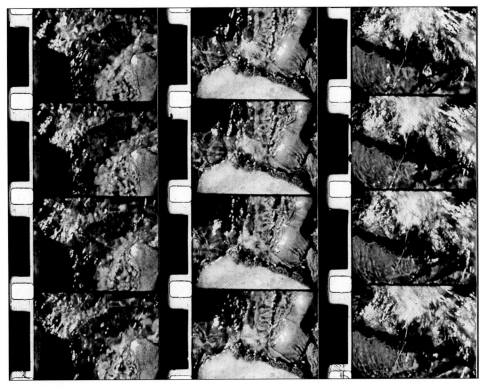

In 1976 Peter Gidal, following in this tradition, described structural materialist film in these words:

Streamline
16mm film, sound, colour, 1976.

> The structuring aspects and the attempt to decipher the structure and anticipate/re-correct it, to clarify and analyze the production process of the specific image at any specific moment, are the root concern of Structural/Materialist Film.[3]

Although structural filmmakers on both sides of the Atlantic began experimenting at that time with landscape imagery, the landscape in these landscape films was usually of secondary importance. As in mainstream narrative cinema and Renaissance painting, where nature is the backdrop to the human drama, the emphasis was primarily on human activity, in this case the filmmaking process. It seemed to me that in these works the processes of film and the processes in nature were still split along Cartesian lines.

An interest in landscape and in the scientific investigation of complex systems in nature, pushed my practice in a very different direction. What interested me about both structural film and complex systems was the possibility of creating work based on the interconnectedness of these systems, where landscape was not secondary to filmmaking process or filmmaking process to land-

29

scape, but process and structure, as revealed in both, could carry information and communicate ideas.

Writing about British experimental films in the summer of 1976, Deke Dusinberre made the following observation about the structural approach to landscape filmmaking:

> The significance of [structural] landscape films arises from the fact that they assert the illusionism of cinema through the sensuality of landscape imagery, and simultaneously assert the material nature of the representational process which sustains the illusionism. It is the interdependence of those assertions which makes the films remarkable – the 'shape' and 'content' interact as a systematic whole.[4]

In my films there is a further significance to this interplay between landscape and filmmaking technology. As Peter Wollen explained:

> The techniques developed by Welsby made it possible for there to be a direct 'indexical' registration of natural phenomena on film. Natural processes were no longer simply recorded from the outside, as objective observation; they could be made to participate in the scheme of observation itself.[5]

In all my films and installations I use the simple structuring capabilities of moving image technologies, such as variable-frame rate, in-camera editing and multiple projection, in combination with natural phenomena such as wind and tides and the rotation of the planet, to produce works in which mind, technology, and nature are not seen as separate things divided along Cartesian lines, but as interconnected parts of one larger dynamic system.

In *Seven Days*, for example, the shape of the film is the result of the interaction between the filmmaker, the equipment, the rotation of the planet and the weather. The camera is aligned with the sun and pans at the same speed as the earth, recording one frame per second from sunrise to sunset. The in-camera editing is governed by cloud cover, by whether the sun is in or out. The final shape of the film is a consequence of the interaction between the more predictable, mechanistic aspects of technology and the less predictable variables of the natural world.

A similar theme emerges in *Park Film*, where the overall pacing is determined by the flow of people along a busy park pathway in London. The flow is determined by the commuter clock (morning and evening rush hours) and by the weather (on a stormy day walking home across the park is considerably less attractive than catching a bus). This is not really a film about a park, or a record of the people passing through the park; the camera is not a passive observer, nor is it used as a surveillance device. In *Park Film* the camera, like the passers-by who trigger its shutter, is an active

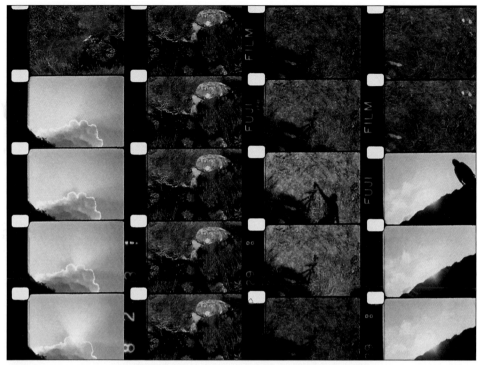

participant, along with the filmmaker and the weather, in the interaction between a park and the city that surrounds it, and it is this interaction that shapes the film. The overall shape created in *Park Film*, and also in *Seven Days*, may be described as an emergent property, a result of the continuous interplay between the cinematic process and the environment.

Seven Days
16mm film, sound, colour, 1974.

The use of technology in my practice is inseparably connected to language. Anthropological research has produced evidence to suggest that tool making and language appeared around the same time in history and that, if so, it is possible that syntax was a product of more complex tool making procedures. When, in my films and installations, I get the wind to crank the camera shutter, use a device to align the camera with the rotation of the earth, or place a video wall on its back, I am dealing not only with tools but also with the language of abstract forms and material processes. These material elements of the film's construction function as syntactic devices that are inseparably connected to the meaning of the work.

Bringing the landscape into a gallery is rather like making a map. The difficulty of representing the limitless expanse of a landscape in the geometric architectural space of the gallery, is conceptually similar to the difficulty experienced by the cartographer who uses the Mercator projection to translate the curvature of the earth onto

31

(Upper): *Windmill #3*, 16mm film, silent, colour, 1974.

(Lower): *Shoreline* 16mm film, sound, colour, six screens, 1977

the flat surface of a chart. In my installation, the process of translation is not registered in lines of latitude and longitude but in the positioning of projectors, screens, and monitors in the gallery.

In the installations, as with the films, both the material process of representation, and the landscape imagery, is crucial to the reading of the work. The recording process in the installations is usually quite simple, perhaps a single, well positioned, continuous take. Instead of fore-grounding the mechanics and positioning of the camera, the equipment used to present the work in the gallery becomes the focus of attention.

In *Shore Line*, for example, a line of six noisy 16mm projectors are prominently mounted on white plinths, where, like an opposing army, they face an image of a pristine line of surf breaking on a sandy beach. The prominence of the projectors, the visibility of the film loops strung from the ceiling, the shadows of the viewer cast on the screen, and the noise of the projectors (the only soundtrack), read in connection with the composite image of the beach, together create a model in which technology, human presence, and the

representation of nature are physical participants in the production of meaning.

Changing Light builds on the model of interactivity that I used in *Park Film*. In this installation motion sensors hooked up to a computer respond to the movement of people in the gallery and this directly affects the surface of a lake, which is projected on a horizontal screen. The DVD recording has eight distinct tracks or 'chapters' corresponding to the eight takes of original footage. The 'chapters' are programmed to alternate in relation to the movement and presence of participant/viewers in the gallery space. In this

(Above): *Shore Line* at the ACME Gallery 16mm film, sound, colour, six screens, 1977.

(Below): *Lost Lake* 16 monitor video wall installation, 1996

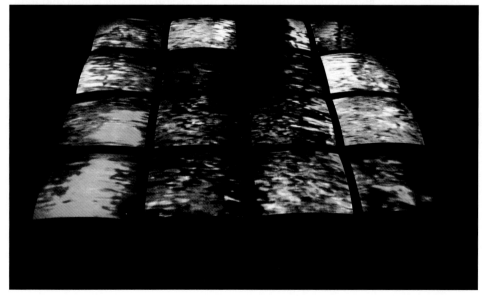

At Sea,
Video projectors,
colour, DVD playback,
4 screen installation,
2003.

installation 'nature', as represented by the lake, is not seen to be separate from the technology that re-produces it or the people who observe it. The viewer is invited to participate in a model in which nature and technology are seen to be one and the same thing, inextricably bound together in a playful dance of colour and light.

In my most recent installation/expanded-cinema piece, *At Sea*, digital technology is used to produce a sort of chart or map, complete with landfalls, lighthouses, channel beacons, and endless expanses of fog and featureless ocean. But there are no fixed points on this map, and any attempt at spatial orientation is made impossible by the relentless shifting of a few ephemeral co-ordinates. My intention was not to create a panorama, a view, or a depiction of homogeneous space, but to create instead a model of mind.

The authors of the Santiago theory propose, 'The world everyone sees ... is not *the world* but a world which we bring forth with others'.[6] In this model of reality, *the world*, Kant's ding an sich, *the world* beyond that which is known by our senses, is not readily available to human perception. It would seem that our perceptions are designed specifically to screen out all but the most essential information and that our only knowledge of *that world* is derived from the internal representation that is continuously being constructed by the cognitive processes that connect our conceptual map to the territory.

In *At Sea*, both filmmaker and viewer participate in the creation of a fictional seascape, in the representation of a subject that is too large to be apprehended in its entirety. It is my hope that this 'bringing forth' of an unknowable subject, in this case the incomprehensible vastness of the ocean, may be read as a metaphor for the process of cognition.

The installations do not bombard the viewer with frenetic action, rapid jump cuts, or bite loads of information. Like the writers of the Kino Eye Manifesto, I prefer to give the viewer the time and the space to consciously engage with the moving image, with its production and with its presentation. With this in mind, I endeavor to create installations where the viewers are encouraged to slow down, take back control of their own thoughts and perceptions; forget about the constraints of beginnings, middles and ends, and enter instead, a state of mind in which reverie and contemplation can play a creative role in the process of conscious thought. It is my hope that in such a space it may still be possible to consider our selves and our technologies, not only in relation to the landscape, but also in relation to the larger more inclusive context of Nature.

Notes

1. Fritjof Capra, *The Hidden Connections* (New York: Anchor Books, 2002), pp. 37–38.

2. P. Adams Sitney, *Visionary Film The American Avant-Garde 1943–1973* (New York: Oxford University Press, Second Edition, 1979), p. 370.

3. Peter Gidal, 'Theory and Definition of Structural/Materialist Film', *Structural Film Anthology* (London: BFI, 1976), p. 1.

4. Deke Dusinberre, 'St. George in the Forest: The English Avant-Garde', *Afterimage* (Afterimage Publishing, London, Summer 1976), p. 11.

5. Peter Wollen, *Chris Welsby: Films/Photographs/Writings* (Arts Council of Great Britain, 1981), p. 2.

6. Fritjof Capra, *The Hidden Connections* (New York: Anchor Books, 2002), p. 54.

Chapter four

A Line Through My Work

Nicky Hamlyn

In this essay I will give an overview of some recurring themes in my films to date. Since each film I make tries to respond specifically to its unique shooting situation, this account cannot be synoptic or exhaustive, but attempts to trace some patterns that have only become apparent retrospectively.

In 1974 I made *Silver Street* whilst a student at Reading University. This four-minute film, which was shot in my room in a house in Reading and the street outside, was based on describing, alternately, a private space and the adjacent public one. The film was organised dualistically around the poles of private/public, enclosed/open, intimate/impersonal, quiet/noisy etc. Its formal problematic arose from the contrasting ways in which the two spaces seemed to demand to be filmed, or, contrarily in this instance, how filming both in the same kind of way would result in very different kinds of shot for inside and outside, and that those differences arose organically from the nature of the two locations. In other words, I came to see the work as arising out of an encounter between a situation or location or subject, and a camera/production strategy – in this case, the same 25mm lens throughout, same framings, parallel cutting between the two spaces – that was suggested by that situation. This led towards the production of a mode of seeing that replaced the anthropocentric point of view of the cinema with the mechanical gaze of the camera. I tried to achieve this in a number of ways, for example, by using identical framings for shots of the same objects. Rather than varying the camera position slightly, which tends to suggest a shifting, and hence human point of view, a repetitive cycle of identical camera positions was intended to suggest a systematically controlled, grid-like, and hence non-anthropocentric point of view. The idea of the film was inspired partly by Robert Morris's reading of Jackson Pollock's paintings as resulting from the interactions of horizontal canvas, liquid paint, stick, gravity, arm mechanics. Morris's behaviouristic take on Pollock rescues it from an expressionistic reading. It points towards an open-ended way of making art, in which, rather than attempting to harness a technology teleologically, it allows the various forces at play in the situation to produce an open-ended outcome whose meaning arises from the light that outcome throws (fortuitously) on questions of matter and perception, here: the experience of 'light moving in time' as the title of William Wees's book on experimental film has it.[1] Paul Sharits, talking about systemic procedures, makes a related statement in his essay 'Words per Page': 'a priori decisions regarding ordering or non-ordering have heuristic value in that surprising forms may emerge from their use which could never be preconceived or developed intuitively'.[2]

In a slightly later three-screen film *Cloister* (1976), these formulations of Morris and Sharits are treated more explicitly. The film permutates a set of triangulated points of view generated by three camera operators; one on roller skates, one running and the third operating a camera on a tripod. The location is a stretch of cloister at the University of Reading's old campus on London Road, and the quadrangle enclosed by it. Each camera points in one of three directions in each of six shots, and shot length is determined by the time it takes to travel the length of the cloister and back again.

Before *Silver Street* I had made a set of films in which a-priori decisions – shooting systems – were used to produce systemic films in which various formal variants of static and moving camera, static and moving subject, were permutated. These were in the form of double-exposed, un-split Standard 8 film (a forerunner of Super 8), which yields four images within the frame when projected as 16mm, and led directly to *FOUR X LOOPS*, (produced in 1974 and presented at 'Experiments in Moving Image'[3] in January 2004). *FOUR X LOOPS* employed a grid form to develop a multi-projector event in which the projector configurations were determined by the possible arrangements of four flashing, diagonal crosses, one to each projector. At the time I saw these films as rather cool and mathematical, in contrast to *Silver Street*, which, with its autobiographical elements, seemed more personal, but now I see them as quite closely aligned, insofar as *Silver Street*, for all that half of it is shot in a personal space, treats its subject disinterestedly, and is not autobiographical, despite the brief appearance of its maker in two shots, since these moments are subsumed by the rhythmic forward march of the film's repetitive ordering and its documentary rationale: a chronological survey of the day in the life of two adjacent spaces.

Nevertheless, from the late 1970s into the early 1990s I made a sequence of relatively long films that, while not explicitly autobiographical, were made in, and inspired by, home. These films; *Inside Out* (1978), *Anagram* (1982), *Ghost Stories* (1983) *That Has Been*

Pistrino,
16mm film, 2003.

(1984), *There Again* (1987–91) and a tape/slide work: *Confessional Fragments* (1983) explored domesticity/domestic spaces in a more extended manner than had been conceivable at the time of *Silver Street*. However, the arbitrarily fictionalising nature of autobiography, and how one might film it, put a stop to this line of work. The stories one constructs about oneself, using shared languages and protocols, the necessarily exclusory, editorial, nature of self-description, combined with the self-censorship incurred by the awareness that one's self-portrait will have a public audience for whom an impression is being created, all seemed to mitigate against anything like an adequate account of self. (In *Experience* (2001), Martin Amis deals with these difficulties by devoting half the book to his dental problems). Ironically, the very quote from *Roland Barthes by Roland Barthes* in which he describes a typical day in his life before going on to denigrate the very idea of autobiography, both appears in *Ghost Stories* and was the text that influenced me to question, and eventually abandon, this kind of filmmaking.[4] After *Ghost Stories* I tried to introduce self-questioning strategies into the work, partly through exploring how representations displace their putative subject. Despite this, however, I felt that I was being drawn into the register of narrative, with its necessary people and characterisation, its mimesis and illusionism, something I wanted to avoid. There

38

are two aspects to this. I was committed to a materialist filmmaking that tries to counter (not avoid) illusionism by challenging its modus operandi. I could not see how that could be made compatible with the world of narrative spaces peopled with ghosts with which one came to form various kinds of identifications. Secondly the manner in which narrative structure follows the rhythm of storyline and dialogue was antithetical to my interest in autonomous structures that could work against, or dynamically with, other elements in a film. There seemed to be no choice between giving in to a camera strategy that simply followed the demands of a narrative, or attempting somehow pseudo-arbitrarily to shoot 'across' the action, sort of ignoring it, but not really. This seemed intellectually incoherent and unjustifiable. I gradually returned to a form of filmmaking in which the relationship between camera and subject is integrated: mutually defining and reflexive.

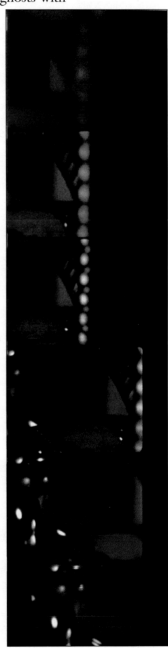

White Light,
16mm film, silent,
1996.

The frame by frame production method of the two Standard 8 films; *Rhythm 1* and *Rhythm 2*, (so named in homage to Hans Richter), and *FOUR X LOOPS* has reappeared in a number of more recent works; *Minutiae* (1990) *White Light* (1996), *Matrix* (1999), *Pistrino* and *Water Water* (both 2003). *Minutiae* was made for the BBC2 arts magazine programme *The Late Show*, which ran from the late 1980s for about six years. It was shot partly frame by frame and with all the dissolves and superimpositions created in-camera. It was made in one four-hour session, on a single roll of 16mm Ektachrome colour reversal film, the kind that was used for shooting news and sport at the BBC until 1983, when current affairs production started to go over to videotape. *Minutiae* partly addressed this history, since it was intended originally that the film would be processed in the BBC's laboratory at Television Centre, edited in one of their cutting rooms and broadcast as an 'on the day', that is, shot and transmitted on the same day.

The work, which is a detailed examination of one of the tubular chrome and black plastic chairs used by the programme for interviews with guests, was programme/site specific, in that it was shot in the studio from which *The Late Show* was broadcast, so that the film would be seen juxtaposed directly with the familiar views generated by the studio cameras when broad-

Rhythm 1,
8mm film, black & white, 1973.

cast. The prioritising of a chair over its (celebrity) occupant was an anti-mimetic gesture, and an affirmation that objects are at least as interesting as people, certainly, at least, in films. In its manner of construction: complex superimpositions, lap dissolves and single frame procedures, *Minutiae* led eventually to *White Light*.

White Light continues the fascination with chrome, its principle subject for twenty-two minutes being a set of chrome-plated bath taps. The film is quite freely structured, but highly controlled, insofar as much of it is made frame by frame. It is a kind of animation, which is partly why there are animated interludes interspersed throughout the film. These are all directly derived (rotoscoped) from the filmed footage, and are intended to be seen as lying somewhere between live action (mechanical images) and drawn animation (hand-made images), in order to pose the question of what kind of drawings are those made by tracing from mechanically generated sources. Additionally, rotoscoped drawings of, say walking humans, have an uncanny quality due to the naturalism of the movements they convey, and I wanted to explore this a little in the context of drawings derived from filmed footage of the visual phenomena generated by inanimate objects, as opposed to the usual people and animals. The idea of the displacement of the putative subject by its representations that drove *That Has Been,* becomes, in *White Light,* a prominent motif in which the displacement is literalised, since the camera lens, in approaching its profilmic object, itself becomes the film's subject.

Matrix returns to *Silver Street's* subject matter of adjacent private and public spaces. The film is constructed in terms of receding planes, of a back garden and the housing beyond it, in which the divide between the private and public sphere, a garden wall topped with wooden trellis, acts as a fulcrum for various spatial elaborations. *Matrix* is both analytical and synthetic. It is analytical in that there is an attempt to explore three-dimensional space through two dimensional planes, invoking Cubist fragmentation, except that the planes are unified around a singular position (not point) of view. The synthetic movement comes about through the re-configuring of the space through shifts in the angle of that point of view, bringing into alignment previously seen elements from earlier, different alignments. The trellis acts as a framing and aligning device, and its form echoes that of the film-strip and the manner in which the film is assembled, that is, in a frame by frame manner.

This film was also an opportunity to question what for me has always seemed a difficult distinction: that between analytic and synthetic as applied to Cubist painting, an approach that has strongly informed films like *Matrix*, with its fragmenting of space into multiple planes and temporal moments. In order to undertake the spatial analysis attempted in *Matrix*, it was necessary to bring into being – to synthesize – images through points of view, camera operations and so on. This is what one is doing in making a shot, unless one subscribes to the naïve view that film simply re-presents its profilmic objects. (Because all painted images are, in a literal sense, synthetic, it is tempting to assume that camera images can be more properly analytical in that that they are not constructed but are disinterestedly, since mechanically, revealing). The 'synthetic' reconfiguring of space, on the other hand, may just as easily be understood as analytical, since the successive formation of new configurations constitutes an exploration of immanent possibilities that yield a further understanding of the space (as profilmic, of course) under consideration. To this extent it may be as much analytical as it is synthetic.

Pistrino is composed entirely of time-lapsed views of a landscape. Most of the shots are medium to extreme close-up, since I was interested not in the kind of large-scale patterns of mundane movement seen in the work of filmmakers like Godfrey Reggio, but in localised movements of light and its interactions with a number of features which manifest themselves as mobile, textured surfaces; sand, weeds, twigs, bushes, stuccoed walls, tree trunks. All the shots are made at the rate of one frame per minute, so that a day lasts for around 28 seconds on screen. The constant shooting rate draws out numerous anomalies: differences of speed and direction of movement that are determined by choice of lens, distance of subject from camera, angle and orientation of objects to the sun and other factors. The shots are framed to maximise the play of off-screen space, or to divide the screen space in various ways. The film tries to push the idea of light moving in time to somehow erode the distinction between objects and the effects they generate. The interactions between the movement of objects and light, shadow and form, evolves continuously. In some shots we see only the shadows cast by off-screen objects, or features whose location, shape and scale appear to alter with the change in light.

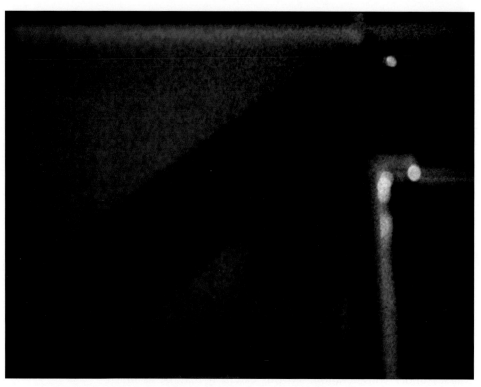

Penumbra,
8mm film, black &
white, 1973.

Thus the film also gestures to, and celebrates, the oldest and simplest form of proto-cinema, shadow play.

If some of this sounds like nothing other than neo-Impressionism, it is important to stress that shots are set-up non-anthropomorphically, in order to forestall any emerging sense of a series of views united around a putative human observer (this anti-anthropomorphism is one of the defining characteristics of many artists'/experimental works). To this end, shot/sequences are separated by black spacing. The camera is programmed uniformly, indifferently recording what is in front of it, so that the film, unlike an Impressionist painting, is not intended, at least, to describe the experience of being in front of a scene, re-presenting that experience of atmosphere through the shifting of colour and light. Instead, the shots are designed to highlight the complexities and ambiguities in any given scene in the world as they arise within a particular set of parameters that includes the apparatus (perhaps this is a difference of emphasis, rather than an absolute distinction). To this end, the film is shot in black and white, diminishing the experience of atmospheric conditions, which depends heavily on colour, and emphasising instead the distribution of light and shadow and the way it gives rise to indeterminacies in the modelling of objects, the way they sit in the landscape, and the degree to which they blend in with their surroundings.

In *Penumbra* (2003), camera strategy and shooting scheme are rigidly determined by the film's subject, a grid of off-white bathroom tiles. The work is formed as a continuously evolving image. In other words it has neither cuts nor dissolves, both of which affect the transition from one shot to another, but exists as a single fixed shot made with a static camera. Thus it invokes the question of what an image is since there is neither a single, fixed image, nor multiple images, insofar as the idea of multiple entails several discreet images. Movement (not motion) occurs through mutations in the image as opposed to camera pans or tilts. In practice these mutations are created through overlapping dissolves that bring in shadows and occasionally objects, which impinge on the uniform, uniformly framed, grid. Informing this idea of movement/mutation are historical examples, such as the zoom in Michael Snow's *Wavelength* (1967) or certain sections of Wilhelm and Birgit Hein's methodical study of filmic pseudo-movement: *Structural Studies* (1974). *Penumbra*'s spatio-temporal grid structure parallels the structure of the film-strip, which is similarly grid-like: spatial in its actual physical form, spatio-temporal in its manner of operation.[5] Here too is a sense in which the work is medium-specific, since video images are presented not as discreet frames, but as an electronic signal composed of a rectangle of horizontal lines of variable luminosity and colour, which are continuously refreshed by an electronic flying spot.

The issue of medium specificity here is raised in a manner that attempts to avoid a concomitant commitment to essentialist characterisations of a medium or a technology. But where a work's concepts and/or structures address, and are informed by, unique features of a given medium, it is surely legitimate to talk about medium specificity. Thus *Penumbra* draws certain parallels between its own form and the form of its medium that would be illegitimate if applied to video. Neither can such a medium-specific approach be dismissed as reductive or essentialist (terms that are often erroneously used interchangeably).

Accusations of reductiveness have often been made by critics whose analysis is itself reductive or in some sense prescriptive and thereby essentialist. Peter Wollen, in his essay 'The Two Avant-Gardes' states: 'The frontier reached by this avant-garde (the 'experimental' as opposed to the poly-semic cinema of Godard et al) has been an ever-narrowing preoccupation with pure film, with film 'about' film, a dissolution of signification into objecthood or tautology.' 'Cinema', Wollen argues, 'is a multiple system'.[6] What Wollen has done here is to identify the alleged abandonment of signification as an innately reductive move. His assertion is based on the proposal that 'Cinema is a multiple system.' Yet films about, notoriously, 'sprocket holes and dirt particles' for example, are always 'about'(or rather, have inscribed in their material forms) many things; light-play, kinesis, rhythm, time and its experience as duration, indexicality, and, so long as a camera is used, representation and reference: 'Film, "motion picture" and "still" film, unlike painting and sculpture, can achieve an autonomous presence without negating iconic reference because the phenomenology of the system includes "recording" as a physical fact'.[7] In other words, all films made with a camera wrestle with questions of representation, even if the film's subject is only a sequence of differently coloured, lightly textured surfaces, as in a work such as Sharits' *Ray Gun Virus* (1966). The second of Wollen's assertions, on which the first is premised, is covertly prescriptive, since it implies that because Cinema is a multiple system, that is what films should be or should aim to be. In other words films should have iconic images, text, soundtracks, representational images, actors etc. But why should films have these things, just because they can and have done? If we abandon the assumption that essentialism entails reduction, Wollen's argument could itself be accused of being tantamount to essentialist, since his prescription that Cinema should be polysemous is based on the fact it has been in films like Godard's *Le Gai Savoir* (1968). This contingent 'has been' is then hardened into necessity, into essence, via prescription. The emphasis on the semiotic is allied here, in the film industry and beyond, to an indifference to the differences between film and video, differences that are technically/procedurally/aesthetically as significant for experimental film and video makers as the difference between water colour, acrylic and oil paint is for painters.

Water Water (2003) revisits the location of *White Light*, consisting of reflections in a single chrome tap. The aim was to make a tightly drawn film, where *White Light* was freely structured. Like *Silver Street*, it is constructed around several opposing forces and formal procedures, some of which map onto each other; pixilation versus mutation, animation versus live action, individually exposed frames versus dissolves, and some which don't: black and white versus colour, movement versus stasis etc. These oppositions are both evident and yet impure in the way they interact with each other. The interactions arise sometimes spontaneously, but also through deliberate permutation of elements – colour, black and white and pixilation for example – and partly through the way the viewer's perception bears on them. One binary opposite is contrary motion which itself arose from an idea about negation, namely, one frame negating its predecessor and/or successor. The presence of mutually negating adjacent frames is also informed by the thought that frames are obliterated, if not destroyed, in the experience of watching flicker films, depending on the kind, or more crucially, degree, of movement or stasis constructed from those individual frames.[8] This constitutes a kind of destructive violence out of which a particular experience is born that is not the experience of frames per se.

What happens to the grid structure here? In paintings the grid is invariably unconcealed, worked-out by the artist as an end in itself or as the foundation for further mark making. Every grid is different, and may be complete and explicit, as in Agnes Martin, implied, as in many of Robert Ryman's paintings, or partial and/or non-uniform, as in Mondrian.[9] In film the grid is an invariant given whose technological/formal characteristics are dictated by industrial conventions. In narrative movies the projected grid unfolds through time, underpinned by a 24 frames per second pulse, but the grid itself is invisible as such, and the pulse barely noticeable because the balance between medium and form is tipped overwhelmingly towards the latter. However, on projection of film that acknowledges the 24 fps base by making it a structuring device in the work, the grid becomes palpably rhythmic – the medium/image is transformed into musical form. In true flicker films, such as Paul Sharits' *Peace Mandala End War* (1965), or passages of *Ray Gun Virus* (1966), the grid underpins the work's form, but at the same time individual frames are obliterated in the perceptual process, subtly affecting the rhythmic pulse. In other words, such works both foreground the grid and engineer disturbances to it, based on an understanding of how the spectator's visual system cannot keep pace with the frame rate. (Given that the presentation of images at the rate of 24 per second is something that does not occur in nature, it is unsurprising that the human visual apparatus has not yet evolved to cope with such phenomena). In Steve Farrer's *Ten Drawings* (1976), in which geometric, abstract drawings were drawn and sprayed onto a large rectangle composed of adjacent strips of 16mm film, the material grid is converted, on projection, into a linear, temporal progression which at the same time refers back to its original spatial form, since it becomes apparent that we are seeing parts of a larger structure unfolding.

In *Water Water*, the grid is made explicit through abrupt, repetitive, incremental shifts between frames, but the frame as part of a grid is not obliterated because the abrupt shifts are small – localised within areas of each frame. The aim is to preserve the visibility of the grid without creating the retinal clashes like those caused by frame shifts in true flicker films.

Hopefully what emerges from this discussion is a notion of films as spatio-temporal grids. Starting from an understanding of film's intrinsically grid-like material form, I have tried to extend this idea into the profilmic in my work. Films become the product of the interactions between the uniform, linear arrangement of frames unfolding through time, and a grid-like profilmic. Seeing the latter as grid-like, often, but not always, depends on identifying recurring or repetitive features in the field of view, which are then used to inform the film's structuring processes. Towels on a washing line, an avenue of trees, windows or a garden trellis can all act as features that prompt a grid-like approach to film structure. Psychological processes, such as habit, and the forming of gestalts, also play an important role here.

Notes

1.   William C. Wees, *Light moving in Time* (University of California Press, 1992).

2.   Paul Sharits, 'Words per Page', *Film Culture 65-66* (Anthology Film Archives, 1978), p. 31.

3.   'Experiments in Moving Image' Old 'Lumiere' Cinema, University of Westminster, Regent St, 25 – 31 January 2004 (London: Epigraph, 2004).

4.   Roland Barthes, *Schedule* in *Roland Barthes by Roland Barthes* (Macmillan, 1977), pp. 81–82. Most of this book is an autobiographical auto/critique of the very idea of autobiography.

5.   The filmmaker Guy Sherwin has pointed out the similarities between *Pistrino*, *FOUR X LOOPS*, Steve Farrer's *Ten Drawings* (1976) and a number of his own *Train Films*. These works were all programmed by Sherwin and screened at Camden Arts Centre, London on 3 November 2004.

6.   Peter Wollen, 'The Two Avant-Gardes', *Studio International*, November/December 1975, reprinted in *The British Avant-Garde Film 1926-1995*, ed. Michael O'Pray (University of Luton press/Arts Council of England, 1996), pp. 137, 141.

7.   Sharits, op. cit., p. 31.

8.   That the illusion of movement in all film depends on the suppression of the frame is the thesis of Garrett Stewart's book *From Frame to Screen: Modernism's Photosynthesis* (University of Chicago Press, 2000). Stewart discusses movies in which photographs and freeze frames appear, drawing attention to the usually unnoticed frame.

9.   Rosalind Krauss discusses these and other examples in her highly polemical essays on the grid in modernist art in 'Grids' and 'The Originality of the Avant-Garde', both in *The Originality of the Avant-Garde and other Modernist Myths* (MIT Press, 1986), pp. 8–22 and pp. 157–162 respectively.

Chapter five

A Few Notes on Filmmaking

Jayne Parker

Although my work is to do with my life, what I film isn't autobiographical. I use film to document images and events, which carry a powerful personal meaning for me. I film things I've seen, or think I've seen. I can't invent these images. They are there already and I must recognise them. Film making for me is about trying to follow through a desire for transformation, and in the end I feel there is really very little I can honestly film.

I use what I understand of film language to express and explore images – everything is image led. I don't use narrative in a conventional way, but I am trying to tell you something. I believe that the visual language of film can show things that I can't find words for.

Most of my work is made on 16mm film. I choose to work on film because of its material qualities – grain, density of black, subtlety of colour and tone and the quality of the projected film image. I like the physicality of film and its mechanical precision. I like the sense of space within the film frame and being able to direct the viewer to what I want them to see.

Until I made my film *K* in 1989, I had always filmed other people. I started being in the films myself when I felt I could no longer ask friends to do the things I wanted them to do. Out of this came the personal importance of witnessing myself doing things. (Now I mainly film other people.)

The documentation of some sort of physical performance or ritual has been at the centre of all my films. I like the drama to come from what I'm filming, to happen in front of the camera. I don't believe I can make an image more interesting than it is by manipulating the film. Things aren't always what they seem. Through filming what is actually there, I hope to discover what lies beneath.

K,
16mm film, 1989.

My whole working process is one of discovery. When I begin filming I don't know what the completed film will look like so I need to keep my options open. This can mean filming a lot of footage – which isn't a very economical way to work – I'm always afraid of failing to notice something. When I begin editing it's almost like beginning again. The film emerges and takes on its meaning, and form, through the process of editing.

Editing has always been very important to me. I like handling the film material, the whole process of cutting the picture image in relation to the sound image, seeing things in close-up detail, the changes in scale of the shots, being able to recreate a sense of 'real

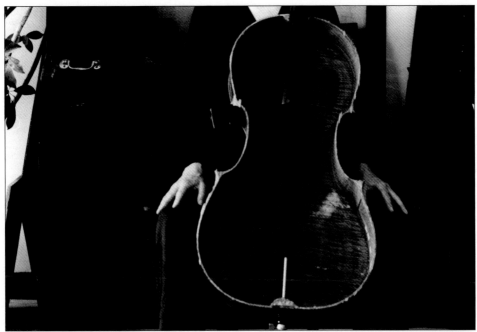

Blues in B Flat, 16mm film, 2000.

Stationary Music, 16mm film, 2005.

521–2 Seconds for a
String Player,
16mm film, 2000.

time', moving between different locations as if they were in the same space, implying dual activities, making connections between seemingly unconnected images or events. I always edit my own films – I couldn't imagine anyone else doing it for me – how could they know what I want?

Music and sound have become increasingly important in my work. For me, music expresses itself visually through the act of being played. I experience a strong similarity between the way music is constructed and the way I try to express ideas through filmmaking. Music allows me to think about film structure in a more formal and abstracted way.

When I first heard pianist Katharina Wolpe play her father Stefan Wolpe's music, I thought it sounded so filmic. There is something I think I recognise in Wolpe's music, which is very close to how I think about film. I would like to do in film what Wolpe does in music.

The drama of musical performance concentrates my act of looking. I am drawn by the act of touch – and then its loss – encapsulated in the sounding of a note. I am trying to make the feel of touch tangible on film. I am entranced by the physical and emotional expression of the musician. The physical act of making music can radically transform someone, visually and emotionally. I am fascinated by the unselfconsciousness of musicians when they are performing, their concentration and vulnerability, often reflected in their faces, and then the moment when they cease to be performers and become themselves again.

(Facing page): *The Whirlpool*, 16mm film, 1997.

Thinking Twice, 16mm black and white, 1997.

I am drawn to the extraordinary visual spectacle that can come about purely because of the musician following or interpreting a composer's score: for example, when cellist Anton Lukoszevieze is required to play with two bows in *Blues in B-flat*, music composed by Volker Heyn. Images occur in music, which I couldn't have imagined.

Question: Can I find a music equivalent, in film?

Chapter six

Film Noise Aesthetics

Rob Gawthrop

Introduction

'... when the spectator hears a so-called realistic sound, he [sic] is not in a position to compare it with the real sound he might hear if he were standing in that actual place. Rather in order to judge its "truth", the spectator refers to his memory of this type of sound, a memory resynthesized from data that are not solely acoustical, and that is itself influenced by films.'[1]

The past thirty years has seen a shift from production to reception and the end of the autonomous object, which had been defined by its intrinsic or formal properties. Cinema, performance and music have interweaving relationships with art, sometimes close but more often diametrically opposed. Noise however, is not an art form but may be positioned within (or outside) an aesthetic/anti-aesthetic dialectic. It is this dialectic and the emergence of noise within post-modernity, and in particular within experimental film,[2] that this essay seeks to address.

Conventionally the presence of noise on film is *unwanted* except when used in specific contexts as semblance. The use of noise however in experimental film had been used both as a neo-dadaist gesture and for making the materiality of the medium perceptually tangible. Here, the process of making was foregrounded and the meaning residing in a theoretical and oppositional conceptual domain, not phenomenological or perceptual. The *experience* of the work however, belied in many cases the makers intent. Much of this earlier work has become, through time and repetition, interesting to listen to for the sound itself, its relation to image and in a broader artistic and theoretical context.

The silent film, or rather film that did not have a combined soundtrack (generally pre 1930s) relied on live music, narration, effects or phonograph records as accompaniments. However the deliberate use of silence, especially in experimental film has been used: a) as a distancing device, for example Peter Gidal's *Room Film*

(1973); and b) to bring closer the consciousness of self, such as Stan Brakhage's *Act of Seeing with One's Own Eyes* (1971). Such deliberately mute films operate similarly to John Cage's seminal *4'33"* (1952) in the sense that the sounds occurring at the time of projection are those that accompany the film. The presence of these ambient sounds would generally be considered as noise, such as traffic rumble, projector noise, speaker hum etc. Interruptions, such as coughing, squeaky seats, doors banging etc., would not normally be considered as part of the work, they would be incidental and unless unduly intrusive, ignored. The contemporary Hollywood feature film makes occasional use of silence but purely for dramatic effect, never as a space for contemplative thought. The complex sound design in contemporary Hollywood films uses a loud mix of music, effects, and natural sounds that accumulate to produce noise to *silence* everything except dialogue. There can be no *listening*, only unconscious and pre-determined emotional response.

Context and history

Until the invention of the phonograph no one had heard reproduced sound before, except through imitation or momentary echoes and reverberations. The profound effect of this has only recently become recognised since easy access to recording devices, and the promotion of sound art and the simultaneous availability of critical texts. The development of what may be called aural culture did have a somewhat inauspicious start. The original 'Grammophon' company of the nineteenth century, had a trade-mark of an angel inscribing grooves on a disc with a quill.

> 'the unmistakable physiognomy of an individual's unique voice; a procedure quite similar to hand written documents produced in a culture centred around writing. It was hardly a coincidence that in 1909 this trademark was retired in favour of the dog Nipper, listening patiently to the mechanical voice of his master. The record had become mass medium – music's servant, not its initiator'.[3]

In the early nineteen twenties Laszlo Moholy-Nagy perceived the potential of the phonograph as an instrument of production and proposed a *groove alphabet* and system of graphic symbols to denote or score the sounds that such grooves would produce. Similar approaches were taken later regarding the optical sound system. Oskar Fischinger (among others) painted paper scrolls and photographically reduced and printed them onto the sound area on 35mm film. The actual sounds produced (along with contemporary modernist composers) were rooted within the overly formalistic traditions of western classical music.[4] Their experiments regarding abstract relations of sound and image were generally derived through misconceived principals based upon theories about synaesthesia.[5] Daphne Oram used the optical sound system in her invention of *Oramics*.[6] This was an early synaesthesia and sampler using 35mm film. Sounds produced by her were used in many TV programmes and feature films.

Walter Ruttman, better known for the abstract *Opus* series and *Berlin Symphony of a City* made *Weekend* (1932), which used optical film recording to document a weekend in Berlin. This concentrated on the noises of the city, edited together to form a poetic soundscape. This imageless film was shown (broadcast) on Berlin radio.[7]

The music concrete composer Pierre Schaeffer reclaimed the term 'acousmatic' from ancient Greece to affirm listening without the distraction of the visible. His intention of using location recordings was more for the purpose of discovering *new* sounds by editing and mixing (using shellac discs at first). The intention of separating the sound from its source was to enable the listener to focus on the abstract qualities of the sound and its musical structure. His *Etude aux Chemins de Fer* (1948) however, never quite loses its source and the title is a bit of a give-away.[8] The use of discs was taken up in the 1960s by the Czech artist Milan Knizak who cut up several discs, painted them and glued them back together in different combinations. More recently Christian Marclay adopted similar strategies, but also with the intention of being able to play them. His *Record Without a Cover* (1985) accumulates dirt and scratches over time, adding to the texture of its own sound.

Dziga Vertov originally studied music and became involved with the Russian avant-garde. Aware of Russolo's *Art of Noises* and the Russian socialist slant on futurism he attempted to utilise both wax and disc recording equipment for recording the audible world but became dissatisfied with the poor sound quality and turned to film.[9] It was when the new film sound recording technology became available that Vertov was able to explore relationships between sound and image particularly in *Enthusiasm – Symphony of the Donbas* (1930). This film, is particularly famous for its location recordings of whistles, horns, hammers, trains, radios etc., and its mix of asynchronous and synchronous sound (or in contemporary terms, acousmatic and diegetic sound). *Enthusiasm* also blurred the divisions between location (natural) sound, noise and music.[10] The politics of making *music* from noises of industrial labour is in direct opposition to the Italian Futurists' celebration of the noises of war and machines. The sounds of labour are integral to many non-western participatory traditions of music and such sounds have influenced much western popular music including the uses of technology in guitar distortion, dub and hip-hop.

Simple things and every-day actions were also central to the loose grouping of artists known as Fluxus. It was Fluxus and its antecedents that brought both the conceptual and the performic to the gallery, the cinema and the concert hall. In La Monte Young's *Poem for Tables Chairs Benches etc*, (1960) the performers' instructions were to make continuous sound by moving the tables, *chairs*, benches etc., across the floor. The resulting scraping is ordinary and direct, with no mystification, but the experience of what is seen and heard is far from ordinary, the cacophonous assault was a shock yet during the work's duration the listener's perceptions shifted to appreciate the sounds themselves. With this, as with many flux events, the score consisted of instructions for an action or actions to be carried out, the *music* produced was *incidental*.

> 'The musicality inherent in the Event, then while critiquing mainstream Western epistemology, also deconstructs the reification, totalization and reductionism of secondary knowledge formations (the disciplines of art history, musicology, philosophy and literature for example).'[11]

The close links between musicians and filmmakers around Fluxus included Tony Conrad, Henry Flynt, Paul Sharits, Yoko Ono, Charlotte Moorman and Nam June Paik. Collaborations such as these were widespread in the underground and the avant-garde generally. As well as being part of *The Theatre of Eternal Music* with La Monte Young and the early incarnations of the *Velvet Underground*, Tony Conrad, John Cale and Angus McClise contributed music for Jack Smith's films and performances. The 'earthquake orgy' scene in *Flaming Creatures* (1962) incorporated screaming, rumbling percussion and tape delay. One of the screamers was the poet Piero Heliczer who, as well as performing in many Warhol films, had also made *Autumn Feast* (1960) in the UK with Jeff Keen. The sound poet Bob Cobbing also worked with Jeff Keen to produce the aural assault of *Marvo Movie* (1967), the noise levels were upped further in the *Blatz/Ray Day* expanded cinema events with collaged live and recorded material using megaphones, signal generators, found sounds, war film soundtracks, newsreels and distorted narration. 'The Destruction In Art Symposium' (D.I.A.S.) London, 1966 organised through Gustav Metzger also included Yoko Ono, Wolf Wostell, Kurt Kren plus many of the Viennese actionists and others. This revolutionary politicisation of destruction, anti-war and anti-capitalism could not be easily dissociated from its noise. Such poetry of destruction echoed the scene in Bunuel/Dali's *L'Age D'Or* (1930) of a violin being kicked down the street or of Nam June Paik's *One for Violin Solo* (1962) where the violin is raised extremely slowly above a table and then brought down with great force. More recently Christian Marclay's *Guitar Drag* used a van with amplifier to drag a connected electric guitar over various surfaces until it disintegrated. In Paul Sharits *T.O.U.C.H.I.N.G* (1968) a subtly changing loop by the poet David Frank seems to shout DESTROY, other phrases seem to emerge out of the noise and the strobing subliminal images. In David Critchley's video *Pieces I Never Did* (1979) he shouts SHUT UP until he is hoarse, in one section he talks about how anything written can be obliterated by writing 'apples' over it and demonstrates by eating an apple while talking.

Reappraisal

'Experiments in Moving Image' (University of Westminster, London, 2004) and 'Expanded Cinema – Film as Spectacle, Event and Performance' (Hartware, Phoenixhalle, Dortmund, 2004) prompted a reappraisal of work. The structural approach to film had tended to be theorised in relation to language, the visual and the problematic of representation. Much work that was frequently lumped within this *structuralist* film bracket was artistically affirmative and not dependent upon such a reductionist anti-narrative polemic. The context of event and the consequent immediacy of the viewing/listening experience were central to the meaning of such work. Sound (noise) and image relations were integral. Sound was not an applied soundtrack used as a comforting adjunct to the visual explorations, it was integral.

Integrated cinema

Wilhelm & Birgit Hein's *Doppelprojektionen V* (1972) uses the live effect – recorded onto film – of a contact mike on a TV screen with a rolling imageless picture. From what appears to be an anti-television, anti aesthetic gesture becomes through repetition and the need to *listen*, compulsive; nuances of sound within the electronic abrasions open up ears previously deafened by the incessant talking heads of mainstream television. Their *Roh Film* (1968), a complex collage of glued scraps of film, hairs and dirt; created the feeling of an aggressive attack on the audience by the projector. It is the noise and rapid incoherence of the imagery that gives the impression of violence. William Raban's *Surface Tension* (1976) appears as fluctuating flickering rectangles of simultaneous oscillating frequencies. Sound as image, image as sound, film as noise as music. Similarly Lis Rhodes *Light Music* (1975) used projections & speakers at opposite ends of the space; film, of mainly horizontal bars of various widths, stationary or moving up or down the picture frame, simultaneously produced tonal noise. Tony Conrad *Ten Years Alive on the Infinite Plain* (1972) projected four loops of alternating (flickering) vertical black & white stripes on a zigzag screen with a live drone played by four musicians. The meaning of this work did not depend on knowledge of its production, it took place before our eyes and ears. Work that used recordings to juxtapose against the image often included noises of nature, the crashing of the sea, fire, thunder and so on. Running water (natural and artificial) has figured in many works: George Brecht's *Drip Music* (1959),[12] Joyce Wieland (with Michael Snow) *Dripping Water* (1969), David Hall (1 of) *7 TV Pieces* (1971) where the TV screen appears to fill with water, Chris Welsby *Streamline* (1976), Joanna Millett *Watercolour* (1982) and Katie Woods *Drip* (2004). This uses ambient sound from a different space to trace the trajectory of each drip (which are seen forming and leaving the ceiling) silenced by the plop of its unseen impact. Taka Ilmura played with our perceptions in *One Frame Duration* (1977): placing a single frame of white between black frames or black between white; with, or without, an audible toneless blip. Our anticipations are confirmed or denied in real time. Wojciech Bruszewski explored sound and image through (de)synchronising with *Test* (1975), where a matchbox is repetitively tapped on a ledge, the synchronisation moved out one frame at a time until the sound and image appear to coincide. In *Yaaa* (1973) a number of yells are edited together to make one continuous sound and *Text Door* (1974) which uses a squeaky door reminiscent of Pierre Henry's music concrete *Variations for Door and a Sigh* (1963).[13] A similar use of rigorous editing and other forms of processing but applied to conventional musical instruments, producing aural and visual relationships, rhythms, unusual harmonics and different timbres; were used in Jenny Okun's *Cows in the Gate, Rounds* (1977) and *Camera Piece for Sunlight and 45 Fingers* (1981); Joanna Millett's *Notes* (1986), *Quartet* (1989), *Grey* (2000), *85 Piano Notes* (2001); and Andrew Quinn's recent work.

Chris Garratt in *Romantic Italy, Versailles* and *Short Ends* (1975–77) reprinted found footage using a lightbox to achieve repetitions of image and corresponding sound. This produced continually shifting relations between the signification of the original material, noise and music. Andy Moss in *Film Sound* (1984) optically printed short looped sections of found film together with their soundtrack areas and overlaid them in varying permutations, much like Steve Reich's early tape pieces, but without regard to tonality or conventional rhythm. Guy Sherwin extended the strategy of printing image onto the soundtrack area by considering what sound the imagery would produce. In *Musical Stairs* (1977) the perspective effect of iron steps making the lines of the steps smaller and closer together when at a greater distance away from the camera caused predicable changes of pitch in the noise produced. Similarly in *Soundtrack* (1977) railway lines merge and separate as the train changes speed and junctions are passed, the sound changing in pitch and loudness accordingly.

Pre digital video lent itself to the audio-visual: the sound and image of fast forward and re-wind, visual snow, white noise, hums, hiss, dropout and feedback. Tony Sinden made much use of this in his *Video Vacuum* performed at *The Video Show*, Serpentine gallery (1975). The work of Woody & Steina Vasulka explored relationships of sound and image through video & electronics, Chris Meigh Andrews in *Horizontal and Vertical* (1978) generated sound and image directly from the equipment. At the time the visual and aural aesthetics of such work was not the primary consideration, and a modernist position (i.e. video as video; film as film), was to the detriment of something that was actually more expansive and profound.

Alvin Lucier's music clearly parallels such strategies, and in particular his *I'm Sitting in a Room* (1970) and *Bird and Person Dying* (1975), were compositions that dealt with the acoustic properties of space using microphones speakers and feedback. Others included Lou Reed's *Metal Machine Music*, Toshimaru Nakamura and his *no input mixing desk* and many other Japanese noise people. The currently fashionable *Glitch Music*[14] has simultaneously focussed attention on sounds not usually listened to, with some works being on the threshold of audibility. Billy Roisz works with noise and glitch musicians and uses live computer processed video feedback in collaborative performances. Pete McPartlan makes use of 'cheap' video and sound equipment, the signals from which effect each other as in *Decay* (2004) where keyboard, camera, monitor and speaker become interdependent.

Personal

In 1976 at the 'Festival of Expanded Cinema' I performed a film event *Eye of the Projector*[15] and now, simultaneous to my work in *Automated Noise Ensemble* with Bob Levene, I am working with the *Ear* of the Projector at various Cinematic Events. Exploring the sounds of worn and partly fogged film with several speakers and contact microphones, investigating visual and aural response differences for live sound with pre-recorded images and making short live noise/music interruption as with *Poplar Cinema* (1998).

Post-script

Noise and its radical use in film has been largely unrecognised but now the emergence of noise, through music and the related theoretical work, has at last started to critically develop our thinking and listening.

'More than colours and forms, it is sounds and their arrangement that fashion societies. With noise is born disorder and its opposite: the world. With music is born power and its opposite: subversion. In noise can be read the code of life, the relations among men.'[17]

Notes

1. Michel Chion, *Audio-Vision – Sound on Screen* (Columbia University Press, 1990), Chapter 5 'The Real and the Rendered'.

2. I have used the terms 'Film' and 'Experimental Film' not only because of them being directly connected to a pre-electronic area of practice but also to pertain to 'artists' film & video', 'cinematic art', 'time-based art', 'media art' etc., I don't want such terms to be either exhaustive nor delimiting.

3. Michael Glasmeier, *Music of the Angels* from *Broken Music* (Artists' Recordworks, 1989), Berliner Künstlerprogramm des DAAD & Gelbe Musik Berlin.

4. The tradition of *prescription* of pitch and harmony developed from Pythagorous through equal temperament and continues with serialism.

5. Misconceptions of synaesthesia in the sense of the applied use of invented equivalents: pitch to colour: or tone to shape for example.

6. See Hugh Davies tribute: http://www.sonicartsnetwork.org/Oram/oram.html

7. This is available on a 3" CD on METAMKINE a label based in Grenoble specialising in music concrète and other experimental music. Metamkine is also a cinematic improvisation trio of Jérôme Noetinger, (electro acoustic composition), Christophe Auger and Xavier Quérel (16mm projectors). Through the use of analogue sound equipment, mirrors and multiple projectors they create live aural and visual noise.

8. Thanks to Mark Sinker for this point in his presentation 'Blips, Blizzards and Biology NoiseTheoryNoise#2', 2004, University of Middlesex.

9. Derived from writings by Dziga Vertov quoted in Douglas Kahn, *Water Noise Meat* (MIT Press, 1999), Chapter 5. This includes detailed information regarding sound and the Russian revolutionary film.

10. There is a not dissimilar blurring in Louis & Bebbe Barron's soundtrack of *Forbidden Planet* (1956), where the electronic music, the soundscape and the sounds of the technology are at times indistinguishable.

11. Hannah Higgins, *Fluxus Experience* (University of California Press, 2002), p. 55.

12. *Drip Music (Drip Event)* For single or multiple performance. A source of dripping water and an empty vessel are arranged so that water falls into the vessel. George Brecht (1959).

13. Harmonia Mundi (1987).

14. *Glitch Music* refers to music that makes use of *unwanted* sounds produced through digitising and processing.

15. See Nicky Hamlyn, *Film Art Phenomena* (BFI, 2003), pp. 32, 65.

16. Ed. Jacques Attali, *Noise: Political Economy of Music* (Minnesota Press, 1985).

Chapter seven

Line Describing A Cone and Related Films

Anthony McCall

This text was originally given as a talk at the Whitney Museum of American Art on December 6, 2001, one of the 'Seminars With Artists' series that accompanied their exhibition 'Into The Light: The Projected Image in American Art 1964–1977'. It was originally published in the winter 2003 issue (no. 103) of the quarterly journal *October* and reprinted in the Mead Gallery catalogue 'Anthony McCall: Film Installations' (2004). This is a shorter version of the original text.

Line Describing a Cone

Line Describing a Cone was made in August 1973, a few months after I sailed from England to the United States. I had been thinking about it for nearly a year in London, I conceived it mid-Atlantic, and I produced it in New York. By 1973, I had already made a number of short 16mm films, but *Line* was the first in which I was able to implement the ideas I had been developing about the relationship between audience and work, and about film as a medium. Here is a slightly edited version of a brief statement I made about the film at the time:

> Line Describing A Cone is what I term a solid light film. It deals with the projected light beam itself, rather than treating the light beam as a mere carrier of coded information, which is decoded when it strikes a flat surface.

The viewer watches the film by standing with his, or her, back toward what would normally be the screen, and looking along the beam toward the projector itself. The film begins as a coherent pencil of light, like a laser beam, and develops through thirty minutes into a complete, hollow cone.

Line Describing a
Cone,
16mm film, 1973.

Line Describing a Cone deals with one of the irreducible, necessary conditions of film: projected light. It deals with this phenomenon directly, independently of any other consideration. It is the first film to exist in real, three-dimensional space.

This film exists only in the present: the moment of projection. It refers to nothing beyond this real time. It contains no illusion. It is a primary experience, not secondary: i.e., the space is real not referential; the time is real, not referential.

No longer is one viewing position as good as any other. For this film, every viewing position presents a different aspect. The viewer therefore has a participatory role in apprehending the event: he or she can, indeed needs, to move around relative to the slowly emerging light-form.[1]

I would add that when the film is watched from start to finish by an audience – more than just a few individuals, say thirty or forty people – then a second level of interaction occurs, this time between members of the audience with one another. Within the dark room, the individual audience members have to negotiate the space in relation to one another so that they can all see the light-form. Paradoxically, the more people that are present, the more 'solid' the form becomes; I am always impressed by how much respect is accorded to the surface of this giant cone so that it is not obscured from sight for someone else. Since what happens at each screening between the different members of the audience is unique, perhaps it isn't really stretching a point to see the screenings as a type of participatory performance.

Until the 'Into the Light' exhibition,[2] *Line Describing a Cone* had always been shown theatrically, which is to say that an audience assembled at a certain precise time to watch the film together. Knowing that one 'has' an audience for a certain complete block of time makes it possible to control the film's disclosure within that time period: the time can be manipulated as a plastic element. This, plus the fact that a group of people are experiencing the event together, creates a unique intensity. However, from the public's point of view, theatrical screenings have the disadvantage of poor access. The solution for 'Into the Light' was to show the film continuously within a dedicated room as an installation. Once the film was over, it started again immediately, and in this way it ran continuously throughout the day. Sometimes there would be one person there, alone, other times five or six at the same time, sometimes nobody at all. This created a more 'ambient' experience, closer to that of individuals coming and going through a museum room to look at a piece of sculpture. In terms of access, this solution was extraordinarily successful. A very large number of people were able to see the film during the three months that the show was up. It meant, of course, that visitors came into the room at entirely different moments during the film's unfolding, and as is conventional in a museum, they chose how long they would give it. Some came and went after a few moments, while others saw it through to completion, and even waited to see it from the start so that they could see it all the way through. At first I viewed this as a distortion of the intended experience. Now I'm not so sure. I think that perhaps it is just another version of the film.

Given a choice of rooms and projector lenses, *Line Describing a Cone* can be projected at any number of sizes. However, I prefer that this occur within certain limits. There are two dimensions to be considered: the length of the form (the distance between the projector and the projection surface) and the width of the cone at its base, where it strikes the wall. Thanks to different types of lenses, these can be considered separately. The length is ideally somewhere between thirty-five and sixty feet long. I prefer the base of the cone to be some eight or nine feet tall, starting at about a foot off the floor. The body is the important measure. Standing inside the cone near its base at the wall, where it is at its tallest dimension, the body should be completely subsumed within it. With outstretched arms it should not be quite possible to touch the upper surface. From there, if one walks down the cone toward the projector, it slowly diminishes in size until the body simply emerges out of it, arriving finally at the apex of the cone at the lens of the projector. Behind the lens, clearly visible on the film as it passes through the gate of the projector, is the miniature two-dimensional circle that generates the three-dimensional form.

These issues of scale and the body, and of moving around a three-dimensional object in a three-dimensional space, are, of course, sculptural issues, and part of the resonance of the experience of looking at them is drawn from this. However, unlike sculptural materials such as steel, lead, wood, latex, felt, etc., light has no solidity, and no gravity. In addition, the explicit control of disclosure over time, the representation of movement, the interchangeability of forms through editing, and the fact that these works have to be viewed in the dark – these are all properties of cinema. In the end, the experience of *Line Describing a Cone*, and the pieces that followed, depends equally on their relationship to both sculpture and to film.

Visibility is also an issue. These pieces are visible in three-dimensional space because the projected light is reflected off tiny particles in the air. In the days when they were made, loft spaces were grittier and dustier than they are now, being then much closer to their earlier lives as sites for manufacturing or warehousing; the same was true of the downtown exhibition spaces. When I projected a film then, I could rely on the dust particles in the air, which would often be augmented by a couple of smokers. Since then exhibition spaces have become cleaner, and smoking has been prohibited. Fortunately, technology has caught up, and we now thicken the air with a small fog machine, which actually does a far more effective job of making visible the planes of light.

In 1974, the year after it was completed, *Line Describing a Cone* was shown a number of times. In New York it was screened at the then quite young Artists Space, as part of their Artists as Filmmakers series curated by Alida Walsh; at The Clocktower, as part of their 'Works: Words' exhibition; at Millennium Film Workshop, in a program shared with David Hall; and at a screening jointly organized by Film Forum and The Collective For Living Cinema. In England that same year, *Line Describing A Cone* was screened at The Royal College of Art Gallery, where Roselee Goldberg was the curator; at the Museum of Modern Art in Oxford, which at the time was directed by Nic Serota; at The London Filmmakers Cooperative, where I shared the program with Carolee Schneemann; and at Garage Art, a contemporary art gallery in Covent Garden, as part of a program which included the films of artists Tim Head and David Dye. These eight institutions provide a good snapshot of how these films, from the very start, straddled two different but intersecting worlds, that of the general artworld and that of avant-garde film.

In recent years, the artworld has paid a lot of attention to work in film and video, yet the dichotomy between avant-garde film- (and video-) makers, and artists 'working in film/video' still seems to be with us. Despite the important role being played by museums such as the Whitney in bridging this divide, the two worlds sometimes seem like Crick and Watson's double helix, spiraling closely around one another without ever quite meeting.

In New York, both Millennium Film Workshop and The Collective were to be particularly hospitable to my work over the next few years. They were the two downtown institutions most devoted to avant-garde film. Millennium was founded by filmmakers Ken and Flo Jacobs in 1966, as a place for both production and exhibition. It continues to this day, slightly expanded to include video. The Collective, founded six or seven years later, was started by a group of young filmmakers who had just completed their studies under Ken Jacobs at Binghampton. The other downtown institution was Anthology Film Archives, founded by Jonas Mekas. As well as showcasing new work, Jonas, and P. Adams Sitney, created Anthology's controversial pantheon of 'essential cinema', which they showed (and still show) in repertory.

The year after making *Line Describing a Cone*, I made three additional films. These were short, either ten or fifteen minute works. *Partial Cone* explored the modulation of the surface of a projected beam of light, creating a range of surface qualities from solid, through glimmering, flickering, and blinking, to flashing. These were created by subtracting a certain number of image frames per second in a series of timed steps. *Cone of Variable Volume* was a conical form, which expanded and contracted in volume, like a lung. The rhythmic movement is imperceptible at first, and progressively accelerates in speed. *Conical Solid* sets up a flat blade of light rotating from a fixed central axis.

All of these films were made using very simple animation techniques. Each of them started with a simple line-drawing, created with white gouache and a ruling pen on black paper. The line-drawing was then placed under the camera, where I shot it, one frame or a few frames at a time, each time moving the line a fraction to the next position. The secret of moving pictures is, of course, that there are no moving pictures. The motion is an illusion. Each second of projected time is made up of twenty-four still images. Projected, the retina of the eye cannot distinguish between them and it combines the separate images into a continuous movement. Animation is simply the process of creating such an illusion of movement using a drawing as an image source.

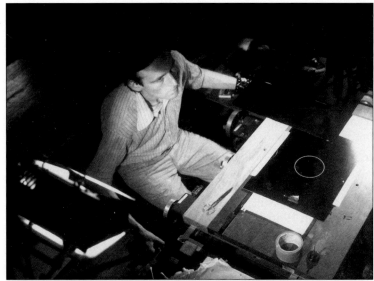

An animation stand has its camera attached to a vertical post, pointing down onto a flat table. The post is calibrated to move up and down, and the table is calibrated to rotate under the camera or move side to side beneath it. In the case of *Conical Solid*, it was easier for me to create my own calibrations. The drawing from which I shot the film was little more than a white line rotating on a pin, with the points of the compass, so to speak, set out around it. The photograph of myself, working at the animation stand, was taken when I was shooting *Cone of Variable Volume* in 1974. In that particular case, the entire film was shot from one single drawn circle; the animation was created by moving the camera toward the drawing and away from it, in minute steps, shooting a precise number of frames at every position. It must be remembered, of course, that in my case, what one sees on the film, and what I drew to shoot from, corresponds only to what one would see on the wall when the film is projected. But when I made it I was really thinking about what was being created in the space between the wall and the projector. The strip of film acts like a kind of stencil, blocking most of the light except for a simple line, or a plain circle, which in three-dimensional space represents a flat triangular blade or a complete volumetric cone.

Long Film For Four Projectors

Toward the end of 1974, I completed *Long Film for Four Projectors*. This was a much larger-scale piece than any of the four *Cone* films. Also, it was conceived not for a theatrical screening to an assembled audience, but as a continuous installation, where individual visitors would come and go in their own time.

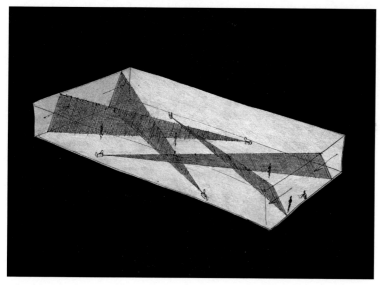

Long Film for Four Projectors, 16mm film, 1974, Installation drawing.

I had been doing live performances for the previous few years in various locations in the countryside, most of them in England. These landscape pieces involved a matrix or grid whose points were defined by small fires. The fires burned for only a few minutes at a time, and they were sequenced to create shifting configurations within the grid. The pieces started off being ten or fifteen minutes long, but I kept gradually increasing their length. I came to realize that the duration of a time-based work could be a determining factor in how the work was looked at. A short performance presupposed an audience that assembled at the same moment to witness it. This in turn created the expectation of a quasi-theatrical event. Extending the temporal structure through the day, on the other hand, defused that expectation and created a set of more or less individual visitors. In addition, opening up the matrix, making it more widely spaced, set up a field that could encompass and surround the visitors. Taken together, these changes created a quieter, lower-key relationship between the execution of the event and the watching of it. I wrote then, that 'The work ceased to be a "performance" with a perceivable beginning and end, with boundaries like an art object, but became rather a condition of the space, as is a high wind, a building, or the activity of a building site'.[3] The last of these pieces, *Fire Cycles*, was the longest, with a duration of twelve hours. It was done in Oxford. After returning to New York, I began preparing for the production of *Long Film for Four Projectors*. I had some of the same ideas in mind.

Long Film is intended as a gallery installation. It requires a large room, preferably one at least seventy feet in length. Installed, the film creates a three-dimensional field out of four, flat, interpenetrating planes of light, which sweep repeatedly through their individual arcs of space and through one another. Spatially, this film is very different from the four *Cone* films. Each of these presents a single volumetric object, which occupies the center of a surrounding space. In *Long Film*, there is a *field* created by the film. It surrounds the visitor. As long as you are in the room, you are within the film. Every point in the room presents a different aspect; it's necessary to walk around, to pass through the planes of light. It can't all be taken in at one glance. The film is in constant motion. It is composed out of the shifting relationships between each of the four planes: their speed of movement, the direction in which they travel, the orientation of each plane to the perpendicular, and the modulation of their surfaces.

One complete cycle of *Long Film for Four Projectors* lasts about six hours. As I noted at the time, this was so as to create 'not an audience as a single, present group occupying a common experiential time, but one that is irregularly spread over the duration of the presentation. Decisions as to when to come, how to approach the work, how long to remain, rest with the individual.'[4] The six-hour length of *Long Film* is built on the repeated showing of only four forty-five-minute reels, one for each projector. There are actually eight forty-five-minute sections to the film (with a pause between each section to change the reels), each slightly different from the other seven. It takes eight reel changes to exhaust the permutations.

The permutations have to do with the nature of a strip of film and its relationship to the film projector. Film frames, twenty-four still images per second, are arranged sequentially down a flat strip. This strip is drawn through the projector gate and past the projector lamp, at an even speed. The light from the lamp passes through each frame, and a lens throws an enlarged version of the image onto the screen. Now, if the image is of a person or place or a written caption, there is a correct way round, and a right way up, for the film strip. For instance, imagine a film sequence that shows, say, a woman walking along carrying a written placard. It will be apparent that something is wrong if the writing on her placard looks like mirror writing; it will seem even worse if she is upside down and walking backward, even if the writing is legible. It will be worse still if she is upside down, walking backward, and carrying mirror writing.

The projector itself is quite indifferent to all this. Mechanically, the ribbon of film can pass through the projector in two directions – from head to tail or from tail to head; and in each direction, the image can be viewed from either of the two sides. So, assuming that the film carries no soundtrack, this translucent strip can be run through the projector in four, equally correct ways. The diagrams will perhaps give an idea of how the repetitions and interchanging of the reels of *Long Film* create different spatial movements.

Long Film for Four Projectors was shown four times: at the London Filmmakers Co-op in 1975, at Millennium Film Workshop and the Neue Galerie, Aachen, in 1976, and at Documenta VI in Kassel, in 1977.

Four Projected Movements

The following year, in 1975, I made *Four Projected Movements*. This used only a single projector. The film was a distillation of the structural idea underlying *Long Film*. This time, there are four different movements, each created by the same fifteen-minute reel of film. The reel is passed through the projector in each of the four possible ways.

This film addressed the architectural space itself. The projector was positioned on the floor, in a corner of the room, so that the adjacent wall and the floor established the boundaries of the space through which the beams would travel. The four drawings show how each slow sweep of the plane of light through ninety degrees acts quite differently on the three-dimensional corner space. What can't be shown is the way these movements act on the body. Representing a slow transition through ninety degrees, from vertical to horizontal, the plane of light variously makes one feel *pushed* in different directions. In the first movement, you feel pushed down from the outside into the floor; in the second, pushed into the wall from above; in the third, pushed down, and out, from the wall; and in

Four Projected Movements (Parts 1–4), 16mm film, 1975, Installation drawing.

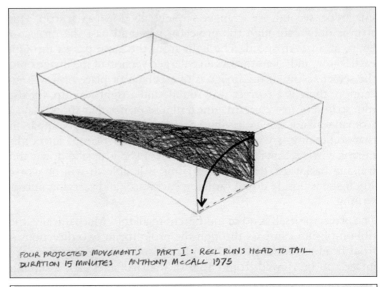

FOUR PROJECTED MOVEMENTS PART I : REEL RUNS HEAD TO TAIL
DURATION 15 MINUTES ANTHONY McCALL 1975

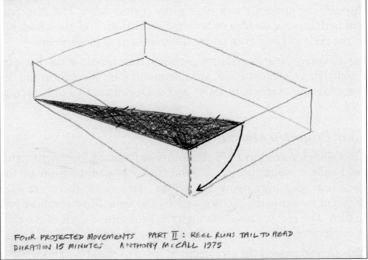

FOUR PROJECTED MOVEMENTS PART II : REEL RUNS TAIL TO HEAD
DURATION 15 MINUTES ANTHONY McCALL 1975

the fourth, pushed out from the wall, from above. This experience is paradoxical, since light – even 'solid' light like this – is, of course, insubstantial.

As with *Long Film for Four Projectors*, the projector is on the ground, situated inside the projection space. The act of threading the projector is incorporated into the piece as an important part of it. When the fifteen-minute reel has run completely through the projector, a small lamp clipped onto the projector is switched on by the projectionist to provide a work light. The projectionist then takes the full reel off the back take-up arm, puts it onto the front

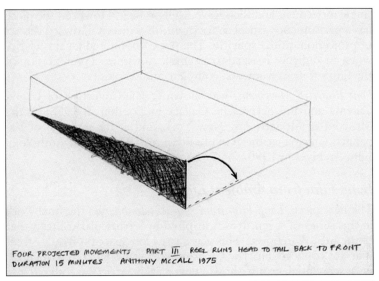

FOUR PROJECTED MOVEMENTS   PART III   REEL RUNS HEAD TO TAIL BACK TO FRONT
DURATION 15 MINUTES   ANTHONY McCALL 1975

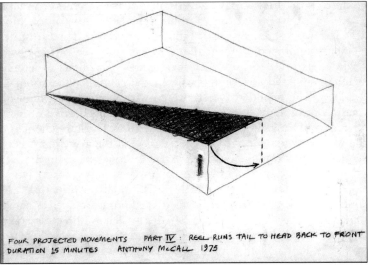

FOUR PROJECTED MOVEMENTS   PART IV : REEL RUNS TAIL TO HEAD BACK TO FRONT
DURATION 15 MINUTES   ANTHONY McCALL 1975

take-up arm, and re-threads the film, switches off the light, and turns the projector on again. This happens four times. The observant will see that the whole physical experience is based on the interplay of the wall, the floor, one projector, and one reel of film.

I described *Four Projected Movements* as being 'seventy-five minutes long with no maximum duration.' The four movements together take sixty minutes to project and I added a few minutes for each reel change. I conceived this, like the previous film, as a continuous installation. Certainly, any four movements experienced back to back describe the complete film. And if many people watch just a single movement and then leave, well, so be it. However, the piece has a performance aspect to it: attention is directed toward the act of projection quite explicitly. The piece undoubtedly gains clarity when an audience is asked to assemble to witness a presentation of the film's four movements, complete and whole.

Four Projected Movements was shown at The Collective for Living Cinema and the Serpentine Gallery in London in 1975; at the Museum of Modern Art, New York, and at the 'Festival of Expanded Cinema' at the ICA, London, in 1976; and at Anthology Film Archives in 1990.

Long Film from Ambient Light

The next piece, *Long Film from Ambient Light*, was the final work in this series of seven. It was inspired by a particular context, that of the Idea Warehouse. This was a large loft space on Reade Street that was connected to The Clocktower. I was invited to participate in a sequential group show, where each artist was offered the complete space for two days. My installation began at noon on June 18, 1975, and finished twenty-four hours later, at noon on June 19. The work used no actual film or projector. Three distinct elements combined to form the 'film', and no one of these was regarded as prior to the other two. These were, first, an altered space: a single electric light hung in the center of the room at eye-level. The windows were covered with white paper, limiting them to being light sources during the day and reflective surfaces ('screens') during the night. Second, there was a time-schema on the wall, which identified the time period of the presentation but suggested its continuity outside the twenty-four hours; third, there was a two-page statement on the opposite wall, 'Notes in Duration'. The notes criticized the hierarchical distinction that was routinely made between the so-called a-temporal arts such as painting and sculpture, and the time-based arts such as film, video, and dance.[5] It maintained that everything that occurs, including the process of looking and thinking, occurs in time and that, therefore, the distinction is absurd. (Of course, the distinction was often made in order to put time-based art in its place, to make the claim that important aesthetic developments were always made – and always would be made – by painting and sculpture.)

As an experience, *Long Film for Ambient Light* seemed at first sight to be a simple installed environment. The shifts that occurred within it, such as the transition the covered windows underwent from being light-sources during the day (a row of projector gates?) to being 'screens' at night (reflecting the light from the electric light bulb), were too gradual to see happening. However, the *film* existed in the space between the room, the statement, and the time-schema, and could be grasped as such. And the visitors who came more than once, who visited at a point during the day and again at a point during the night, were able to confirm for themselves the turn-around that had occurred in the space during their absence. The installation sat precisely on a threshold, on one side of which was 'time-based' art, and on the other, 'non time-based' art.[6]

Notes

1. From my artist's statement to the judges of the 'Fifth International Experimental Film Competition', 1974, Casino Knokke-Heist, Belgium. Held approximately every five years, the judges of the competition that year were P. Adams Sitney, Stephen Dwoskin, Ed Emschwiller, Dusan Makavejev, and Harald Szeemann. *Line Describing a Cone* won the Marie-Josi Prize. The statement was re-printed in *The Avant-Garde Film: A Reader of Theory and Criticism*, Ed. P. Adams Sitney (Anthology Film Archives Series 3/New York University Press New York, 1978).

2. 'Into The Light: The Projected Image in American Art 1964–1977' exhibition at the Whitney Museum of American Art, New York, 2001–2002.

3. Felipe Ehrenberg, 'On Conditions', *Art and Artists* 7, no. 12 (March 1973), pp. 38–43.

4. *Long Film for Four Projectors* notes, November 1974.

5. The following comment by Mel Bochner in an article about Malevich expresses the position succinctly: 'When you're interested in art, you're interested in the exchange that occurs when you stand in front of a work, alone, and look at it. It is atemporal. That's not what happens when you see a film, or a dance or video, or any of the other performance arts' (*Artforum*, June 1974).

6. *Long Film for Ambient Light* was also exhibited at Galerie St Petri in Lund, Sweden, in 1975, and at the Neue Galerie, Aachen, in 1976.

Section II

Languages of Representation in Film and Video: Thresholds of Materiality

Lis Rhodes
Trilogical Distractions

Sarah Pucill
The 'autoethnographic' in Chantal Akerman's News from
Home, *and an Analysis of* Almost Out *and*
Stages of Mourning

Nina Danino and Susan Poole
*Film, The Body, The Fold, an Interview with Nina Danino
on* Now I am Yours

Katherine Meynell
Attitudes 1-8

David Critchley
Video Works 1973–1983

Chris Meigh-Andrews
Early Videotapes 1978–1987

Gareth Evans and Andrew Kötting
*What he does, how he does it and the context in which it
has been done: An alphabetarium of Kötting*

continued over

Daniel Reeves
Ardent for Some Desperate Glory, Revisiting Smothering Dreams

Cate Elwes
War Stories, or Why I Make Videos About Old Soldiers

Vicky Smith
Moving Parts: The Divergence of Practice

Chapter eight

Trilogical Distractions

Lis Rhodes

Introduction

Some things are very disturbing. That is how they are meant to be.[1] Movement was never intended in a one-way system – though in the fast lane they say market forces move things in and out with impunity. (Caught in the wind on a blustery day?) The sale had been essential – it was said – for progress – or was it profit?[2] To avoid the distraction of explanation – which is only to visit a depository of assumptions – who are you going to believe? – Certainly not me or your own eyes. The moving image would be unlikely to induce anything but mistrust even in the event of the material moving in front of you. In the real there is very little movement in an image except in the sense of deterioration and loss. That an image appears to move – that images are made to move – to construct a deliberate illusion of movement – is this what we have been doing these past few years?

Reality is a belief

Is this illusion of movement a faint replica of precisely the happenings that have happened right in front of our eyes? The illusion of democracy covertly deflects attention from corporate monopoly.[3] If there has been movement – and certainly nothing is ever still even if some things never move – it has surely been back to front and inside out. If there is something that moves with the speed of light it is speculative capital – the virtual casino of capital markets. Without doubt nobody on the outside has gained like those few souls on the inside. Transparently in fact.

When nobody has crossed the road in living memory what was initially prevented is now impossible. It would be difficult to deny that insecurity – debt – the fear of and distraction of histories reduce all into compliance. This indeed might be the case except that illusion and belief rely on consistent irrationality[4] – on the smooth

Just About Now,
Video, 1993.

– on the glitch free transfer of irrationality into the familiar – an endless occupation and destruction of rationality. Lying is prone to inconsistency – not of doubt but of certainty – this is the recent script which omits oil and imperialism but includes belief and the illusory – a beggaring of belief itself. The compliant do not comply. But pressure is there – it is here.

Belief is an entertainment

The absurdity of actuality is a distraction in itself.[5] The actuality of absurdity is extraordinary violence. Such violence may be entertained by belief in its sentimental necessity. It is said if there is no conflict – no competition – there is no reality. Certainly it is resisted by consideration. But illusion is material to the absurdity of actuality. In having to make image conform to a certain economic doctrine and context any opposition is entertained. 'Entertained' not as in the OED definition 'occupying attention agreeably' (1612) but as 'taken into service' (1662) and 'paid wages' (1709). This latter definition is basic to the corporate relationship (of image and capital). Either way we are included – there is no choice – we are distracted from whatever we might do into what we are distracted into doing. This needs inversion if not redefinition of entertainment altogether.

Image is not distracted by capital in order entertain. Image and capital entertain each other in the accumulation and reproduction of profit. They do not respond to something that is not one or the other since this would imply that the relationship between them had been changed. This cannot be the case because the constant relationship between image and capital is profitability. They are closer than we might think – but as far apart as ever.

Just About Now, Video, 1993.

Certain images are wanted or not wanted by capital. Images preferred by capital are only those which endorse narratives agreeable to capital and which implement its beliefs. The collaboration of image and capital is possible in that they both use illusion. Coincidently images – in the sense of representation though not of perception – depend on illusion. But in the world of capital images are in the end selected in terms of profitability.

In theory image distracts capital. In fact capital controls image. But because of image's capability to transcend theory – to perplex and confuse – capital cannot afford to relax in its attempts to control. Capital is always at risk of losing control. This loss of control is evaded by the insistence on recognition and neo-familiarity.[6] There must be a sale. This is the market place of image and capital with which we are only too familiar.

79

Entertainment is a collaboration

The collaboration is not ethical but ideological and economic. Profitability is made to be seen as natural – common sense – rather than economic artifice or manipulation. The ransom which must be paid for refusing this collaboration is debilitating – which is precisely what it is intended to be. Debt – an offence requiring expiation – and extortion follow as night follows day.[7] You are no longer the individual subject. You are part of someone else's interest.

Nothing can deal with the apprehension of truth distinct from its political moment. In defining meaning image will be made to be collaborational or dissenting. Either way the corruption and recuperation of its original aims and intentions are likely. It will be taken away from itself and blamed for being unwrapped. (Is the subject of the sentence ever the subject of the sentence?) Before being released – as this or that deception or self-deception – I am permitted to believe. I have learned to imitate.

Collaboration is a distraction

It is an offence to imply a taxonomy or deceptive classification. The above might be just that if it were only that. This is not so. Distraction has another purpose.

In the sense that to distract can mean 'to perplex or confuse' – 'to cause dissension or disorder' (1597) – the OED – image distracts

Cold Draft,
16mm film, 1988.

capital. Capital has to resolve this distraction with a spectrum of erasure – select / delete / ignore / erase – in order to establish its control over image.[8] Capital controls image while image constantly tries to distract it. Image distracts capital while capital constantly tries to control it. All else is destabilised.

To stand still at an angle to expectation is to resist – to walk away is a permitted offence. The ensuing silence and invisibility leave the stage in the hands of the ideological censor. Distracted by the censor's investigation the relativity of moral scales is not always noticed. They are because they are not them. There was not here – here had gone too.

The art of distraction

To intervene between capital and its mirror (image) is extremely dangerous. Perhaps image and capital could be prised apart as it were intellectually but not in actuality – now. There is only one interface between image and capital – risk. Someone must lose.[9]

That image is more distracted by capital than capital is by image is probably why nobody can imagine the absence of capital. It cannot be seen and so cannot be represented. Absence is necessary to ensure absence of alternative. Movement was never intended in a one-way system.

This is not an immutable state of things – an unchanging condition. It is a particular artifice disseminated worldwide.[10] The moving

81

image still. Still fabricated and drawn from the margins and posted in uniform editions – flag wrapped limbs may be returned but not to sender.

Some things are very disturbing. That is how they are meant to be. The image is still – habitually still – captured between then and on the other hand.

Did history end?[11] Meanwhile the news.

The days before yesterday were still on the horizon – tomorrow's rain sweeping light before dark – switching under the motorway – laugh she whispered watch the dial and pretend not to kill. The city multiplies in steel shadows – certainly fabrication contains a deal of truth.[12]

I wait for precision that will be violence exactly – flowers strewn on the road. Were you wearing gloves in the winter when the fish was frying?

To distract so as not to be distracted is the art of distraction trilogically. Who can do more than warn and less than subvert?

Notes

1. The grander the scale the more theatrical the action – the greater the carnage judiciously done.
2. With a shift of perspective similar actions are differently judged.
3. The rape of perception is a certain measure. – Rewind carefully.
4. Fast forward and pause – power is dependent on the belief that it is not. – Replay slowly.
5. That which appears as evident may disappear as evidence when viewed from a different point of view.
6. So repression is commemorated and memories contained by resemblance.
7. Values are attributed to established points of reference and then assumed to drip with equity on all.
8. Can it not be seen that power depends on submission?
9. Giving is only the present continuous of having been Taken.
10. The more we have – the more of the same we do have.
11. The Cleaner of the Courts commented – that yesterday was much the same as today.
12. That is how history is made.

(Considerations of the *Deadline Trilogy – Cold Draft, Deadline, Just About Now*, 1988–1993)

Chapter nine

The 'autoethnographic' in Chantal Akerman's News From Home, and an Analysis of Almost Out and Stages of Mourning

Sarah Pucill

In this essay I explore Catherine Russell's writing on 'impure'[1] Structural Film and the autoethnograhic,[2] which I draw on in my discussion of three works, Chantal Akerman's, *News From Home*, (1976), Jayne Parker's *Almost Out*, (1984) and my own film *Stages of Mourning* (2004).

In the 1970s, whilst the high Modernist Structural film movement sought to eradicate any trace of the personal or the subject as author, in the wider frame of Fine Art, the feminist art movement was making famous the slogan 'The Personal is Political'. In fact the impact of feminism in art criticism was major, and feminist critique and practice succeeded in shifting the parameters for what could be valued as art. The consequence was that the frames of reference for artistic debate expanded, so emphasising the intersection between the 'personal' and the wider social and political context. An important point here was that the shift was as much in the criticism as in the practice.

In her book *Experimental Ethnography*, Catherine Russell compares the relationship between ethnographic cinema and avant-garde film practices, the key connection of which is the question of looking. She proposes that Structural Film be read in the wider context of the history of representation and visual culture, and re-visits Structural film from the perspective of post-modern ethnography.[3] She acknowledges the challenge that the Structural Materialist film theories of Peter Gidal[4] and Malcolm Le Grice[5] pose in terms of unsettling the passivity of the spectators' otherwise voyeuristic gaze. This challenge to provoke a more fluid viewing experience where the spectator becomes both passive and active, as seeing subject and observer, she incorporates and develops in her critique of 'impure' Structural Film. Gidal and Le Grice's discourse to blur the distinction between theory and practice, intellectualising and perceiving, subject and object of the gaze, is echoed in her writing on the autoethnographic. Following on from Constance Penley[6] she argues that because of the desire invested in looking, the spectator of Structural Materialist Film is not 'freed' from the technology of the gaze. Russell extends Structural Materialist Film theory where the subject is understood in universal terms (and therefore the subjects' viewing experience) to embrace a confrontation with looking that is not divorced from the socially differentiated 'embodied' subject. In her chapter on Structural Film, she describes the work of a group of filmmakers that she sees as marginal to Structural Film because voyeurism is confronted literally as 'content' or as a mode of representation, rather than as a 'disciplinary technology'[7] that she ascribes to the endeavour of Structural Materialist Film. Ackerman's *News From Home* is given primary place in her analysis of 'impure' structural film works.

The experimental autobiographical work that arose in the 1980s and 1990s in film and video in the US, Russell has defined as autoethnographic or domestic ethnographic. In general this work has diaristic elements but the author and his/her claim to truth or objectivity is put into question, as is the idea of a self as 'whole', self-knowable and fixed. Understanding moving image practice as the medium best suited to explore questions of a de-centred subjectivity, she points to the critical value of a practice that tests the limits of self representation as the autobiographic becomes *autoethnographic*. This is at the point where the film or video maker understands his or her personal history as implicated in the wider social and historical framework. As distinct from autobiographic work that retains an essential self that is fixed and is revealed as a singular and known 'truth', the autoethnographic instead stages the self as a performance, the self is objectified and as such is acknowledged within the social world. In this staging of subjectivity, the subject is fragmented as a consequence of the inherent quality of the medium. It is a simultaneous crossing between the spheres of the private and the public world where the subjects of documentation are the artists themselves (often also their family or friends). The framing of this 'self' acknowledges that the 'other' within the self already undermines self-awareness. This idea of the 'other' within the self, as the splitting of self between image/sound, subject/object, and past/present is explored within this self-reflexive approach to autobiographic artists film and video.

In *News From Home*, the voice-over of the filmmaker's mother's letters to her while she was away from her home in Belgium, is overlaid with extended duration static shots of New York streets and subway. Following from her previous films *Jeanne Dielman, 23 Quai de Commerce, 1080 Bruxelles* (1975), the marginal world of the women's household work is a key element. The letters recount the mundanity of daily routine, medical ailments and economic worries which are interspersed with the mother's declarations of love and sadness at being separated from her daughter asking her to write back and return soon. The mother's emotional outpouring is in marked contrast to the anonymity of the public space of New York street life, which serves to intensify the sense of a mother's closeness. The personal is shared with the viewer and is thus made public. The presence of the mother becomes all pervasive. The reader barely pauses for breath, the continuousness of the reading being paralleled with the continuousness of the actual and 'real' time of the profilmic and the viewing experience. The voice-over alternates with a silence, which in turn is set against the presence and absence of traffic sounds and of filmed streets that alternate between busy and empty, of people or of traffic. Extremes of closeness and distance are conflated so that uncertainty is evoked; is it the relationship with the mother that is alienating or the New York metropolis? A sense of being in transit is literally shown on screen but is also expressed symbolically by the letters. Throughout the film, it is the profilmic that is literally in transit (the people, the traffic), the displacement of the filmmaker is only suggested in the underpinning autobiographic narrative i.e. via the letters. However, in the final shot, the filmmaker's transience is literalised as the camera/filmmaker very slowly pulls away from the shore, and in a long tracking shot pulls away in real time in the boat, until Manhattan is far in the distance.

What the film addresses above all is a collision between the private and public that questions the assumption of what is subjective and objective, but also of who is at home and who is foreign. The passers by on the New York streets are of diverse racial heritage. Binary power structures in terms of both gender and race are here exposed in terms of expectations of traditional ethnographic film, that is, the voice-over as objective and at home, which is re-enforced with what the camera shows, that is 'other' and not at home. Here camera and voice-over are disjunctive. The anonymity of the cameraperson is partially maintained, until in the final very long take where the person behind the camera is, we realise, on a boat, and we assume is leaving the city she has been living in to return home to her mother. The film's resolution brings the autobiographic and the professional together as it is the person behind the camera who is in transit and displaced, and who is exposed in terms of her private and social autobiography. The question of displacement that the film addresses resonates in terms of the filmmaker's Jewish heritage.

Similarly, in *Almost Out* (1984), by Jayne Parker, the video centres primarily on a relationship between the video maker and her mother who sit in full view in an editing suite naked, and talk. The issue of looking is central to the video. Modernist elements of reflexivity are evident as image (the editing suite) and as voiced dialogue. A cameraman is present in the first half hour or so, as voice only, and his camerawork is discussed between the three. There is a laying bare of the video making process as the performers react and respond to camera frame and zoom during the process of shooting. The video was made at a time when nakedness in feminist quarters had become a taboo so this video was a bold attempt to challenge the then ideologue which was that women were necessarily dis-empowered by being naked for a camera. These specific issues are discussed as the cameraman for example comes in close on the artist's breast, saying that the camera can be brutal, and the question of whether the camera can hurt is discussed. The filmmaker's success here is not in simplistically negating this point but in moving beyond the problem by talking through it, i.e. talking through the potential 'harm' a camera can do to a body simultaneously as the camera frames. The artist here is crucially both objectified body as well as speaking subject who directs the cameraman.

The durational element is important for the ultimate reading of the video, which sets up a contest between seeing and listening to a body/subject. The viewer's relation to the womens' nakedness changes during the viewing and listening as the initial shock of nudity subsides. As the video progresses, the discussion becomes solely between the mother and daughter. The question of trust is raised as the mother explains why she has chosen to be naked in front of a camera for her daughter. Her reason is that she wants to give whatever she can to her daughter and that she understands it is important for her. Her trust and generosity cannot at this point be separated from the way in which we see the mother's naked flesh. The discussion continues more specifically on their relationship.

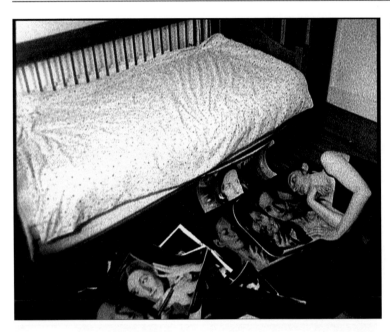

Stages of Mourning, 16mm film, colour , 2003.

Whilst the mother is given the space to question the questions which she does at times, it is the daughter asking and the mother answering, offering her time, her body, her honesty, her thoughts. There is a sense that the filmmaker's lines are semi scripted and that the mother's are not. Also, that the questioner wants to draw something from her mother, as if something is being tested. The harder and more direct the questions become, the harder it is to listen, yet the harder also to stop watching. The closer the intimacy between the mother and daughter, the greater the involvement of the viewer. The daughter asks the mother where she came from, and the mother shows the camera and daughter her abdomen. At this point the separation between the material body and the psychical seem the most disparate. At the same time the sense of necessary failure in being able to return to the place of ones origins is most crystallised. The illusion of unity that the language of video brings in the suture between image and sound is brought to the fore in this moment of failure for the evidence to satisfy.

My recent film *Stages of Mourning,* was made soon after the death of my late partner the filmmaker Sandra Lahire.[8] The film is a compilation of footage and photographs that I had lying around after her death (some were shot as private footage, some for a public audience). The twenty-minute film consists of me performing in front of the camera in silence in a home cluttered with large and small photographs, a 16mm projector, video and a computer that all bear images of the recently deceased. My intention for the film

Stages of Mourning,
16mm film, colour,,
2003.

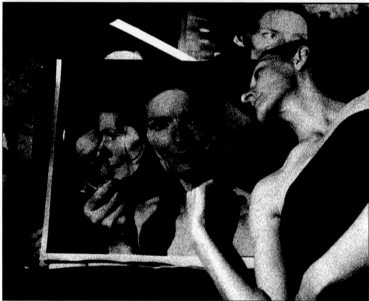

was to highlight the sense of fragmentation that occurs when confronted with death. In the film I enact through the representational mediums of photography, film and video, processes of a splitting of the self as image, images that split between subject/object, past/present, and private and public. The question of authenticity in terms of the truth between representation and real object

Stages of Mourning,
16mm film, colour,
2003.

was a key underlying concern; the truth of the performance, which is both staged and authentic, and of the truth in terms of the self which here is scattered. The sense of a coherent, stable and boundaried self is put to question. A sense of fragmentation is played out to the camera as I re-stage a pose in a photograph, move inside the photo or film projection, or sit at a computer screen as I orchestrate my late partner's performance at the click of a mouse. Whilst the film is also an emotional lament about my lost lover, there is at the same time a self-conscious striving, that is staged to camera to pull the scattered fragments together to re-live the past in the present.

Unlike the previous two works *Stages of Mourning* lays bare the life circumstance of the filmmaker, and bereavement as a period of crisis. The film opens with written text that is addressed to the deceased in the second person (you). In this way the viewer is implicated in a position that is awkward and uncertain; shut out, as voyeur, or as empathetic bystander. The film title *Stages of Mourning* is ambiguous in the sense that a stage is something both for a public audience as in the theatre and is an internal and private process of for example, mourning. I wanted the film to encompass both senses of the word, as for an artist what is private and what is public is often not separate. For the viewer, the mourning is real, but it is being staged at the same time. As I perform with the ghost (my late partners image) in the lens-based material, I perform my desire for her image to be real; to elicit a truth from the image of her as if a trace of her could be a part of her. In the moment of acting out this searching, the futility of the exercise is made apparent; the illusion is both real and not, it conveys a presence that is believable, even if at the same time this believability is a cheat.

The film stages an examination of the self, split between the here as viewer and there as screen, the here as living and the there as memory. An oscillation is experienced in the shifts between different frames of time and spatial frames. The viewer watches and maybe identifies with the performer as filmmaker and griever who is also looking at the image and late partner. Self and other are played out in multiple forms; present/past, self/representation, self/lover. The close identification of the filmmaker and performer with the deceased lover suggests a collapsing of self / 'other' in this time of recent loss.

As a meditation on the nature of the materiality of film, the film draws influence from the Structural Film concern of reflexivity. The experience of repeatedly seeing two faces (myself and my late partner) for twenty minutes draws attention to the 'stuff' of the medium, as texture and as physical entity, as computer terminal, projector or, to the physicality of the photograph in terms of scale and colour. As in *Almost Out* the performance is both actual and scripted. I stage a performance for the camera whilst grief is being lived, so destabilising the distinctions between what is actual and what is staged. The desire to re-live the past I enact on film whilst also interrogating questions of the experience of the present, of self, and of making a film. My roles as a human being, as an artist, performer, camerawoman and editor are thus conflated and exposed.

In the works I have discussed, the artists are engaged with the canonical avant-garde film and video debates, and the autobiographic, and with their subjectivity in terms of difference (as woman, Jew, lesbian) so that a bridging between the personal and social and philosophical is acknowledged and incorporated into the body of the work. In these works, it is in the moment of the most personal or actual, in the moment of the most intimate and therefore subjective, that the self is opened up to the viewer most forcefully as a shared experience. So what is apparently confined to the domestic and private, here switches place with the public. These works exemplify the autoethnographic mode in the way that the intellectual and emotional are not separated out and the way in which the fragmentary nature of the medium is laid bare; in *News from Home*, dislocation of voice-over with image, in *Almost Out*, the split between speaker, seer and seen and between an other and the self, and in *Stages of Mourning*, also the split between seer and seen, and between an other and self but with an important emphasis on the present and the past. In each work there is an internalisation of an 'other' that is embraced as a part of the self. Each work reveals elements of uncertainty between self and other, the staged and the actual, often creating a sense of disorientation in the intermixing of different registers of communication, that is between symbolic and literal, abstract, and indexical. The films also undertake an element of risk in exposing what is culturally designated as private. But also in the risk of the process of making, that is, of combining artistic 'objectivity' from the emotional attachment that is inevitable in one's 'subjective' relationship with one's life. And so it is in the interstices of uncertainty, in the confrontation of the unknown within oneself that the Other, which is both within and outside oneself, is most fully shared with the spectator, in the risk to expose what is close but also uncertain.

Notes

1. Catherine Russell, 'Framing People: Structural Film Revisited', *Experimental Ethnography; the Work of Film in the Age of Video* (Durham and London: Duke University Press, 1999).

2. Catherine Russell, 'Autoethnography: Journeys of the Self', op. cit.

3. Russell quotes from Stephen Tyler, who advocates for post-modern ethnography: to make 'no break between describing and what is being described'. Catherine Russell, 'Framing People: Structural Film Revisited', *Experimental Ethnography; the Work of Film in the Age of Video* (Durham and London: Duke University Press, 1999), p. 162.

4. Peter Gidal, ed., *Structural Film Anthology* (London: British Film Institute, 1976).

5. Malcolm Le Grice, *Abstract Film and Beyond* (Cambridge: MIT Press, 1977); *Materialist Film* (London: Routledge, 1989).

6. Constance Penley, 'The Avant-Garde and Its Imaginary', *Camera Obscura 2* (Autumn 1977), pp. 3–33. Also Constance Penley and Janet Bergstrom, 'The Avant-Garde: Histories and Theories' *Screen 19 no 3* (Autumn 1978) cited in Russell, Catherine 'Framing People: Structural Film Revisited', *Experimental Ethnography; the Work of Film in the Age of Video* (Durham and London: Duke University Press 1999), p. 160.

7. Ibid., pp. 159–160.

8. Sandra Lahire, Filmmaker 1950–2001.

Chapter ten

Film, The Body, The Fold

An Interview with Nina Danino on Now I Am Yours

Susanna Poole

SP: In your film *Now I am Yours* you filmed Bernini's sculpture of St Teresa.

How did you come to St Teresa as a text?

ND: There were a number of paths that drove me to the sculpture and to her writing, one was through Lacan's seminar on the feminine and jouissance. Since I've been working with film, I've always been interested in the question of the feminine, of absence.

SP: Lacan's Seminar *XX*, *Encore*.[1]

ND: Lacan's seminar talks about the woman as absence and as fantasy as well, but it seems also, as the feminine as a vector, which has more access to jouissance. Those were the beginnings of it. Also through feminist theories of psychoanalysis such as Cixous' notion of *l'écriture féminine*, and Kristeva's notion of the semiotic and the *chora*. I've been interested in the borderline of what you can express but cannot be said exactly through language. So that, the feminine is that which can't be said through language because it is in excess of language according to Lacan. So that captured various streams of thought that I was involved with – which is the question of the feminine and how one can talk about it and the question of absence from representation which all my work has been about. How do you set up presence through absence. And in language what cannot be said? I went to St Teresa as an author by studying her writings for themselves and through literary criticism which provided some grounds for the way in which as a woman her rhetorical style was developed to cope with and is shaped by, political and gender constraints – however, I was not approaching her as a biographical subject, but as an interface through which various aspects of my interest could be developed. And then I went to Bernini's sculpture – because that was actually the most memorable site of Lacan's speculative seminar – and looked at it. And it was the inverse of what I've always been interested in. It's absolute pure representation. And yet what it represents is not actually what it's representing. It's pointing toward something else.

SP: Lacan's idea is that women cannot fully express themselves in language because our experience is constituted outside language.

ND: He is saying that woman or the feminine are outside or not exactly inside but it seems to me that this is something that at the same time cannot entirely be colonised by language.

SP: There are many women artists that feel inside this constraint of language. Especially women artists that choose means of expression other than through written language. Experimental film was an alternative to linear language and was used very much in this sense. For instance, a filmmaker like Tanya Syed would say that she doesn't want to use verbal language at all, because it can be so limiting. So this issue is present in women filmmakers.

ND: My own work has stemmed from words and speech. I've always felt that the voice is a potential that's very neglected. There was a dogma in experimental, avant-garde or artists' film where silent images are always hierarchically placed to take predominance over any work that has sound. And I really can't see why that should be the case. I always wanted to deal with that. The reason why representation for me is related to the position of the woman, is that I wanted to use film and language to represent absence without using the representation of the woman. There was a lot of debate in feminist visual practice in the 80s about how women are represented in circuits of power, and how women should take control – if not of the means of power – then of their own forms of representation. This didn't touch on the intangible area of the feminine which I was interested in. I had the possibility of using image, absence of image, sound or no sound to create narrative possibilities, which again, was contrary to the dominant model of avant-garde film, which was against any form of narrative. I was experimenting with sound coming from the voice which does have the potential to radicalise the image, not least because the voice of the woman in cinema is the least heard. Kaja Silverman talks about how the disembodied voice in cinema is usually male, it's usually over the image, and it's usually quite powerful.[2] I tried to work very directly with this, as a response to all the male voices. The woman's voice can be used to locate or dislocate the image in exactly the same radical way as silence can. The voice is as plastic as the image.

Now I Am Yours,
16mm film, 1993.

If you don't use conventions of fiction drama using actors or art using performance or people, but if you're using images in non-linear ways, then you may have to start to read images metaphorically. I want to keep away from using the image as a metaphor. Providing you are clear about the position of sound to the image and the image to silence, you can create a form of indirect representation. So the voice, for me is very important, not just in what it says, but in the fact that it's there as an element.

SP: The issue of the body exists in many different ways in women's art, and also in women's lives. There is the assumption that we are not just mind or soul but that there is a body there. Whenever there is a voice that speaks, a camera that is moving, or whenever there is a word that is written, there is a body that is not there and it's a gendered body. We all have experience of the body, so it comes to the fore in women's writing. It affects the possibility of creating a different film language, and also, through what Kristeva says of the semiotic, about what in language is more physical, which is so important in poetry.

ND: The 'pulsions' of language.

SP: That can't be fixed directly to a meaning through words but are more ambiguous, more material. One can't say that this means this exactly.

ND: In that context, it's not what is said by the voice, but it's been important to find a way of speaking. Those undercurrents which are contained in the way something is said, not only in the content of the speech, but in the texture of what one is saying, whether it's pace or rhythm, or fastness or slowness. So that it's as much in the body of what one is saying as in what is said. That for me has always been a line between the way that the voice is close up to the microphone, but you're not an actor reading, and you're not supposed to believe the emotions, but at the same time it's on that border where there is a tension between the possibility of the subject that feels, and the text that is written.

SP: How do you work with this reading?

ND: I started to use my voice in a method quite intuitively in my first film. The voice is kept deliberately on the edge of detachment and the conventions of drama are always being pushed away. At the same time the voice, especially the woman's voice, is a very emotive, sensual thing, and so the subject is there. Marguerite Duras, is a filmmaker who reads in this way and she uses her own voice in her films. But I found my way of doing it that has suited what I'm trying to do. In *Now I am Yours* there is a lot of speaking because it's connected to the urgency of delivery and to the necessity to say, to the act of speech.

SP: In *Now I am Yours* at one point there is a sudden change from the single voice to many different voices coming together in a more deep, possessed, devilish voice. It reminded me of *The Exorcist*, of hysterical women's voices, and of the hysterical body in psychoanalysis. This is the body that speaks, produces symbols and takes hold of the whole subject, who is not in control any more. And of course, in the case of the saint, or the mystic, it's God that is supposed to be speaking through her body, while in the case of *The Exorcist* it's the Devil. But in a way it's a similar idea. Were you thinking about the body of the saint in this way, as the site of challenge, the desire for dissolution, an urge to break out of the boundaries of the body?

ND: It's a dramatic point where language can't suffice. For Teresa at that point, in her own account, the body is at a liminal point. The body was a very difficult experience for her because she was assailed by ill health all her life. In ecstasy the experience of the body has a duality to it, a 'sweet pain' so the body is never erased entirely. The soundtrack sections you refer to are performed voices by the singer Shelley Hirsch. There are several tracks of voices playing at the same time. It's a dramatic point of a plastic filmic/sonic experience. The image is turbulent, the sound is turbulent. The image is full of curves and folds that are all overflowing. And the language through the multi-track voice performance is a response to it. Shelley performed the music 'live' in response to the picture. She laid one track, then another. She worked with a harmoniser, where the voice is caught, repeated or looped and laid down as a pulse or a rhythm and then another track is laid down, perhaps of words or

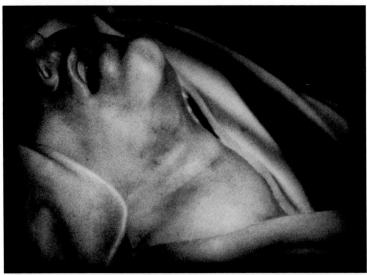

Now I Am Yours,
16mm film, 1993.

lines – in response to that one and so on, building it up and giving it 'body' so that five or six tracks form one piece. The sound is a response to the turbulence of the folds of the image. I don't think it's an escape from the body. Is it like a possession of the body? I don't think so. It's like a release from the body really. It's the opposite, a kind of celebration of excess.

SP: There's more the sense of pleasure than of pain?

ND: Yes, but it is slightly demonic as well. There are several other

97

moments like that in the film, which are all different. But they are only a representation of what can't really be said and is performed excess – it's a performance. It's a performed camera work and it's a performance for voice too. In another part of the soundtrack there's a spoken track and a voice that comes up from under and overtakes it. This under voice – which is Shelley Hirsch's performance – is that other voice which is in non-verbal language. So, call it the metaphor of poetry – I don't know. But it's like a performance of what isn't really exactly linear. It attempts language, but it's defeated by language. It comes in and out of the body of the film; it swims in and out and becomes several voices. But it's the same person and it's one piece of music.

SP: Of course for each image you know the work that was behind it and also the physicality of the work involved in it.

ND: Yes, it was physical, even to bring alive the turbulence, through the folds. Those folds, they were filmed by half-dancing in front of the sculpture. Also, the image was further manipulated in post-production to make the sculpture come 'alive'. So it was a physical film in that sense, yes.

SP: How did you gain access to shoot the Bernini statue?

ND: We got permission to film in Sta. Maria della Vittoria for three days only when the church was closed to the public twice a day. We had to set up a high scaffold, to the level of the face of the sculpture and take it down and set it up again for the next session. We had to shoot quickly. The other parts of the film of the garden or the cemetery is footage which I shot by myself in places which I visited and revisited and spent a lot of time in, whereas the sculpture sections were shot in a limited amount of time.

SP: What crew did you work with?

ND: We had a lighting cameraman Chris Hughes on 16mm and I filmed with S8 camera at the same time. There was a camera assistant and a lighting electrician and his assistant. Of course we needed to light the interior – the Cornaro chapel is quite brown and dark.

SP: So you don't have that kind of feeling that you have in the film?

ND: Not at all. It's very static and it's very dark and gloomy. It's a sepulchral chapel. That was another path, because the film was about death and how film can bring the body to life. It expresses the need to ward off death, to struggle with the forces of life and death. The body is resurrected but it's an illusion, done in a cinematic theatre. The film is in response to my own father's death and an act of mourning. Hence the section at the end of the film about the necessity to try to stop the erosion of memory through the work of remembering. It ends at the cemetery where the body can no longer be seen, the shots are of the marble surface, which covers the surface of the earth and commemorates the body.

SP: The last part of the film with shots of the black and white photographs and your own voice reciting verses from the *Song of Solomon* has a personal quality There are also shots of the cemetery, which is also a beautiful garden and close-up of flowers, which are symbolic of love and death. This section introduces the feeling of melancholy, mourning and the ultimate tragedy of losing the body of the beloved. Nevertheless, at that point in the film the fluid backward and forward movements of the camera together with the music and the rhythm of the voice communicate a living pulse, a sense of rapture in which is strongly felt the presence of a person, of a living body, it might be the body which I, as a spectator, have a desire to re-create behind that voice and the moving gaze of the camera.

ND: We are talking about the physical body but there is also the 'body of the film' and the energy it unleashes be it intellectual or physical. Giles Deleuze writing on Leibniz talks about this energy in the baroque and the fold and the body. This quote is from chapter nine, 'The New Harmony': 'If the Baroque is defined by the fold that goes out to infinity, how can it be recognised in its most simple form? The fold can be recognised first of all in the textile model of the kind implied by garments: fabric or clothing has to free its own folds from its usual subordination to the finite body it covers. If there is an inherently Baroque costume, it is broad, in distending waves ... surrounding the body with its independent folds, ever-multiplying, never betraying those of the body beneath' but engulfing the wearer in thousands of folds of garments which 'overcome their bodily contradictions and (to) make their heads look like those of swimmers bobbing in the waves'.[3] The Baroque fold is 'radiating force' a response to the rectilinear Renaissance space. The editing in *Now I am Yours* creates points of rectilinear space, for example the look of the Witnesses of the Cornaro Chapel is edited to look at St. Teresa, or the footsteps on the soundtrack match the shots in the garden but the dominant space is not bound by stabilising fixed points of view but exists in unfixed time or physical space. The sound and image create the waves of emotion, which drive the film. Of course this is mirrored by the central image of Teresa and the tunic which is bursting in a 'liberation of folds that are no longer merely reproducing the finite body' but 'a go-between, or go-betweens (-are) placed between clothing and the body. These are the Elements. We need not recall that water and its rivers, air and its clouds; earth and its caverns and light and its fires are themselves infinite folds.'[4]

'But the essence of the Baroque entails neither falling into nor emerging from illusion but rather realising something in illusion itself, or of tying it to a spiritual presence...' 'That is how the voice and the image create a kind of presence' '...that endows its spaces and fragments with a collective unity'.[5] The voice and the image form a collective unity, which constitutes a presence, but that presence is realising something in illusion. It is the space of the image, which doesn't exist other than through cinema. 'The Baroque artists know well that hallucination does not feign presence but that presence is hallucinatory.'[6]

SP: How do films create their own presence and if they don't have a narrative how do people respond to that?

ND: What is really important is to talk about presence as force as Leibniz says 'Force is presence and not action'.[7] What constitutes presence is what could be thought of as the body of the film. It's the way in which a film acquires its own body, creates its own body through time as it unfolds. I think of films as having a body. In the way that the body occupies its own ground, its own identity, its own feeling, its own matter. It begins, when you make a film – you're creating something that has its own plasticity, its own folds, its own shapes, its own stature, its own verticality, its own sense of its standing on its own self. And its own voice as well. That's the body of the film, not the body behind the camera, or the subject of the film, but the film as a kind of body. As a piece of cloth, a form that is created out of its own material. The material of course is the material of film and cinema, which includes the elements of sound and image and time. That's how you construct the body of a film, which has the ability to speak – it has its own volition sometimes as well. And once you finish a film it is almost like having another presence there that comes into presence when you project.

SP: But one that doesn't belong to you any more.

ND: It doesn't belong to you any more. It came out of me but it has its own body, in time, whenever it gets projected.

SP: This idea of the film having a body and becoming an autonomous being from you fits very much with your preoccupation not to set up metaphors.

ND: Yes, that's why I want to insist on the film having a reality, which does not rely on the metaphor of the image. Illusion is a form of presence. The illusion of cinema creates a cinematic presence. Maybe that might sound a bit essentialist but I think that's actually what happens, or what can happen in the conditions of cinema. Certain films draw on this and have the ability to impact themselves on our memory and create desire. Sometimes if someone has liked the film they have said 'I want to keep it, can I have it?' But of course, you can never have a film because the point about it is that it always institutes a kind of loss. That's really what that presence insists on, that it's only a presence through its own absence. It's transient – but has a lasting impact. That impact of presence is instituted through force and its own finality.

SP: Every art piece has this kind of mortality in it. Even Bernini's statue, which is the most present and material, you go to see it and when you go away, you experience this kind of loss because you can't possess it completely. Every time you see it, it is different because the light is different and then it's finished, it has duration.

ND: Although the medium of film, has a particular ability to make us feel absence and loss. It is particular to cinema and cinema can do it very well. It's particular to projection, for example, and to the fact that the image doesn't exist in reality.

SP: And to the fact that cinema has this technical capacity of reproducing reality so well, more than any other form of art, which is why we feel this contradiction so sharply.

ND: This is why for me the need to get away from metaphor is important in order to work with that contradiction. The image is not anything other than itself. It is not a poetic reading only but also an image of something that exists or has existed out there, or is existing right now at the very moment of projection again, for you, for itself.

SP: And your using the statue as the subject of your film *Now I am Yours,* fits in with the idea of the fold, because you're not filming 'live action', but a statue that in itself is …

ND: Absolutely dead. It's static. It's petrified.

SP: It's mirroring something else.

ND: Yes.

This interview was first recorded on video for the documentary *The Touching Camera* directed by Susanna Poole, 1998. Edited sections are in the documentary. This is the first publication of the full interview. My thanks to Susanna Poole for making available the original recordings.

Notes

1. Jacques Lacan, 'God and the Jouissance of The Woman', Seminar XX Encore trans. Jacqueline Rose in *Feminine Sexuality*, eds., Juliet Mitchell and Jacqueline Rose (London: Macmillan, 1982).

2. Kaja Silverman, *The Acoustic Mirror* (Bloomington and Indianapolis: Indiana University Press, 1988).

3. Gilles Deleuze, *The Fold; Leibniz and the Baroque,* trans. Tom Conley (Minneapolis: University of Minnesota Press, 1993), p. 121.

4. Ibid., p. 122.

5. Ibid., p. 125.

6. Ibid., p. 125.

7. Ibid., p. 119.

Chapter eleven

Attitudes 1–8

Katherine Meynell

The Impetus

This video installation was intended as contemplation on how we understand the residue left by performance. The work references Emma Hamilton's 'attitudes' of the late 18th century, though not representationally or illustratively as in a costume drama. More generally it continues the dialogue about records, memory and precedent, with the aim of contributing to an iconography of women's live art practice.

An account of Emma Hamilton

Later, she becomes best known for being Nelson's mistress, although the first mention of her career was an account of her posing semi dressed as a 'nymph of health' in the surgery of a doctor who cured impotence. Throughout Emma Hamilton's life she used her intelligence and sexual charisma to her advantage. Her work, based on classical antiquities and figures from myth and literature, was ostensibly to please a much older husband, Sir William. So in conformity to his taste, she would dress in an antique costume of white tunic and belt, performing at high society soirees in Naples. In this context Emma Hamilton developed her 'attitudes' as a new art form, possibly as a result of modelling for George Romney. In 1787 Goethe wrote '... with a few shawls (she) gives so much variety to her poses, gestures, expressions etc., that the spectator can hardly believe his eyes. He sees what thousands of artists would have liked to express realised before him in movements and surprising transformations ... This much is certain: as a performance it's like nothing you ever saw before in your life'.[1] In another contemporary account Mrs Gram Holmstrom wrote 'It is noteworthy that this mimoplastic art is not an emanation from the contemporary English Theatre'.[2] Historically, these performances have been suggested as the precursor to living room charades. Although regarded by some as illustrating classical themes, in a savage cartoon of 1791,

Attitudes 1–8,
Video, 1998.

Rowlandson suggested that these were little more than a sex show. At her height, Hamilton was a muse and inspiration. There are many surviving images of her from this period, not only by Romney, but also Vigee LeBrun and Rehberg-Piroli. These were used directly, for the shooting script of *Attitudes 1-8*.

The making of this work

I chose Hayley Newman as the performer of these attitudes, to strike a pose and hold it – as the expression of emotion. The performer was asked to have sluttish overtones and I accentuated the breathing 'live-ness' of her still poses, by having a single fixed position camera for each of the attitudes. The majority of the footage was shot by Sarah Turner, at the British Museum in Room 70, using the backdrop of artefacts from the collection of William Hamilton, to provide a framing of high culture. I returned to shoot (several times) during the day with a small hand-held camera to shoot additional footage; a Portland vase; walking around a small Cupid, panning across a line of busts; a crocodile-skin suit of armour.

I post produced the sound, with crossed microphones for binaural effect. And finally the material was made into eight looped sources: short episodes to be played simultaneously, each monitor showing a different 'attitude'. It formed a sixteen-track sound-scape within the room, each pair of tracks describing an action that may or may not be visible to the viewer.

The display

The eight monitors were arranged on plinths in the Royal College of Art 'Link Gallery'. This is an awkward corridor (linking) space, on two levels. I built the plinths at different heights so that the

103

distance from the ceiling, the sight line of the work, would be continuous throughout the gallery. Four monitors were placed against the side-walls facing in at either end of the gallery, and four monitors were placed (incorporating the steps between levels) in a square, facing each other in the centre of the room.

On entering the Gallery no single vantage point was possible, I walked between the monitors sometimes catching glimpses and incomplete reflections of other monitor sources on the shiny surface of the screen. The sound was minimal and divided as different parts: breathing, sighing, cloth rustling, a tambourine, footsteps, grapes being slurpily eaten... each sound source synched to a

Attitudes 1–8,
Video, colour, 1998.

specific image, acoustically both connected and disconnected, depending on how the sound was isolated or fused with the particular image visible at that moment.

This work exists between time frames, suggested by quoting the visual accounts of Hamilton and by quoting the museum itself as backdrop. It self consciously throws the authority of museological conventions into the current frame, as constructs, which I appropriated for the purpose of providing a fictional history of live art. Fictional because such a thing or (non-thing) is literally not possible and also fictional because all histories become the interpretation of those who seek to represent them. I do not understand *Attitudes*

105

1-8 as a 'trace' or recovering of events, but as a new and current work.

Taking the eight monitors as vitrines, much as a museum might display artefacts as evidence, each monitor images the performer as well as real artefacts from the British Museum. In a series of very slow actions, Newman performs a present (the time of the work) against the evidence of the historical past. A sense of the authority of the museum has been exposed (whilst still admired for its style, a style which might have some vestige of reflected glory). Newman wears her own clothes. In one monitor she walks in iridescent high heels, clicking her feet. In another monitor she sits with her ample breast exposed, a pile of grapes slips awkwardly from her bacchante head and she looses her composure, looking at the camera in recognition, that 'fourth look' ensuring the viewer's understanding of the processes of this construction. She masquerades as herself, identifiable as the young woman who performs; she is an artist herself. Although some of the considerations of class and gender have altered in two centuries, a sexy and successful working woman still requires other signifiers to establish her worth. Dress and valuables help. In such exaggerated circumstances as the British Museum irony is intended.

With careful attention to dramatic (filmic) lighting, black and white picture and high production values, expectations of narrative drama are invoked but do not occur. All reasonable efforts were taken to ensure that the end result looked 'classy'. As there was no place from which the screens were simultaneously visible, it was to remain explicitly partial and understood as different fragments. Conversely, the sound perceptible from anywhere in the room at any given moment, was only visually connectable in parts to an individual monitor, so causing a coexistent separation and connection of sound and image, oscillating between accepting and refusing a conventional position. These *Attitudes 1-8* do not have an order (although partly narrative, in that they pictorially describe a scene) instead they offer a structure that is without semantic specificity, repeating, re-rolling and seemingly continuous, each viewing moment a potentially different position in the room.

In this work I have attempted to represent woman as historically marked and incomplete, imaged in *Attitudes 1-8* within a range of poises, postures and costumes.

Notes

1. Gram Holström, Monodrama Kirsten, *Attitudes, Tableaux Vivants – Studies on Some Trends in Theatrical Fashion 1770–1815* (Stockholm: Almquist & Wiksell, 1967).

2. Iveagh Bequest, *Lady Hamilton* (London: Arts Council of Great Britain/G.L.A., 1972); Susan Sontag *The Volcano Lover* (London: Johnathan Cape, 1992).

Chapter twelve

Video Works 1973–1983

David Critchley

B etween 1973 and 1983 I made twelve single screen video art tapes, two multi-screen video installations and a multi-media performance using video. Until 1975 I thought of myself primarily as a performance artist and made many performance pieces using live action, live and recorded sound, slides, film and photography. There was often a self-fulfilling prophecy element in the works, such as eating until I was sick, drinking a whole bottle of whisky (until drunk of course) impaling myself in various ways, stripping, dancing, and working in the style of early 1970s artists, such as Stuart Brisley, Robert Morris and Vito Acconci. I often collaborated with others, and we explored our personal identities as performance art.

The notion of moving away from being a studio based solitary artist, towards collaboration or performance, and producing art-works that were not object based, were art political issues in the 1970s. Now this appears to be the norm, with entire retrospective exhibitions presented in major galleries using, for example, video and multi-media. However, it was important then to justify one's collaborative, time-based, non-object practice, artistically, philo-sophically and technically.

In 1973, when I made *Changing*, my first performance to be recorded on video, I had never seen a piece of Video Art. Using a portable quarter-inch reel-to-reel recorder, a static camera shot of me changing piecemeal through every item of clothing I owned was recorded in a single forty-minute take with sync-sound. This was a complete revelation to me at that time, as a Super 8mm cassette lasted around four minutes, a 16mm reel two minutes, and as for sound, well that was complicated, or non-existent. However, the first problem of this new medium had raised its head in that a forty-minute static camera shot could be very boring for an audi-ence, especially in black and white on a fourteen-inch monitor.

With a view to livening up the presentation and dynamism of ideas

Pieces I Never Did,
Video U-matic Low
Band, 1979.

on video, my next piece *Yet Another Triangle*, was a three-monitor installation showing three camera views of three performers undertaking an impossible to fulfil instruction – 'keep the other two performers in frame'. This action piece resulted in a dynamic twenty-minute game (the length of a portapak tape) with Stuart Marshall, Keith Frake and myself in a gym at Newcastle Polytechnic. The three tapes were shown on monitors facing inwards from the points of an equilateral triangle, sides about five metres, placing a viewer in the same predicament as the performers – only any two

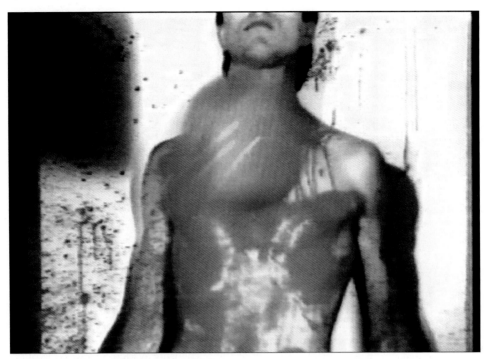

monitors being watchable at one time. A re-shot *Yet Another Triangle* with David Hall and Tony Sinden was screened in 1975 at the exhibition, 'The Video Show', at the Serpentine Gallery.

Pieces I Never Did,
Video U-matic Low
Band, 1979.

Moving to London in 1975 I met and joined in with the group of

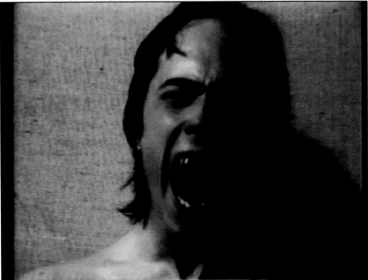

109

Pieces I Never Did,
Video U-matic Low
Band, 1979.

artists who rented 2B Butlers Wharf.[1] Over the next three years we ran it as a venue for performance art and time based media of all kinds. Alongside this, and in close contact, was another group of artists who having met at the Serpentine 'Video Show', continued to meet exhibit and develop ideas, and became founding members of London Video Arts[2] (which was eventually merged with the London Filmmakers Coop to become the LUX). LVA began operating screenings and video art distribution in 1978.

Trialogue, Video
½-reel to reel and
U-matic, Black and
White, 1976.

Static Acceleration,
Video ½ reel to reel
and U-matic, Black
and White, 1976.

Zeno Reaches Zero,
Video ½ reel to reel
and U-matic, Black
and White, 1975.

By the mid 1970s I had seen plenty of video art and was working in a structured analytical way, using the properties inherent in half-inch reel-to-reel black and white video equipment, coupled with a minimalist performance element. Screens were typically 19inch Sony Trinitrons, so I used a close up shot of my head as an expressive icon in six of the early tapes to have approximately one-to-one human scale to work with. Time and space conundrums still provided me with starting points for most of the pieces, and are expressed through the titles *Zeno Reaches Zero* (1976), *Static*

Acceleration (1976), *Trialogue* (1977), *Pieces I Never Did* (1979), and *No Record* (1983). These works throw out contradictions related to their subject matter and its realisation in video.

By 1979 when I made *Pieces I Never Did*, colour cameras, U-matic cassettes and a wider range of monitors were available. Consequently I was able to visit many performance, film, video and audio ideas and present each channel synchronised on three players and monitors. I was able to resurrect areas of personal performance that had been edged out by the structuralism of early video art, such as shouting the words SHUT UP until I lost my voice, having objects thrown at me until I changed colour, and proposing to end the piece by blowing myself up.

My last three works from this period were much looser, playful, visual and verbal narratives. By 1983 the advances in home video, cheaper equipment and my wider familiarity with the technology meant that the issues of the 1970s had been played-out. Another generation of video artists were at work with a more political, populist, and televisually oriented agenda. It was time for me to do something else.

Notes

1.　John Kippin, Belinda Williams, Alison Winckle, Martin Hearne, Mick Duckworth, Kevin Atherton, Kieran Lyons, Steve James, Dave Hanson, Alan Stott.

2.　London Video Art founding members: David Hall, Stuart Marshall, Tamara Krikorian, Stephen Partridge, Pete Livingstone, Roger Barnard, Jonnie Turpie, Marceline Mori, Wendy Brown, Brian Hoey, David Critchley.

Chapter thirteen

Early Video Tapes: 1978–1987

Chris Meigh-Andrews

M y earliest exhibited video tapes – *Continuum, The Viewer's Receptive Capacity* and *3:4* ,[1] were collaborations, produced in the TV studio. My first solo tape, *Horizontal and Vertical* (1978),[2] explored video image manipulation using the 'Videokalos Image Processor', a self-contained video mixing and image-processing device.[3] During post-production the 'raw' video was rescanned and fed into the Videokalos. Using a 'best take' process the colours and transitions (mixes and wipes) were gradually introduced across the duration of the tape. Working in this way I was influenced both by the configuration of the Videokalos and by the practice of its designers. As with a number of the video imaging tools built by Steina and Woody Steina Vasulka, for example, the origins of the image-processor as an outgrowth of practices derived from audio technology (including the overall 'architecture') and 'live' broadcast television were inherent in the Videokalos.

Video as an Electronic Medium

Conscious of the electronic nature of video, I was increasingly interested in the relationship between the 'natural world' and the technology I was using. At the time video equipment was far less portable, with much of the image manipulation accomplished in post-production. Many technical manipulations specific to video – an enhanced perception of the video raster and scan lines, the shifting colours, video 'wipes' and mixes, and the punctuating rhythm of a deliberately maladjusted vertical hold, had an aesthetic significance.[4] Using a slow contemplative pace with a gradual shifting of movement, colour and time, I sought to make landscape works, which through their use of duration and the manipulation of basic video elements made reference to a mediated experience of

Continuum,
Two-screen/monitors
Video, Black and
White, 1977.

landscape, and to the subjectivity of the viewer. I also wanted works that referred to their medium of transmission, developing a language particular to video with reference to the landscape elements being represented. I sought to make a work, that whilst entirely and obviously video, bore no relation to broadcast television in content or form. I wanted to make works, which were emphatically 'video' but were just as clearly *not* TV.

The use of horizontal and vertical wipes in *Horizontal and Vertical*, was an attempt to develop a set of formal codes that were specific and particular to video. Although influenced by David Hall in works such as *This is a Television Receiver* (1974), I was seeking a more lyrical and subjective result and was more attracted to the ideas of filmmakers such as Malcolm Le Grice as evidenced in *Berlin Horse*, (1971).

Michael Snow's film *Wavelength* (1967), was also a major influence. *Wavelength* used the formal device of the zoom to frame and provide the tension for a quasi-narrative structure. The film also had a transcendental and metaphoric dimension, neither of which was particularly in favour in English avant-garde film and video circles of the time, but one which was in tune with Peter Donebauer's notions of time-based art, and one that I was sympathetic to.

In terms of the development of a purely medium-based language for film, the work of Stan Brakhage was of major significance to

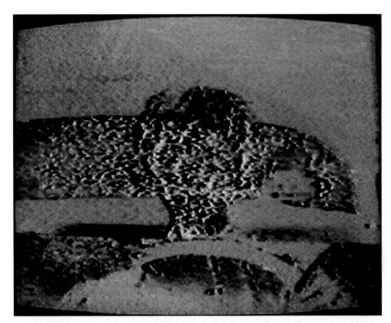

The Distracted Driver,
Video, 1980.

me. Working with the Videokalos was a way of gaining control of elements within the video 'frame'. Filmmakers including Le Grice working with the optical printer, and Brakhage, who drew directly on to the film surface were able to control the level of signification within the frame. I had yet to see the work of the Vasulkas who had developed ways of delving within the video frame in works such as *Caligrams* (1970) and *Matrix* (1976).[5] Seeking a line-by-line method of working with the video image, the Videokalos offered me the closest possibility at that time. Gaining control of image brightness, contrast, colour changes, and in later work such as *The Distracted Driver* (1980), and *The Chance Meeting* (1981), image keying, I was able to manipulate the unfolding of the video image across time, beyond the basic cutting that I had been able to achieve in the edit suite.

The Distracted Driver (1980)

The Distracted Driver (1980) was constructed from a monochrome original, shot at night using an image-intensifying camera. *The Distracted Driver* has a clear narrative, there is a 'story' told directly via the soundtrack. In contrast to the landscape pieces, I worked with saturated colours, utilising the full range of multiple luminance keying levels. Attempting to extend the literal narrative into the application of the colourisation of the monochrome original, my intention was to introduce colours into the image to suggest the subjective experience of the central character – the 'distracted driver' of the title, actively investigating ways of representing subjective experience.

Much of the narrative in *Distracted Driver* is tied to the soundtrack. The core idea was to conjure up complex memories in the mind of the viewer which were to be experienced running in parallel with the video images. My interest in the relationship between memory and moving imagery did not begin with this work, but it is the first piece in which I tried to make it explicitly part of the 'narrative' of the work. The story of the film *Psycho* (Dir. Alfred Hitchcock, 1960) as recounted by the car's passenger makes reference to a number of visual elements from the Hitchcock film, appealing to the viewer's memory and establishing an ironic contrast to the image on the video screen. My choice of colours was arbitrary, as I was primarily concerned to use colour to represent the driver without attempting to present any particular aspect of 'character' – the subjective perspective of the camera representing the driver's viewpoint.

The establishment of my independent practice: 'Three Quarter Inch Video/Productions' (1980–1988)

For the most part, artists' video in England in the late 1970s and early 1980s was tied to the art school system and to production funding from the Arts Council of Great Britain. London Video Arts was at this time solely a distribution organisation – there was no video equivalent of the London Filmmakers Coop, with its tradition of accessible workshop resources. In 1980 I formed a partnership with two LVA colleagues to purchase some second-hand video equipment.[6] Occupying two rooms in 79A Wardour Street, Soho, 'Three Quarter Inch Video' hired out the equipment to cover costs, providing us with access to facilities for our own work. After this initial equipment purchase, the nature of the facilities developed considerably reflecting changes in the technology, our finances, and technical requirements. Although the partnership was dissolved in 1982, the enterprise continued and these facilities formed the core of my studio for the next six years.

The Edit Suite

The most significant impact of the new studio on the development of my work was made by the regular and uninterrupted access to picture and sound editing. *The Room with a View* (1982) initiated a working process that characterised my approach to video. Working almost daily with the video image, I produced a series of drafts or versions of an idea, editing and re-editing, adding images and/ or sequences, testing out alternative permutations and juxtapositions, different soundtracks, building up layers of image and sound

The Room With a View, Video, Black and White, 1982.

combinations. This approach, traditional to painters and musicians but less common to video artists at this time, gave me the confidence to explore ideas and sketch out new works on a trial basis. This way of working directly with the materials of the medium would not have been possible if I had had to present ideas for proposals to potential funding agencies or had worked only when I could gain access to 'outside' facilities. This procedure allowed me to produce works with alternative uses of the same material, to make alterations or test out new permutations quickly and economically. Work of this period was fluid because I was able to work more freely, and felt less tied to a particular version of a tape or approach to an idea.

The Room with a View

The Room with a View is about the view that photography gives us of ourselves, the way in which time, memory and image are intertwined. Notions of identity and self-image were a major theme in my video work of this period, leading directly to later tapes and installations in which this self-reflexive aspect of the human mind becomes central. Initial ideas for this tape came out of readings of *Camera Lucida* (1981) by Roland Barthes, and the work of Jo Spence[7] and Cindy Sherman. Experimental films in which the still image was a primary device were also highly influential, particularly Hollis Frampton's *Nostalgia* (1971) and *La Jetée* (1962) by Chris Marker.

The Room with a View presents a sequence of family snapshots in chronological order, continuing until the point at which I have a clear memory of the event untainted by the view imposed onto that event by the camera. These are pictures that made a significant contribution to my 'sense of self' – images of growing up that are infused and elaborated by parental reminiscences – ordinary events magnified by the very fact of being preserved, frozen out of the flux of life, and made iconic. I wanted to make work that was personal, but also 'public', my choice of holiday 'snaps' based on a certainty that they resembled countless other personal images. This video assemblage of snapshots is intercut by images of the sea and sky originally recorded for a three channel video installation *Field Study* (1980). Additional video material was combined with captions, diagrams and simple line drawings.[8]

The Prototype Videokalos Image Processor: 1982–87

I intuitively felt that the early work I had done with the Videokalos was a starting point, and I needed to further explore its potential. Between January and May 1982, I worked under Peter Donebauer's supervision to repair and restore the prototype Videokalos synthesiser.

Although the Videokalos did not offer any entirely new possibilities for video production, it combined facilities that were otherwise not available in a self-contained unit. The acquisition of the working prototype considerably extended the range of image-control processes available in my studio. This innovative and unique instrument was influential on my developing attitude to the medium, reinforcing my understanding of the instantaneous and fluid nature of the video image, its production processes paralleling those of audio recording. The rebuilt prototype Videokalos was, until the addition of a digital frame store in 1987, the image-processing core of my studio. It gave me significant control over the video picture providing me with a sense of video as analogous to the audio signal-controllable in a fluid and malleable way. I understood video not as framework of discrete 'units' of time to be cut and pasted, but as a shifting stream of signals which could be controlled as a musician controlled sound from an instrument. Video – like music, was instant, interactive, direct and fluid.

This perception of video as accessible, fluid and personal was in marked contrast to work that was being made for broadcast television at the time. In an interview for a Channel Four documentary series on British Video Art, I was very clear about my understanding of the potential for video as an art medium.[9] To me, it was like asking a musician about the relationship between music and the radio! An important contributing factor to this view was my parallel freelance activities, which included animation work for children's television.[10] Although free to experiment visually, I was working to a brief with a budget and a production schedule, with a specific target audience. This was a very different set of constraints, and it made me acutely aware of the demands and requirements of broadcast television, which formed a marked contrast to my fine art practice.

The issue of 'audience' for my work was one of the most significant factors. In the early 1980s, it was difficult to know if there *was* an audience for this kind of work other than within the small artistic community that had formed around LVA, the ICA and the art schools. The Arts Council had extended their 'Film-Makers on Tour' scheme to include video artists in 1980, and I made a number of presentations in venues around the UK as part of this scheme, which gave me some measure. Critical writing on video art was limited, and came mainly from other artists who were seeking to develop their own practices. David Hall, Stuart Marshall, Catherine Elwes, Jeremy Welsh, Mick Hartney, Tamara Krikorian, all practitioners themselves, were writing about work that for the most part, reinforced their own ideas about what constituted video art practice. In this period distribution was centred entirely on London Video Arts, who, by the mid-1980s were selecting work on the basis of criteria drawn up by a small panel of volunteers, all of whom were artists.

Time Travelling/A True Story (1982)

Having worked with photography as an influence on memory, I decided to develop a tape about the relationship between memory and the moving image. I was particularly interested in the role of 'narrative', and the tendency of the mind to organise experiences and events into narratives, making life into a kind of story, ignoring events that do not fit, or are ambiguous, smoothing out inconsistencies. *Time Travelling/A True Story* organises fragments of personal 8mm film footage into a story, using a soundtrack as the structuring device.

The tape has two distinct sections; the first presenting the rescanned film footage edited to a modified voice-over from Jean-Paul Sartre's novel *Nausea*. Experimenting with old film footage was itself like the process of playing with memory. The images on the film were of places from my own past – 'authentic' fragments and material evidence of an early fascination with the moving image; a record of my earliest interest in cinema. This was another aspect of the 'self' that could be put alongside the childhood photos in *The Room with a View*. Being able to electronically manipulate, reorganise and re-present these fragments became a major theme of the work; creating a fiction from them was the second level. This, I

The Viewer's
Receptive Capacity,
installation, 1978.

felt, was the strength and uniqueness of video technology in its personal dimension. Video had become a 'support medium' and a contemporary frame for the representation of an 8mm past. These moving images could be framed and contextualised by video as the family album framed the snapshot.

The second section of *Time-Travelling / A True Story* is a kind of reprise. Another fiction, presented in a contemporary idiom, a very obviously manipulated and electronic 'present', which comments on the past by reprising written phrases from the first voice-over as electronically-generated captions. I wanted to make a work composed of as many different layers of image-making as possible. Referring to a kind of inter-textual 'present', I was attempting to weave as complex an image as I could, presenting the video screen as an imaginary space in which these layers could briefly and temporarily mix and condense.

Interlude (Homage to Bugs Bunny) (1983)

Interlude (Homage to Bugs Bunny) was a personal experiment, a soundtrack experiment with patterns made by the repeating musical phrase derived from a 'pirated'[11] sequence from a Bugs Bunny cartoon. The accuracy of my editing (and my edit suite) was tested, and in this sense I saw it initially as a kind of technical exercise. Fascinated by the work of the American 'minimalist' composer Steve Reich, I had became increasingly interested in the visual structure suggested by the relationship between the repeating musical rhythms and the looping cycle of the cartoon characters; the musical structure influencing decisions about where and when to 'cut' the sequence.

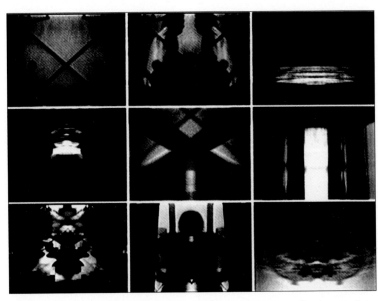

An Imaginary Landscape, Video, 1986.

These ideas notwithstanding, I had also had some preliminary plans to make a piece of work that was 'about' the experience of watching television. An avid Bugs Bunny fan, I had seen this particular episode many times.[12] *Interlude (Homage to Bugs Bunny)* was significant to me because the image became 'physical', both because of the use of duration, which I had learned from the structuralist film-makers, and rhythmical because of what I had learned from listening to Reich. It was also nostalgic, because it referenced childhood television viewing, and conceptually interesting to me because it referred to the 'flow' of programming which by now seemed to define the medium of television so specifically.

An Imaginary Landscape (1986)

An Imaginary Landscape makes reference to a series of musical compositions by John Cage. Cage's influence through Nam June Paik and the Fluxus movement on early video art is fundamental, although the connections to John Cage in my video piece are less direct. I wanted to create an imaginary electronic space – a 'landscape' inhabited purely by reference to the image. The tape describes a space that is completely electronic – existing exclusively within the space of the screen. The landscape is 'imaginary' in the sense that the viewer is taken there through the unfolding of the (tele)visual experience. The progression on the screen from 'real' perspectival/architectural space is presented as a way of arriving there through perceptual means (i.e. by watching the tape unfold as it transforms between a recognisable visual space to one which is purely electronic).

121

The Stream,
Video, 1997.

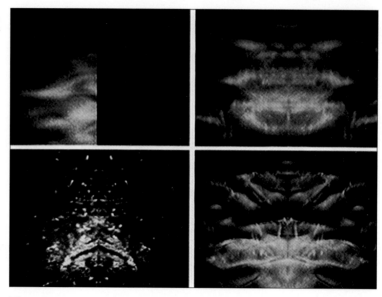

The sequences were processed using an early digital time-base corrector, the Gemini II, a twin-channel frame-store with a limited range of digital effects. To me, this digital storage and retrieval of image-sequences suggested an entirely new approach to the presentation of moving images which problematised durational video work. The issues that arose from this new possibility were not simply in relation to the viewer/artwork relationship, (e.g. in terms of how the work was presented and how meaning was expressed and perceived) but had profound implications on the conception of the work itself. David Dunn and Woody Vasulka have written about this in their article 'Digital Space: A Summary':

> What becomes apparent from the structural demands of this technology is that there is an ability and even an affinity for discrete genre to interact through the binary code in ways which transcend linear cause and effect relationships, revealing new compositional concepts with regard to space, perspective and morphology.[13]

The introduction of digital image-processing into my repertoire heralded a shift in my work and highlighted a creative problem leading to a growing dissatisfaction with pure durational work. In my video tapes of this period I had began to explore ideas about a potential parallel perceptual space created by the viewer/tape relationship. In my subsequent video tape, *The Stream*, I attempted to make this notion more explicit. I believe that the implicit non-linearity of my tape work at this point lead directly into the sculptural video installation work of the next period.[14]

An Imaginary Landscape was most often shown in its single-screen configuration, but was intended as a two-screen piece. In the twin screen version of the work, two identical processed and edited single-screen video tapes are presented side-by-side, running in opposite directions – one 'forward' and one 'reversed', so that one image-sequence begins as a representation of the space it is recorded in, and the other begins as a digital abstraction. As the sequences unfold, the positions reverse, so that they end in opposite positions within the screen. My intention was that there would be no 'real' forward or reverse in the piece. In a sense, this also implies that there is no 'end' to the work either, simply a set of cyclical relationships, a sort of 'moebius strip' of fluid images. This approach to linear presentation would later lead me to abandon durational tape making and begin to concentrate on installations in which the image sequences would be made from repeating loop structures.

The Stream (1985–87)

The Stream is about dialectics – a presentation of opposing parallels, co-existencies and interdependencies, presenting fluid electronic images of flowing matter in relation to a reference to the flow of human cognition. I drew inspiration from the work of David Bohm (1917-1994) who posited the notion of a crucial relationship between mind and matter in *Wholeness and the Implicate Order*. *The Stream* begins with a quotation from the book:

> As careful attention shows, thought itself is in an actual process of movement. That is to say, one can feel a sense of flow in the 'stream of consciousness' not dissimilar to the sense of flow in the movement of matter in general. May not thought itself thus be a part of reality as a whole? But then, what could it mean for one part of reality to 'know' another, and to what extent would this be possible? Does the content of thought merely give us abstract and simplified 'snapshots' of reality, or can it go further, somehow grasp the very essence of the living movement that we sense in actual experience?[15]

The influence of Steve Reich's music is also important to the development of *The Stream*. After attending a lecture about *The Desert Music* (1984) in which Reich spoke of his attempts to set the verses of William Carlos Williams, I decided I would try to produce a 'video setting' of *Music for Large Ensemble* (1977). The tape was not simply a set of images to accompany Reich's music, but an attempt to present something much more complex, both abstract and philosophical. The fluid video images should be seen to hold metaphoric and poetic significance, to be understood not simply as the record of something that existed in nature, but

On Being,
Video, colour, 1985.

Still Life With a Monitor,
Video, 1983.

mediated via a technological process which ordered them for an entirely different purpose other than to simply re-present them. The images of the flowing river had, like the music, an abstract relationship to nature. I wanted to suggest that the parallel between thought and image in nature was mirrored in the language of the moving electronic image. My intention was to merge the physical, rhythmic experience of the music with the mind's visual and visceral memory of flowing water, to make a work which established a set of interdependent relationships between the movement of the music, the flowing water, the video imagery and the flux of thought process of memory and cognition.

In many of my video tapes in the 1980s I had been interested in notions of flow, both in terms of the 'flow of information' and with regard to the inherent properties of the video medium, such as how the signal is produced, recorded and displayed, but in *The Stream* this was combined with an interest in philosophical issues about the nature of matter itself. From *The Stream* onwards, flow is much more tied into an enquiry into the nature of thought processes and consciousness in relation to the substances and materials that comprise the video image and the physical world it is part of. This tape led directly on to a series of sculptural installations I produced in the 1990s in which the relationship between the two dimensional image on the screens and the objects in the space becomes the principle arena of meaning.

Notes

1. Made in collaboration with Gabrielle Brown.

2. And subsequent tapes in the same series, *Scanning, On the Pier*, and *Clockwise and Counter Clockwise*, (1978–1979).

3. The 'Videokalos Image Processor' was designed and built by British video artist Peter Donebauer in collaboration with Richard Monkhouse. See Peter Donebauer, 'A Personal Journey Through a New Medium', ed. Julia Knight, *Diverse Practices, A Critical Reader on British Video Art* (University of London Press, Arts Council of England, 1996).

4. Influenced by Joan Jonas' *Vertical Roll* (1972).

5. See www.meigh-andrews.com for an interview with Steina and Woody Vasulka.

6. The original partners were Alexandra Meigh, Peter Livingstone and myself.

7. See *Putting Myself in the Picture* (London: Camden Press, 1986).

8. Exhibitions of *The Room With a View* included: 'New British Video', Museum of Long Beach, California, 1983; 'Video/Performance', The Photographer's Gallery, 1984, the ICA, London, 1982; The Basement, Newcastle, 1982).

9. *The Eleventh Hour*; 'Video One', 'Video Two' and 'Video Three', directed by Terry Flaxton and produced by Penny Dedman of 'Triple Vision', commissioning Editor Rod Stoneman. Broadcast on Channel 4 in September 1985.

10. Between 1981–88, I worked freelance for BBC TV, producing over 100 short films and video animations for *Take Hart, Hart Beat* and *Know How*.

11. The pun here was intentional, this tape was made before the brief vogue for 'Scratch Video', but was in fact, shown as part of a survey of British scratch video work in 1986 ('New British Video' Atelilier de Pedegogie et d'animation, Strasbourg, France).

12. *Irate Pirate*, dir. Chuck Jones.

13. David Dunn and Woody Vasulka, 'Digital Space: A Summary', http://www.art-scilab.org/pages/digital space.html, pp 1–5.

14. For further information, see my essay 'Sculptural Video Installations 1989–95' in *Experiments in Moving Image* (London: Epigraph Publications, 2004).

15. David Bohm, *Wholeness and the Implicate Order* (London: Routledge and Kegan Paul, 1980), 'Introduction', p. ix.

Chapter fourteen

Andrew Kötting

What he does, how he does it and the context in which it has been done: An Alphabetarium of Kötting

Gareth Evans and Andrew Kötting

E is for …

Experimental moving image – i.e. technological, narrative, expanded, performative, theatrical, sculptural, structural, formal, participatory – and the opening up of writing possibilities. **Explicitly** Kötting as intoned through the cipher that was **Evans'** theoretical debate on his oeuvre and subtext.

Eden. From the garden back to the garden; it is perhaps not overstating the case to say that the fact of Eden and the unique insights she has bought to Kötting's life and work have led his explorations into areas. She offers thresholds for ventures into the very core of consciousness and perception. Eden, as (dis)abled daughter, agent, collaborator and catalyst, is essential to appreciating how Kötting works, why he works, how he deploys and values time and how he is not afraid. How he is opened out and into celebration by a 'situation' normally deemed to be one that 'reduces' possibility. Eden embodying and generating an instinctual tolerance.

English/ness. Albion the longer, older, wilder island, Anglican Gothic, but England is the place into which the work is lovingly tossed. The amour/hate relation with what makes us is the tick-tock here: an ironic celebration of things Anglo that allows for absurd affections to dance a pier-end afternoon waltz with occasional vehemence towards insular narrow-mind, but more likely amused observance of island ways and folk. Time Based Media as hymns to 'Ancient and Modern' madness.

Experience. Sleeves rolled up and forearms plunged into the pulsing tissue of existence. Work it like a Cornish tin miner, your very life part of the seam. Hands inside a sentient being, head in the air and not up its own cinematic colon:

F is for **Family**. Tribal without the fences. They acknowledge extension, the social constituency of being, that then allows the private visions to blossom from the head out, meeting the wider air, changing and being changed. Where there is dys-family, let it be used.

Fence (up over it). Vistas larger there: a refuge and safe-haven outside the Gulag that is the mainstream pantomime. But it's not just choice. It's necessity, a stratagem by which to reach the future of one's own life. Avant-Garde and wanton experimentalists. If the halls of access are sealed against them, then they shall (do) wander this world with the evidence and the report. They project the films on ravaged sheets and weather-beaten walls. And those who value such reports shall be there also, waiting first, then watching, then transported… evaluating the impact and role of the artist's community and now writing their *anthologies of*.

(Self)-**Funding**. The British cultural machine feels self-satisfyingly well oiled enough without these larky sparkers running amok with their crazy rants. Now, it seems, at best, from film fund end, these works are tolerated, almost with embarrassment (by some backers even), like a loud relative on the gin at a funeral. But more often, such relevant outrider visions – and others in their tribe – are seen as barbarian deviations that somehow got in when the windy lookout was un-staffed. That they were made at all on this rocky pile is enough for awe. Bums-on-seats, it's a low-end shot for certain, but not in the ambition. Like the cockroach after the blast, perhaps the justice comes when the struggle they've been through to arrive at all, means that they can survive as documents and testaments to other ways of telling. Someone giving it out – or not – does not determine the making. A man lives, he thinks and feels. He makes. Somehow.

Funny ha-ha & **funny peculiar**. Exactly.

G is for…

Gallivant. The first proper long one. Are you shore? The desire and faith to explore family and autobiography. The littoral truths of an island are perambulated in a shaggy circuit activated by family across three generations, (well de/scribed in Iain Sinclair's *Sight and Sound* dispatch 'Big **Granny** and Little Eden'.) What must be mused upon however is the democracy of looking. The wide ear and eye, both for folk, their ways and for signage. Make the personal a generous filter into the social.

H is for ... **He** is not alone. There are and have been many of them and **Happenstance** and bricollage. Structuralist, post structuralist, essayist, non-sequiturist, modernist, post modernist, late modernist and **hyper**-modernist, actionist, narrativist, anti-narrativist, implied narrativist and thus **Hybrid**. n. An animal or plant resulting from a cross between genetically unlike individuals. Hybrids between different species are usually sterile. Not always....always room for the not-always.

I is for ... **Imagination**. The more you imagine, the more difficult it is to find words for what you're imagining.

J is for Derek **Jarman**. Proof positive and evidence of a commitment to experiment with the moving image outside of the industrialised pantomime. An index and register of the Kötting (**Jackofalltradesandmasterofnone**) (vulgar?) project. For why? Because they are too interested in things; they are both irreverent and kneel at the altar of a life-given seriousness, a creative urgency-imperative; they work in all disciplines, media and weathers; they build no fence between life and work; they thread a personal mythos with that of a hybrid nation; they dig into place but think wide; they layer intent; they are shredders of linear time; they hymn the margins; they speak in 'folk' languages; they are found challenging, a threat even, by much of the state cultural apparatus; funding is not a given; family and friends are central to their practice and project; they are the glue and they have both taken a fine photo.

K is for ... **Klipperty Klopp.** A man running around in a field. Obsessive, arcane, manic. Performance in the Great Out Of Doors. We'll never know with him ... where he was going until he was coming back ... and then he'll swear blind half the time it wasn't him that went.

L is for ... **Language**, lingo, gramlot, verbiage: formulation of the current in relation to the historical. Word as a new strain of image making. Visuals in the sonic as in the seen. Respect for place, personality and the social. The constantly mutating rituals of the daily. Let it all out of the mouth and in at the ear. Never Oxford English, but multilingual ease. Lived **lipwork**. Biodiversity of the tongue.

Leila Dorcas McMillan, without whom… and whose menstrual blood ignited a fire. The Sibyl to the BadbLoOd &.

M is for … **Making** (do). And **Modus** operandi for him, like so many others. **Mother** Thatcher the bully, the great 'inspirer', no more funding so to the getting-on-with-it. Stretch the life one finds oneself within, like skin, into fresh forms. Hands on haptic. Turn the lack of and inadequate to advantage and celebrate the difficulties. One word in French: faire – to do *and* make. Fair play to them, if it's not one thing it's another. **Making** (it up) as they go along. **Map**. Normally folded around the stretches covering London, the South (Coast) and French Pyrenees. The axis of action. The trigonometry of incipient desires.

Mapping Perception. Pan-**media** expanded cinema. The beating core of how brain makes mind makes consciousness makes things and makes the work, work? Makes it **matter**, makes critical text? How it **magpies** things for use. There is, in mind and work, a constant re-incorporation of the stuff across time and place. Experimental scientific love poem to a daughter. **Margins** are central. Edge lands are normal.

Man-in-the-mountain dereliction. **Mongrel**. Nowhere is more mongrel, more nomadic than 'terra cinema', (eArthouse) in its stories, yarns, hybrids, mixed-race in form and content; in its frames and personnel, in the influences that wander like rogue crew members between shoots or the formats that find their way in. Deploy **multiple** styling for the multiple realities, audio/visual dysfunction, fissures in sequence, cutaway from the linear, everything is possible.

N is for **never** a finite **Narrative,** neither one thing nor another, hither and dither within the neverneverlands of spillage, post polemics and critical histories, **new**.

Nomadic. Keep innovative production alive in this country. From the outskirts (but at the centre of experience) keep the creative human story turning. Tell tales from the end zones, fire yarns for gathered folk to stave off night (but dig into it also, like darkest peat, damp to touch). Mongrel futures are the only workable ideal. Reclaim the current in relation to the historical, mine the deep strains of popular experience and folk memory, re-present them for the digital age.

O is for … ö, Umlaut and Kraut. He doesn't know where he originated from but he's been sound in his family for years and years and years. **Occitania**, Cathars and the French folk of **Oc**. A radicalism of people, culture, lifestyle, belief, geography. Peripatetic bandit country. Tunnels, subterranean and the *underground*. An influence on the work. **Orient** and exotic; alternative film

Mapping Perception, 35mm film, colour, 1996.

Acumen, 16mm film, colour, 1991.

culture as early Moorish spices and Turkish delight instead of boiled potatoes and Bakewell tart.

P places contemporary moving image practice and **polemical** discourse within the historical context. Post Cathar and pre-eminent evaluation of the impact and role of the artist; always has been

130

Hububinthebaobabs, 16mm film, Black & White, 1987.

and always will be. The placeless **place** and the co-ordinated zone share the projection when it comes to territory. We move through it on our ceaseless journey towards understanding. Some people carry it, like a burden or a memory, or both. They bring other places to other people, who then take a little of the weight and mix it with their own longing to create narrative. So not really place as land-scape at all, but more of Manley Hopkins' *inscape*, consciousness as it might look if it were dimensioned into say video or film. Searching for works that have been to the edges and looked over, shamanic flights returning from the far reaches with word of the void's whistling rim.

Pan's people. *The school of* anarchic Arcadian genius loci Pan. Work can challenge pretty Pastoral, never the Merchant Ivory, always a streak of debauched fertility and the wildness of outlaw woodland. Non-urban and definitely not happy-clappy; rather it's where the bestial occupies folk and bloodletting. **Performance**. Artifice as an index of certain truths. It might start with the body's business and work out. From 8mm onwards, reels soaked in Live Art and multi-media japery, the staging of self and others, perhaps as an acknowledgement of certain confessional tics in the social order and **Politics**. It does not have to be placard politics but the vision must be inherently committed to degrees of dispossession and the reverse – reclamation. Less the megaphone, more the hope of 'politics' and ever the **Prank**. n. A mischievous trick or joke, esp. one in which something is done rather than said, or is it?

Process. The work is as much process as framed product. In constant flux, images and sounds migrate, are curious about the elsewhere, are remixed, lose titles and gain new labels briefly; fixity is not the spine here; things arrive into being are held like water in the hand, and then pass on. Are flawed, unfinished. This is how the work is like the life. It holds light like mercury. It pools and spreads.

Q is for …

(nowt so) **Queer as folk**. People are the bedrock of the landscape, from which grow flowers and trees of ideas. Family, friends, strangers all bring worlds, more or less delved in. In the *eARTHOUSE Manifesto*, it is counselled that there be an obligation to spend time with arms or feet inside another sentient being, alive or dead. This is a more or less accurate description of relations with folk as much as fauna. The stories and histories are inhabited by, and live within, people. The world breathes through people. Through what they do and fail to do; what they reach and fail to reach. From home-movie to Imax spectacle.

R is for …

Regional. No place is less than any other place. In potential. And **Ritual**. The functional symbolic. The acts that explain lineage, thresholds, group identities and their reasons; to themselves if nobody else. The oeuvre, and the actions of those drawn into its web, is one of accumulating, acquired and observed ritual. Ritual is the psycho-geography of personality and community. It layers identity so that it can be read and mis-read. The **reflection** as an attempt to **rationalise** and locate the work within an historical canon.

Richard **Rorty** and his Final Vocabulary – forever impressed – pre-empting Bauman's Liquid Modernity, thus few closures in the work … He's crossing the river to get to the other side, don't ask him why, the river's not wide.' *(Hoi Polloi)* set in the Pyrenees – **Realm of Old Oc**. Here is the generating locus for fifteen years of production. Here the house site of much work but more, the escape route into the real work. The high ground of all the ideas. Conception and working up. Its isolation. Running, walking and sitting there, mulling it into being.

So to **Scale**. Scale shifts, accompanied by similar strategies in sound and thematic. They are central to the operation. The spectrum of sensual awareness that acknowledges continuous flux from macro to micro is seen as simply being the case of things. It is less an aesthetic choice (while being one) than an accurate response to things on the ground. It's in the nature of attention.

Structuralism? Gently does it, John Smith-style. A little doesn't hurt but don't forget the humour. **Self, Soil and Society**. The seamless story. The moebius strip of relations. The hall of mirrors. What one starts with, goes on with … picture after picture after picture, whatever the per second.

So to the **Sound** the world makes. Not just music, not just

Gallivant, 16mm film, colour, 1996.

ambience, not just voices, not just found sound, archive echoes, signal spillage, technical accidents, hiss, guffaws, foley and radio. But all of it and also the silence and also, what cannot be heard. It's the sound the world makes. Without sound, vision is stumbling in the dark. And anyway, there's a bonus: *Noise Drives the Devil Away*.

Stock. Anything. From 8mm to 35mm, pic to pixel, digital to découpage. Whatever's available, whatever works, a bricolage and right carry on.

T is for ... **Time**. Hurry up gents; it's body time vs. geological time, the rock against the public clock, the seasons stirring it up with 'living memory'. Sculpting in time is the aim of the game, whether in council house close or with continental reach. The timepiece has human hands, its face is the sky at dusk and its numbers a tree's banded years, ringing in the changes.

Things for the experimental moving image; Objects. Bodies. Matter. Clutter. Flotsam. Jetsam. Consumer ephemerals. Landfill. Mindfill. Stuff. The Real. Where ideas live. Whether it be a borrowing from John Berger's *Pig Earth* or digging deep into Zola's *La Terre*. Film lives absolutely in a material world – bull and man, sperm on the hands, pigs in branches, rooms like caves or armpits, piss in graveyards, phlegm, pus, shit, rock, rain, mud, mud. Institutions are built of walls. A vision for the differently sighted. **Traces** and smidgeons, a little bit of this and a little bit of that. Picking them up, leaving them. **Transportative**: 'I'm going to take you to a place where you have not been before' *(Klipperty Klopp)*.

Tree. Lumberjack (of all trades and master of none); trees as plankage *and* life force. A mountain think-tank bang in Ariège **timber territory**. From the under-tree, the root expanse, artesian influences feeding in through the practise itself. Trunk, to the work's arching network of boughs, branches, foliage. Hubbub in the Baobabs: shelter and story. Often weather-shaped *and* shaping, focusing, patterning the surrounding area, it acknowledges dependence while simultaneously standing clear. For John Fowles, the tree is the prime imago of creative endeavour.

U is for ... anti **Ubermensch** and **Useful**. 'It's in the most unlikely places you're likely to find things.' *(Gallivant Pilot)* and **Undermine** (the self). 'They took his body and drank his blood and didn't feel very good.' *(Anvil Head the Hun)*. Ongoing tension between seriousness and nonsense. Serious nonsense. Certain doubts should prevail in the work. They help humanise those lofty intentions that make the project, they protect from those that take everything that little bit too seriously.

Therefore **V** is for **Vagabond**. Hither and dither, upstairs and downstairs and in the lady's chamber. The rationale is not to locate the work within any historical bloodline. The **Videosyncratic** or Vaudeville Cow Opera?

Virus (benign), it's cross-media: the idea is out and spreading. Hosts are numerous and the virus can survive in the harshest environments. In fact, there's a sense it can turn adversity to its breeding advantage infiltrating diverse paradigms and tested in experimental moving image.

Voices. In the head, throat and chest, on the tongue like varieties of honey. Archive accents, society sounds. The nanny noises of radio revelations, institutional informing through information. Knocking up against local crackle, the chatter of place and profession. Stories told in the timbre they happened in. An island's audio bank of tales tall and true. The *(Hoi Polloi)* poetry of necessary phrasing. Listen closely and you're halfway there ... **watching** carefully ... I wonder how many of you did?

W is (other) **Words** that are important and that can be gathered here as time goes on ...**Work**. **Written**, this, in the shadow of The Long Man, at Myrtle Cottage (c.1550), Wilmington, East Sussex, Stoke Newington, London and Gensing Road, St Leonards on Sea, back in East Sussex. And **within** the rarefied atmosphere of the thing that is; the past forty years of practice led polemics.

X and **Y**: 'You** don't ask to be born, do you? You're born, **you** live, you die. You're here, you're not, **you** are and you're not. And that's the end of it.' *(Visionary Landscapes)*

and **Z** not yet attained? Digital futures and highDef disasters.

A is for ... for the beginning and the buzzing of the bees. **An anthology of ...**

Acumen n. the ability to judge well; keen discernment, insight and (not *that* concise) compendium of a whole stack of tics, washed in a Paradjanovian symbolic sheen and a Sean Lockian black comedy with a logic all of its own. What might be its covert moral? Are we fish out of water? We live in the lives we live in. Somehow, there is a surreal making do, a strange survival. A world in which **ambiguity** might reign supreme.

Aphorism as an historical context. An aristocratic genre of creativity? The wisdom of concise thinking, of experience compacted into essence. This might be at the heart of the work. The fragmentary and 'unfinished', the fleeting and the found. Set these to dance with digression, wilful extension, waffle, natural curiosity, distraction and a sometime reluctance to discard and you have the oeuvre we might be considering.

Academics and **Advisors**, Could**avists** and Should**avists**, Historians. They are there not because they have special access to truth but because they have been around and can read on.

B is for ... **Body**. Ur text. Vessel and votive, subject and object. The physicality of the work, text, image, language, subjects, cannot be understood separate from an appreciation of how the maker views flesh. From micro to man-tall, sphincter to six foot, its trajectory, provocation, context and fallout are the streaming plots at the root of all manifested. And there is a democracy to **bodies**. From the *Act of seeing with one's own eyes* to Stelarc *Suspensions*. They fuck and fart, bleed, pus, puke. They also come in all sizes and with all adornments. They are never mocked, always given equal footing. And those that are loved – Leila's, Eden's – are acknowledged openly and often as being indispensable to the continuation, nay, the very **being** of the project.

Being the layered reading of territories, urban and other, via signs of all kinds and without prejudice as to the source or status of the prompt. **Being** the eyes and all senses of a conscious drift through space, time, architecture, experience, history, the latent future. A Psyche and its geography.

Collaboration - David Burnand, John Cheetham, Jem Finer, Eden Kötting, Andrew Lindsay, Sean Lock, Mark Lythgoe, Leila McMillan, Toby McMillan, Andrew Mitchell, Gary Parker, Russel Stopford, Nick Gordon Smith, Mark Wheatley, Ben Woolford, and, and, and … Soul-aids to a persons work. Without others the self that is known might stop. Thematically, solitary figures in the oeuvre are de-centred. They only stabilise into (eccentric) order in the orbit of others. They collaborate on the business of being. On surviving existence.

Commas, semi-colons; colons even: springboards of suspense, breath held a beat. But full stops. Never … rather a trinity of stepping-stones to futures. Assimilation, collation and then the regurgitation, contingency a must.

Creation myths. Films as the shared, seen dreams of tribe, family and selves. Fables of the de/re-construction. Looping lines of narrative out of ordered time and territory. Undoing things to make new things, new arrangements of people, place, power and priority.

Cut-ups are closer to reality. No singular grain of truth. Bits and pieces gleaned from a set of **contexts** and practices. They are no longer bound to any prescriptive reading of the term, but instead exist on the edges of the discipline. There has been a **'change'** and an undermining of the perimeter fence that separated experimental film and video with that of mainstream **cinema** we have seen a breeding of diversity.

Kötting is of that diversity. Time-based work may have wanted to disrupt the meanings and values of **contemporary culture** but these are no longer grounded in the foundational certainties associated with 'modernist' experimental film and video. There has been too much 'seepage' and there is no longer a 'given' or 'self-evident' context. Fluids travel easily.

Thus **D** is for … **Difference**. The work as a difference engine. A vehicle into otherness and revelation. Aesthetically, bodily, mentally. Everything Normal? No.

Digression. If you don't leave the path, you won't see the waterfall.

Chapter fifteen

Ardent for Some Desperate Glory: Revisiting Smothering Dreams

Daniel Reeves

In 1978, after returning from a lengthy stay in India, I began to work with the video medium for the first time. I had taken time off for some travel and study of meditation and yoga after completing a degree in cinema the previous year. The sudden realization of how subtle, plastic and immediate the video editing process was came at the most perfect moment for me. All of the fluidity and spontaneity offered by the medium was as a complete revelation. I was thirty years old and hungry to grapple with issues that my poetry and sculpture could not reach. An immediate convert, I saw clearly that I would no longer have to struggle with the a/b roll, work print, confirmation process and subsequent delayed vision of film editing that had hindered my aspiration to deal directly with motion imagery in the making of transformational art. Shortly after collaborating with Jon Hilton to make *Thousands Watch*, a short video work concerned with the proliferation of nuclear weaponry as a metaphor for suicide, in February 1979 I comprised a short list of experimental works that I hoped to create in years to come. A few of these projects were meant to deal with personal and societal issues of organised violence, trauma, memory and denial. Two of the works were in time successfully produced from my wish list: *Smothering Dreams* (1981) and *Obsessive Becoming* (1995). It is the earlier work that will be explored in this brief essay. In doing so I will touch on issues of funding,

137

dissemination, aesthetics and technique. Both of these productions are first person narrative works created with a clear intention to conjure a doorway in an almost alchemical manner for the viewer to explore her or his own grief, confusion, anger and loss. I also sensed intuitively that the process of making both films would have a cathartic charge for me as well.

Smothering Dreams looked directly at the childhood myths of war that were an important strand in the nurturing and cultivation of my generation that came of age in the 1960s. At the same time, it juxtaposed and contrasted these mythologies with the realities of combat faced by young men who were for the most part teenagers dressed for the role. My naïve expectations were completely shattered by my year in combat. On the 20th of January 1968 I somehow survived an ambush of my platoon just south of the DMZ in the opening days of the Tet Offensive in Viet Nam. Despite our training and experience we were completely unprepared and nearly overwhelmed. Over half the platoon of thirty-one, including our commanding officer, were killed after we were trapped behind an armoured vehicle for a good part of an afternoon, after being ambushed by a much larger force of North Vietnamese soldiers. Some of those who died that day had arrived in Viet Nam only a few days before. I was a young Marine radio operator and later during my six-month stay in a military hospital, I was awarded the Silver Star for gallantry in action, the Vietnamese Cross of Gallantry, and the Purple Heart Medal for wounds received in combat. These have not been a source of pride for me, and in fact I am not sure where they are anymore. It is not that I am ashamed of them, but my memory of war in those early years was characterised by remorse and despair. The medals only aggravated my sense of guilt at having survived. What I remember most about my year in Viet Nam and the ensuing years of psychological and emotional recovery was a feeling of betrayal, anguish and an overwhelming sense of sorrow for the lives on both sides that were tossed away for such an enormous folly. I had signed a waiver in order to leave for Viet Nam at seventeen years of age, and had my eighteenth birthday on a troop ship somewhere on the Pacific Ocean. Until I arrived on the beaches of Quaing Tri province, I had fervently believed that; not only was our cause just and our goals noble but that we were offering up our lives for the good of others. When I awakened to what we were really doing in Viet Nam and understood how terribly the people of the countryside were suffering and realised that they were dying needlessly in a war with no meaning, it was as if my eyes were open for the first time. Yet by then it was also too late. For a number of years after surviving I would revisit the incident of the ambush in a chronic recurring nightmare. This return to horror kept me running in all the wrong directions at times. After my release from the military I began to make art as if on autopilot. In an attempt to reconstruct my life in solitude, I lived in a small cabin in the woods of Maine without running water and electricity for three years. To survive, I isolated myself completely from a world of commerce and the quotidian *business as usual* approach to life that for me was the very engine that propelled my country and myself into such savagery and madness.

> A young officer stares into my fear as we rock back and forth in the warping air. Where his mouth should be he becomes a thick red waterfall that won't be turned aside with any field expedient tourniquet or fervent prayer known to anyone on board. I never have enough strength to leap beyond my own horror and touch him anywhere to let him know that it will surely be alright.
>
> Surely be fine –
> Even though all my heart keeps wailing over and over is:
> no mouth
> no teeth
> no tongue
> no fucking way they will ever fix this shit.
>
> From *I Have This One Afternoon*
> Daniel Reeves, 1988[1]

After finishing college under a disabled veterans rehabilitation program in 1977, I went to see the Hollywood film *The Deer Hunter* the following year. It had been touted as a defining cinematic statement on the war in Viet Nam but I left the cinema half way through the screening when I understood how wrong-headed and ignorant the portrayal of the North Vietnamese soldiers was. It troubled me intensely that popular culture was offering up visions of armed conflict that obscured the potential for insight and reconciliation, and perpetuated worn out myths of racial and cultural inferiority. It wasn't such a cerebral reaction at first, but more a visceral feeling of a strong disgust mixed with anger. This extremely popular film, although replete with cinematic skill, craft and virtuosity of performance, served up the same sensational projection of the otherness and brute nature of an Asian enemy that characterised films about the Japanese in the Pacific that were common fare in theatres when I was a boy. At one point in *The Deer Hunter*, North Vietnamese soldiers are shown forcing prisoners to play a drawn out version of Russian roulette with all the typical arch villain monstrousness depicted in Hollywood films produced during the 1940s. I perceived this as a kind of cultural brainwashing and evidence of a subtle, pervasive and seductive amnesia that sets in when a notion of war surfaces in popular culture. In my dismay, I

139

All images in this chapter taken from *Smothering Dreams*, Video, 1981.

resolved to try to offer up something from my own experience that would respond directly to this pervasive militarization of consciousness. More importantly for my psychic life was the intention to break through the boundaries of my own despair by creating a powerful eulogy.

After receiving a National Endowment for the Arts fellowship in 1980, I set out to make the work that was eventually to be entitled *Smothering Dreams*. My total budget for a working process of nearly two years was approximately $20,000. If it had not been for the commitment, dedication and personal sacrifice of a great number of contributors this would never have been possible. The start up monies came through The Television Workshop in New York, NY, the major experimental broadcast television in the US at the time. Having always taken an artists approach to production, I wrote, recorded and edited the work. Because I was not adverse to using film, the work became a hybrid video production that made use of one inch type C video tape as a master format in the field and in post production, but also employed 35 mm and 16mm film from both archival and field recorded imagery sources. During this period my process was not in the least way traditional (no scenarios, story boards, scripts and cumbersome links to producers). I generated imagined and recreated scenes both metaphorical and actual, researched and gathered archival materials, music and historical voice actualities while keeping up an active reading and writing regimen that I hoped would inform and enrich the final work. During this time I was also interviewed for a PBS documentary entitled *Soldiers of a Recent Forgotten War* by the artist Philip Mallory Jones. Philip eventually allowed me to use the audio outtakes from my interviews that ultimately provided the somewhat ambiguous first person narrative track for *Smothering Dreams*.

It had always been my intention to avoid making the work MY STORY writ large in order to open the work more fully to the viewer participant. In the immediate years after the war, the suicide, addiction and incarceration statistics for Viet Nam combat veterans had become an unfolding catastrophe. The middle of the road media were only interested in the sensational aspects of this terrible haemorrhage for a few flickering moments. I was aware of a responsibility to speak for those who had little or no public voice. It had become important to me in the process of creation to construct a substantial persona that would gradually emerge in the texture of the storyline. Yet, I considered it equally important to fashion an emotional modality and non-specific identity for this voice, to provide a kind of transparency that would also allow other refrains of memory from another point of view into the mix. A good example of this is the mother who states that she *'felt like she was going blind'* when she was told that her son was dead. It is an oblique reference to my own mother who fainted and fell off the back porch when an official car pulled into the dooryard after I had been wounded; but it also serves as a kind of armature for the universal and personal memory of the abrupt arrival of the most tragic news. In fact none of the voices are identified during the tape, although it is clear that continuity is provided by a certain single voice among the others.

By using my voice from an interview that was generated in a real exchange, as opposed to a prepared narrative text, a strength of presence characterised by natural tonality, spontaneity and earnestness threads sparsely yet clearly through the piece. I also used the voice of Ron Kovic, the author of *Born on the Fourth of July* who was wounded and paralysed for life during the same battle. We hear a fragment of his speech in front of the Congress building in Washington overlaid with the sound of weeping taken from an army instructional film used for training those whose job it is to notify the relatives of the dead.

> I am the living death.
> The Memorial Day on wheels.
> I am your Yankee Doodle Dandy
> Your John Wayne come home
> Your Fourth of July firecracker
>   exploding in the grave.[2]
>
> Ron Kovic

Earlier in the work, over a montage of clips from popular cultural and archival images from documentary, training and promotional films from the government, I make a first-person statement addressing the same issues from another vantage point:

> I was a cowboy, a knight, bomber pilot ... fastest gun in the west ... a winner in any gun fight ... silent, strong, loyal, and shedding not a tear ... running from one movie dream to another ... we played it by the book, repeating hand-me-down war stories told by blind men.
>
> Daniel Reeves
> *Smothering Dreams*, 1981

My continuing efforts to uncover archival materials was aided by civilian workers at the U.S. Army Film Library which at that time was on a small military base in rural Pennsylvania. After going through the normal protocols and restrictions, things began to change due to the persuasiveness of intention and integrity. After the staff noticed what I was trying to do with my visual research they were happy to let me go through everything that was not in the Top Secret vault. This restricted repository had, until the late

1960s, held all the Japanese motion picture materials gathered immediately after the bombings of Hiroshima and Nagasaki. The government kept this stunning and revelatory footage hidden until the great film historian at Columbia University, Eric Barnouw, pressed for it's release and eventually made the powerful short documentary *Hiroshima – Nagasaki – August 1945* (1970) with footage kept secret for over twenty five years. In any case, I was permitted to have access to everything and allowed to take hundreds of hours of 16mm film materials back to Cornell University where I was working to make film transfers to one inch videotape masters. In contrast, when I completed a few days of archival research at the Marine Corps Film Library in Virginia, my request to duplicate selected materials was firmly denied. Curiously enough the stated reason was the potential for emotional stress for the loved ones of the wounded and dying Marines depicted. This policy has been firmly codified in law. The United States Government now reserves the right to send your son or daughter back home on a closed coffin but completely restricts the right of all citizens to view the corporeal evidence of its military misadventures. Since November of 1991 the Pentagon has banned the media or public citizens from filming or photographing the return of flag draped coffins from war zones. In 1996, a Federal Court of Appeals upheld the ban and it has been reinforced extensively by the Bush administration during the war in Iraq.[3]

After being shut down by the Marine Corps, I knew that I still had sufficient materials from other sources including the Army, so I did not waste time pressing a case that might be won but would demand much more expense and effort than I could afford if I was to get the film completed in time for broadcast on September 6, 1981. My plan from the start had been to try to achieve a sort of fractured gestalt of imagery and sound centred on the actual ambush. I desired to reconstruct both reality and dream reflection strengthened by a quality of heightened verisimilitude that suggested the fragmented hallucinatory nature of such intense violence. My intention was driven by a sense that fewer people would support calls for war by default or design if they had any idea of the full dimension of the terror and suffering involved. At some point well in to the second year of production, after completing a short work entitled *Body Count*, that served as a study for the larger work it became clear to me that I would have to stage a dramatic recreation of the ambush. There simply was no footage available that came close to the intensity that I demanded. Clearly combat cinematographers for the most part just stop filming when things fall apart.

> I didn't want to have to shoot those scenes, to recreate the afternoon. It was frightening and too close to the real thing. I was very fortunate because what came out of it was so much more compelling. It was shot in a way that allowed-real energy to come through people. Crew and actors were really terrified, actors were crying without reserve, and the final condensed period of filming took place in such a short period of time that everyone came close to reliving that same experience.[4]

Eventually by late May of 1981 I had assembled a cast of sixteen or so young acting students from Ithaca College with one older professional to play the Lieutenant. I also managed to put together a completely skilled but unpaid crew of engineers, line producers, pyrotechnic people, audio engineers, and professional film and video makers to operate the extra cameras for the two full takes of the actual combat scenes. Altogether we were about thirty-three cast and crew, approximately the number of the original platoon. Because my strategy was intended to foster a deep bonding and understanding amongst us all I chose from the outset to spend a great deal of time in preparation leading up to two very full days of shooting during the longest days of late June. After several long sessions of presentation and discussion I asked everyone involved to read two pertinent but radically different books on the Viet Nam war; *Dispatches* by Michael Herr and *Winners and Losers* by Gloria Emerson. After several weeks of preparation we recorded material over a two-day period culminating in two running takes recorded in the falling light of the late afternoon of the second day. Each take lasted about ten minutes as there was only enough blank ammunition and other supplies available to sustain the momentum. Over the shooting period the actors were required to stay completely in character to build up the emotive and psychological resonance that they would carry into the denouement of the final ambush. To a certain extent this moment was designed to come as a surprise. The group knew approximately where it would unfold but not precisely when it would occur. I had determined through my own camera practice that I would record with a heavy RCA 3 tube colour camera linked to the first generation of Sony's one inch field recorders carried by another operator in order to record the highest quality possible. Partly due to the weight of the camera but mostly informed by my wish to have the most fluid and subjective view of the action possible, I chose to keep the lens at its widest angle dangling and soaring the camera slowly and steadily through the action, at times passing only inches from the faces of the actors. This meant that there would be no reference view either through viewfinder or monitor, but by then I had developed a style that would be reliable and strong as long as there were no technical catastrophes. Also on account of the somewhat modified cinéma verité style and the relative expense of the dramatic recreation it was decided that there would be two 16mm cameras recording along with an additional professional ¾ inch camera and recorder. These additional camera views were invaluable in the final edit for segments that required a different feel or vantage.

> *Smothering Dreams* ambushes images of Vietnam, both re-staged memories and archival shots and narrative films, to unravel how they detour pain into male fantasies. *Smothering Dreams*, then, exorcises these images from their masculinist frameworks in order for Reeves to reclaim his physical pain as a combat veteran. It is through the wound that Reeves moves toward a recognition of how boyhood, violence, and nationalist wars conspire to destroy the senses. The tape tries to re-create the psychic space of combat pain for the spectator as well, not in the sense of having the spectator identify with Reeves, but in the sense of having the senses rewired to see war as destructive of the human psyche in a collective sense, a movement from the outside images of battle to the inside image-scapes of subjectivity. Near the end of the tape, Reeves clarifies this strategy: 'I don't think the average person has any idea of what combat is like'.[5]

When it was all over and the smoke drifted along the surface of the swamp water stained red from stage blood, I remember everyone being completely overwhelmed emotionally. A kind of terrible yet benevolent fury of grace had descended on our activities. People were holding on to one another and weeping as if what had transpired were utterly real. One actor, a good friend, had put ear plugs in his ears and did not hear the signal to cut so he was lying in the water clutching his chest and writhing with spasms as if in agony. We thought he was having a heart attack and were immensely relieved when he sat up removed his plugs and said he was fine. I was absolutely sure during those final minutes that if I could hold it all together over the next two months of round-the-clock editing, the work would achieve the level of strength I aspired to.

> *Smothering Dreams* begins with imagery of bodies in a swamp, and ends with a young boy wandering through the same scene. Walking as if in a dream, yet more curious than horrified, the boy is established not only as Reeves's perception of himself as a child, by also as the embodiment of a kind of glaring innocence and naive cultural view of war. Shot in slight soft-focus and almost painterly with the bloodstained water and refined composition, this opening shot also establishes the stylistic realm of the work, graphic yet artfully composed. A poem by Wilfred Owen forms the soundtrack: 'If in some smothering dreams, you too could pace behind the wagon that we flung him in, and watch the white eyes writhing in his face, you would not tell with such high zest to children ardent for some desperate glory, the old lie – how sweet, fitting it is to die for one's country'.[6]

I did persevere through that long summer although at one point lightning struck my house when I had progressed about three minutes into the edit stretching the tape and forcing me to start over from scratch. In those days I would create a master edit in ¾ inch in my own studio and then bump up to one inch for additional effects, titles and a final sound mix at The Television Laboratory at WNET Public Television in New York.[7] Previous to beginning the formal edit I had gone down to New York City to create effects reels using a variety of digital optical devices including Quantel, one of the first commercially available digital optical devices for real time image processing.[8] I was keenly interested in the digital equipment that was just then becoming available on account of my chronic desire to find ways of restructuring, processing and reforming the spatial and temporal texture of the video image. Until the advent of affordable PC and Macintosh based digital editing systems artists depended on all sorts of hybrid funding strategies and borrowed time from the fringes of the corporate world.

Smothering Dreams, at just over twenty-three minutes in length, ended up being a phenomenal success in every respect. After a

Labor Day weekend broadcast on WNET-13, the Public Broadcasting Affiliate in the New York Metropolitan region it was lauded by the television critic John J. O'Connor in the New York Times, who wrote: 'Where *Apocalypse Now* was bloated and pretentious, *Smothering Dreams* is lean and harrowingly to the point'.[9] That winter I was the recipient of three EMMY awards for directing, videography and editing. The work was then rebroadcast nationally in the US, Britain, France, Germany and many other countries. It won First Prize at the first Sundance Film Festival and is included

in dozens of museum collections including the Museum of Modern Art, New York. More to the point, it was used in post-traumatic stress disorder treatment in hundreds of Veterans Administration outreach centres in the United States, and then again in Russia after the tragic events in Afghanistan. Writing this essay now, twenty-five years later, I am certain that what I know and feel about the business of patriotism, xenophobia and war would lead me to make an altogether different work, yet this document served its intention.

In a recent interview, the Vietnamese poet, Zen master and peace activist Thich Nhat Hanh offered the image of a candle flame as a metaphor for a soldiers responsibility and conditioning:

> 'An act of cruelty is born of many conditions coming together. When we hold retreats for war veterans I tell them they are the flame at the tip of the candle, they are the ones who feel the heat, but the whole candle is burning, not only the flame, all of us are responsible. When we kill because we think that the other person is evil, that we are killing for the sake of peace, that we are doing a good thing, this is not right mindfulness. If we are mindful, we will see not only the present situation, but also the root and the consequence of our act in that moment. Mindfulness also helps a soldier to see that he or she may just be an instrument for killing used by his or her government.'[10]

In truth, this is insight that reaches to the deep roots of the problem of organized violence and the perpetual reappearance of war in our time. With the events that have risen to make the early years of this new century a time of great fear, uncertainty and suffering I feel a completely renewed commitment to this kind of work. It is clear that when governments misrepresent the truth and lie to the people who they claim to represent it is time for the governed to seek out the truth free from hesitation and fear. Media artists have the tools to reclaim the truth.

As an artist, my own work is turning more and more back into this stream of intention and commitment. I am currently working on a three channel installation entitled *End-to-End* that focuses on human folly, madness and the will to destroy. *End-to-End* is a triptych 'video painting' employing High Definition video, DVD-Rom playback and state of the art plasma screen displays. A large electronic painting shown on three large screens will slowly shift in a subtle metamorphic transition over a period of time allowing the figures, objects and landscape to come full circle in the duration of play. In the production of *End-to-End* I have been striving to create a truly hybrid form using professional actors in a constructed dramatic environment that is both a real and virtual space. Using green screen keying technology coupled with High Definition simultaneous recording of three linked HD cameras, the output serves to optimise the display quality and characteristics of digital motion imagery to a very high degree. With an elaborate and finessed lighting scheme and choreographed movement of actors in the foreground space I have been able to employ the keyed virtual space to create a total surround suggestive of magic realism. I am also currently gearing up to begin the final segments of an independent feature entitled *Perdu* in collaboration with Sean Kilcoyne the performance artist and founding member of Swords to Ploughshares a California based Veterans activist organisation. *Perdu*, a hybrid work that has been made on digital video with the aim of transfer to 35mm film for release, relates the dramatic narrative of two men who survived both battles of the Somme in the First World War and their efforts to reconstruct their lives. Lastly I will soon be collecting interview materials from young disabled veterans from the nightmare that Iraq has become with the intention of creating a documentary for broadcast. These are the faces and stories behind the repetitive blurbs of news fragments that mask the realities of our present state of perpetual war.

Notes

1. See: www.poetsagainstthewar.org

2. Read by Ron Kovic in an address to the Democratic National Convention at Madison Square Gardens, New York, 1976. Also see: *Born on the Fourth of July* by Ron Kovic (New York: McGraw-Hill, 1976).

3. See: www.memoryhole.com

4. Daniel Reeves, quoted in Marita Sturken, 'What is Grace in All This Madness: The Videotapes of Dan Reeves', *Afterimage*, Summer 1985, Vol 13, no. 1 and 2, pp. 24–27.

5. Patricia R Zimmerman, *States of Emergency: Documentaries, Wars, Democracies* (Minneapolis: University of Minnesota Press, 2000), pp. 80–84.

6. Marita Sturken, 'What is Grace in All This Madness: The Videotapes of Dan Reeves', *Afterimage*, Summer 1985, Vol 13, no. 1 and 2, pp 24–27.

7. The TV LAB at Thirteen/WNET, New York, NY, 1972–84, nurtured video art, created innovative television made with everything from half inch portable video equipment to high-end broadcast quality editing and processing, and offered fresh local and global perspectives from new independent media makers.

8. Quantel-and-digital technology. In 1973, the company now known as Quantel developed the first practical analogue-to-digital converter for television applications. That innovation not only gave Quantel its name (QUANtified TELevision), but, revolutionized the ability to transform analogue video signals in real time. It is important to note that other innovations came from direct artist/engineer collaborations at video pioneering organizations such as the Experimental Television Center in Owego, New York, created and run by Ralph Hocking and Sherry Miller, among others.

9. *New York Times*, 4 September 1981.

10. Included in an interview by Lisa Schneider 'This is What War Looks Like', see: www.beliefnet.com

Chapter sixteen

War Stories, or Why I Make Videos About Old Soldiers

Cate Elwes

In the course of a career as a writer, video-maker and curator I have developed a series of works that examine masculinity as it crystallises and dissolves within the praxis of the military and the emblematic image of the war veteran. Such a project begs many questions and although I am not alone in my obsession with military conflict, a lifetime of introspection leads me to interrogate, if not resolve some of the issues that arise in considering this body of work based on war.

BURNING QUESTIONS

I have often asked myself why I harbour such a fascination with the reminiscences of war veterans. I cannot attribute it to any specific empathy with the victims of war. Although they undoubtedly suffered, none of my subjects are reducible to the collateral damage of military conflict; 'my' soldiers were mostly SAS combatants, volunteers and modest heroes in their own time. I have a declared but fugitive interest in heroism and if this is the main attraction, I could have chosen better and more competent subjects. Within the wider drama of WW2, these soldiers were by no means major players, leaders to whom the outcomes of battles can be accredited. As Roger Hourdin says of his time in the French SAS: 'I was more of a Boy Scout than a soldier. We were amateurs. We weren't career soldiers, we were civilians disguised as soldiers.' And yet these volunteers had undergone the rigorous SAS training, and, once back in their homeland, waged their own little wars, often outside the reach of higher authorities. Although their guerrilla warfare is

of anecdotal and historical interest, I cannot say that their impro-
vised soldiering and independence of spirit has been what most
attracted me to their stories.

Further, there would appear to be no overriding reason for giving
more space to military aspects of masculine violence, however
justified, so heavily promoted within popular culture. In fact, it
would seem incompatible with my natural pacifism and declared
feminism to be legitimising militarism in the current climate of
reprehensible Western expansionism. What personal and political
motivation could be driving a defection from the traditions of
woman-identified feminist art in favour of what might, at first
glance, constitute yet another celebration of men and their lethal
war games?

POSSIBLE ANSWERS

The Personal

As has always been the case in my own practice, the 'War Stories'
were triggered by a personal event. In January 1994, Lt. Colonel
Oswald Cary-Elwes died. In the previous eight weeks, hospitalised
by his third and final stroke, this man, my father, had drifted in and
out of consciousness. On the rare occasions when he spoke, turbulent images of his experiences during WW2 emerged that, to me at
least, were something of a revelation. I certainly knew that he had
been in the SAS and parachuted into occupied France towards the
end of the war, but what distressed me most was the realisation
that this was only the second time I had heard him speak about his
war. The only other occasion occurred one Sunday when a visitor
to the family table, emboldened by my father's generosity with the
wine, had questioned him about his experiences. Once we brushed
aside Oswald's protestations that it was all frightfully boring really,
this usually reserved man spoke at length about his wartime adven-
tures in the SAS. I remember nothing of what he said, only the
astonished silence of his assembled children. THE WAR had long
been a mysterious presence in the family, producing a sense of
inherited memory along with a class and culture represented by a
uniform in the attic, a framed photograph of Oswald accepting the
Médaille de la Ville from Jacques Chirac and his dress sword leaning
in a corner of his room. However, no concrete narratives had ever
accumulated around these objects.

After this long-forgotten lunch party, my father once more fell
silent on the subject of war and to my eternal shame and regret, it
never occurred to me to ask him to flesh out his one polite summary
of army life. My failure was not entirely due to a lack of imagination
or indifference to my father; it was also political. I was a late child

Paul's Story, installation, Video and printed panels, 2004.

The Six Lives of Erich Ackermann, sound installation with photographs taken by Ackermann in 1944, 2004.

of the 1960s and, and by the 1970s I had become as entrenched in my left-wing, pacifist-feminist views as the Colonel was in what I regarded as his rampant conservatism and male chauvinism. We each stood for what the other most despised. And by 1994, it was too late. Although we became close friends in his later years, the political gulf between us was never breached. In that miserable January, I watched Oswald slip away from me, a familiar and much-loved parent, but also a silent witness to a life that would be forever closed to me.

Devastated as much by the loss of his 'other' life as by the disappearance of the father I had cherished, I began a pilgrimage to the edges of his story that took me as far away as the South Pacific and drew me into the lives of people who had known him and fought

alongside him in those critical war years. Although my motives in producing a series of works around 'War Stories' were initially driven by a need to recreate aspects of my father's life, I soon found myself responding to a sense of obligation towards all the stories of conflict that were entrusted to me in the course of my quest. This sense of duty, the belief that we owe something to the generation that resisted Fascism, is widespread in the culture although, in my own experience, it is also marked by that generation's silence. My father's discretion was due to a natural reticence as well as the English adherence to the Official Secrets Act, long after it was

Above: *The Six Lives of Erich Ackermann*, sound installation with photographs taken by Ackermann in 1944, 2004.

Below: *Paul's Story*, installation, Video and printed panels, installation still, 2004.

155

necessary to avoid 'careless talk'. The English culture of secrecy does not exist in France where veterans are more than willing to talk. The problem there is that, even now, no one wants to listen. There is no French equivalent to the contemporary British SAS to make heroes of the men who joined the regiment during the war. Many of them will tell you that the work they carried out, as well as the activities of the Resistance, was, for many years, disregarded if not suppressed. The individuals who took up the reigns of power in the post-war years were drawn from the ranks of those who had built civilian careers under German occupation while others risked their lives for freedom. Post-war, France needed the experience of doctors, teachers, police and local administrators, not the doubtful abilities of guerrillas, the *sanguinaires* who knew more about blowing up bridges than local tax. De Gaulle's inspiring image of France as a nation of *résistants* who, with a little help from their American friends, cast out the evil invaders was far-fetched, to say the least. The truth was less glorious, my veterans say, and there existed many war-damaged individuals who, after the liberation, silently accused some members of the new post-war establishment of having been collaborators. In spite of the mythologising of the Resistance, the rank and file of the Maquis and the French SAS, were, for the most part, silenced through the neglect of those who, for whatever reason, did not fight.

Another kind of silence afflicted a more recent subject of my 'War Stories' series. After his death, I gained access to the diaries of my father-in-law, an ex-Luftwaffe pilot. For him, silence was a question of survival in post-war Europe particularly in East Germany where Erich Ackermann and his family found themselves subject to a new form of tyranny. With the initial impetus from an emotional response to loss, a succession of hidden stories of conflict came to populate my imagination and I used them to create a series of tapes and installations that remain ongoing.

Masculinity and aggression

For many years, my commitment to feminism had resulted in work founded on the principle that 'The Personal Is Political'. This entailed an engagement with female experience in order to articulate what had, until then, remained hidden and to locate that experience in the context of a wider analysis of Patriarchy and its workings. Until the birth of my son, I had not been interested in masculinity, and even then, the work that I made with Bruno related more to my experience of motherhood than attempting an investigation of how masculinity was forming within this individual child. The death of my father marked a new awareness of the complexities of masculinity, not in the socialisation of a male child but as it manifests in an individual representative of an extreme form of maleness, that of institutional militarism. This led me to consider aggression and my own assumption that all the ills of the world stem from men's inability to control their own violence. However, war, as the epitome of aggressiveness, is not, on the whole, waged in anger nor is this form of violence common to all men. Less than 20 per cent of the male population at any one time will have experienced combat and in the post-war period even fewer adult males will seen any form of military action.[1] As Sue Mansfield has written, this 'seems hardly likely to qualify (the waging of war) as an instinctive drive or basic human need'.[2] I have since learned from the veteran Paul Robineau what most military leaders know: it is very hard to persuade men to kill even in the heat of battle. The fact that he, my father, my husband's father and many of their colleagues overcame their natural inhibitions towards violence and killed, has disturbed and puzzled me all these years.

Latterly, I have become aware that I too, share an aggressive instinct, born, I often feel, not only from my status as human animal, but also from the traditional subjugation of my sex. There may also be a residual competitiveness in me that betrays a childhood spent scrambling for attention in a large family. Indeed the instinctive talent for guile, feigned attack and manipulation that I developed as a child would appear to equip me well for a career as a military strategist. Not only that, but my status as a mother would mean that I would be likely to fight to the death if my blood line were threatened even, as Mansfield observes, 'where parental flight is possible'. My tendency to family bonding would also stand me in good stead – it has been shown that units governed by compassionate leaders encouraging fraternity among the ranks are more successful than those based on the 'sadomasochistic hierarchy of the men's house'.[3] If I add to these persuasive arguments the fact that my army childhood and genetic inheritance might have produced in me, not the furious rejection of all things military, but a predisposition towards organised conflict, then excavating my father's stories and those of his generation of soldiers would be just another way of examining myself, albeit a self well masked by my profound horror of violence.

Self-portraiture

Some twenty-five years ago, at the time of the Women's Exhibitions at the ICA in London, it became widely accepted that images of men fashioned by women were, at one level, self-portraits. Rozsika Parker declared that women imaging men reveal women's 'fantasies and desires, fears and defences rather than provide a concrete picture of the men they purport to describe'.[4] In addition, there has been a tradition in both art and literature of women representing flawed, damaged or invalid males and the 'War Stories' would appear to be consistent with this tendency: Roger Hourdin is psychologically damaged by war; Paul Robineau is blinded and scarred by conflict, Erich Ackermann suffers appalling injuries – the crashed planes standing in for his battered body – and my father is simply dead. In their reduced physical and mental states, these men, symbols of male authority and power, are cut down to a more manageable size. The differences between conventional masculinity and femininity are also reduced in the depiction of injured men. They take on a sensitivity and vulnerability more often found in women while the artist-daughter assumes the mastery that building a memorial in art entails. In this way, the power imbalance is, if not reversed, then, at least, modified.

Building the memorial – the role of the listener

> The storyteller is Death's secretary.
> John Berger

The four works that I have so far produced in the series are essentially documentary and biographical in character – the subjects speak of their experiences in long, uninterrupted sequences. *The Liaison Officer* (1997) is the most conventional documentary, a video-film charting the events of 'Operation Lost' in which my father was sent into Brittany to locate bands of SAS dispersed by a German attack. In *The Boy Scout Soldier* (2000), Roger Hourdin tells his war stories in French across six monitors, arranged as a low, sculptural memorial, combining translations of the text with flowing images of processing veterans. Hourdin's colleague Paul Robineau forms the central subject of *Paul's Story* (2004) and the story of his blinding by a piece of shrapnel is told with voice-over video of the eye in question, wall texts and graphic representations based on the Cross of Lorraine. The 'other' side of the conflict is represented by my father-in-law in *The Six Lives of Erich Ackermann* (2004). Erich's war diaries and photographs of the crashed planes he walked away from are reproduced and his recollections are read by his son Uwe. These thumbnail sketches of the works omit my own presence, which is deliberately muted. I am perhaps most conspicuous by my absence. I rarely appear in the works and if I do, only as a voice occasionally posing a question or as a fleeting background reflection. Sometimes my hand is seen touching that of a subject and in the case of *The Liaison Officer* both my hands sort through my father's belongings. Where I am most present is in what Stuart Brisley described as the 'Mmm' factor. He was referring to my regular interjections of 'Mmms' – echoing confirmations of the speakers' testaments. Hélène Cixous would interpret these encouraging humm-ings as a reference to the pre-lingual body, the body in an infantile, purely expressive state 'singing from a time before Law',[5] before language clamped down meaning and relegated us to our ordained places in the symbolic order. The body is a primitive sound box and voice as material 'resonates through and connects bodies' – in my case linking that of the questioner with her father and those who have, over time, stood in for him. Beyond their pre-lingual references, my utterances, whether intelligible or purely expressive confirm my central role in the work as witness and listener. This is not, in fact, outside prescribed female roles within a male-oriented, society. As Jean Fisher points out, being a 'listener' places the woman in a supportive role to a male subject, akin to the 'typist, stenographer, nurse, psychic, medium, psychoanalyst, – all ears and typically connected to the technologies of (tele)communication'.[6] But I am not only a listener, I am also, as Fisher would say, a 'transmitter'. In the leading questions I pose, the organising and re-editing of what my subjects tell me, I not only transmit what they wish to say, but also draw out repressed aspects of their stories that they inadvertently communicate as well as less conscious levels of meaning that relate to my own subjectivity.

In my role as privileged listener, off-camera interrogator and post-producing re-formulator, I assume a disembodied femininity, a de-eroticized subjectivity. In terms of female representation, I am transposed from a visual economy to an 'economy of the ear'[7] as well as operating a subtly interpretive structuring device within the work. The videos and installations united under *War Stories* constitute biographies infused with elements of autobiography as well as an enactment and interrogation of traditional male and female relationships within the western culture subtending descriptive works of art.

Biographical Art and Reality Wars

> 'Confessional television conflates the personal with the universal and normalises trauma as part of the human condition rather than a product of social ills.'
> Unknown contributor to a London conference on Memory, 2000.

From Kutlug Ataman's interviews with women in wigs to Ann-Sofi Siden's videos of East European prostitutes, all biographical work exists in relation to television documentary and Reality TV. My own work is no exception. However, there are many significant differences between video art and television confessionals that go beyond the contrasting viewing conditions of galleries and TV consumed in the home. Within a television documentary, it is rare for an individual to tell his own story uninterrupted by voice-over commentary, cheap dramatic re-enactments of events or the testaments of a multitude of eyewitnesses interrupting the narrative flow. As a result, the viewer loses empathetic contact with an individual subject and comes away with only a generalised but coherent sense of an historical moment and, inadvertently, the opinions of an anonymous and invisible producer. In contrast to this rationalised vision of history, artists like Ataman and Siden allow individual subjects to speak uninterrupted for long periods of time, establishing a specific vision but within the raw data of unedited speech, keeping all its complexities, disjunctions and contradictions intact. With external events continually intersecting with the narrative, the unfolding of personal experience is cast in its social and political framework and is never reduced to the a-political 'privileged tinkering with the self'[8] that has become the hallmark of confessional television. If the viewer cares to listen, a strong sense of individual subjectivity can arise in durational biographical video, suggesting an egalitarian, one-to-one relationship with the viewer as an individual rather than as an anonymous member of an amorphous 'audience'.

PROVISIONAL CONCLUSIONS

In common with Ataman and Siden, I have contrived to let my subjects speak uninterrupted in spite of the mediation of my questioning and the imposition of structuring devices. When I have attempted to represent conflict, I have tried to avoid explosions, actors, uniforms or male voice-overs directing interpretation of what is essentially military fiction – whether mine, my subjects' or those promulgated by television documentaries. Whatever their intentions, television re-constructions of war create habituation and promote acceptance of actual conflict. Even soldiers themselves use war films by Kubrick, Stone et al to psyche themselves up ahead of engagement with an enemy. As Anthony Swofford admitted, before the first Gulf war, he and his fellow marines watched war films 'and were excited by them, because they celebrate the terrible and despicable beauty of our fighting skills'.[9] Although I try to avoid the worst pitfalls of television documentary, I do not pretend that I make anti-war art. As Swofford has demonstrated, it is virtually impossible to do so and I cannot disavow the fascination I hold with the history of my father's war. I would not even pretend to be immune to nostalgia, although I would hope to eschew what Jane Wright has described as 'the death of history and the rise of nostalgia as a worldview'. By means of durational testaments, contemplative installation formats, declared authorship, auto-biographical co-mingling and a minimalist approach to imagery, I hope to resist my own propensity for nostalgia and oppose the processes that promote military conflict in the mass media.

EPILOGUE

The processes that endorse violence as a means of resolving conflict have included in 1994 the publication in Conservative newspapers of glowing obituaries for my father designed to bolster patriotic feeling just as the Falklands debacle was unfolding. They also manifest in the institutional pressure I was subjected to when I lent Roger Hourdin's photographs for a Channel 5 documentary on the SAS. I was finally persuaded to withdraw them on the grounds that images of WW2 SAS operations were being used to discredit the current activities of the regiment. I more successfully resisted the television convention of war reporting that only tells stories that can be supported by combat footage or sensationalist photographs of carnage. I deplore the cynical manipulation of subjects by Reality TV in order to induce angry or tearful outbursts and 'parade fake emotions in public'.[10] My veterans speak in calm retrospect, their feelings framed by the carefully-wrought constructs that constitute their memories. I do not invite the viewers to 'holiday in their misery' as Julian Stallabrass would put it, nor seek for my subjects aid in healing the scars of the past through some Freudian sense of a talking cure. The veterans show no urge to resolve their experiences or to exorcise and forget. The stories are exhumed, circulated, and returned to their narrative setting. They only ask of us that we bear witness and come to our own conclusions. Finally, I allow the customarily 'hidden' relationship of interrogator and subject, of female listener-interpreter and male protagonist to take its place as a central, problematic theme in the work. In terms of an ethical stance, I oppose the reduction of war to a narrative of goodies and baddies, what Uwe Ackermann calls the 'Nintendo approach to conflict' and Walter Benjamin, the 'narratives of the victorious'. The testaments of my subjects challenge the authority of official memory and as Rosemary Betterton observed: 'The stories recounted by Paul and Erich ... go against the grain of post-war stereotypes: the traumatic injuries suffered by a French soldier and the courage and comradeship of a German pilot do not fit with current nostalgic wartime fantasies'.[11] My subjects are caught up in unthinkable events beyond their control and their responses leave us with a universal, peacetime question around moral and physical courage: what would we have done in their place? What manner of man would this Colonel's daughter have made?

Notes

1.   Martin Woollacott believes that the contemporary fascination with militarism and war is due to the fact that so few of us have ever experienced it.

2. Sue Mansfield, *The Rites of War, An Analysis of Institutionalized Warfare*, (London: Bellew Publishing, 1991 edition).

3. Ibid.

4. Rozsika Parker, 'Images of Men', *Women's Images of Men*, eds. S. Kent & J. Morreau (Writers and Readers, 1985).

5. Hélène Cixous quoted by Jean Fisher in 'Reflections on Echo – sound by women artists in Britain', *Signs of the Times* catalogue, MOMA, Oxford, 1990.

6. Ibid.

7. Ibid.

8. The artist Martha Rosler's term.

9. Anthony Swofford, 'The Sniper's Tale', *Guardian Weekend*, 10 March, 2003.

10. Ros Coward writing in the *Guardian*, January 2000.

11. Rosemary Betterton, 'Out of Conflict' in *Out of Conflict* catalogue, ArtSway publication, 2004.

Chapter seventeen

Moving Parts: The Divergence of Practice

Vicky Smith

Reading Felicity Sparrow's article in *Filmwaves* (Issue 22, Summer/Autumn 2003) about Steve Farrer's contribution to the 1976 LFMC 10th birthday celebration I was reminded of some of the unique features of the London Filmmakers Co-op. Farrer filmed the audience as they entered the cinema door. The film was immediately processed in the lab and fed through next door into the projection booth. In this film feedback event the audience were able to watch themselves, framed twice, in the door and the projector gate, both subject and object of the film. Farrer's piece which celebrated film machinery and the immediacy of the film medium was made possible by the special facilities of the London Filmmakers Co-op, which housed a cinema and workshop with a film lab under one roof.

With its arsenal of equipment, resources and adaptable space, the LFMC inspired numerous artists to exploit their experience as artisans in control of all stages of film production, '… handing over … aspects of authorship to the apparatus and the event …'.[1] During the 1990s the LFMC hosted expositions by Loophole Cinema, Kino club, and Jurgen Reble. Loophole in particular explicitly fore-grounded their fetishistic relationship with the film matter/apparatus. On stage, behind and in front of screens the machine was the main protagonist as bodies, silhouettes, projections and sound collided in an accretion of layers. The fascination with 'two way shadows' emerged partly out of Loophole's Greg Pope and his experience as a projectionist. Jurgen Reble staged a live editing event by charming a giant 16mm film loop, which escaped the projection booth and crossed the cinema, into the Auditorium. Film was there to be enjoyed in its most sensory aspect, interacted upon directly by the audience, a constantly evolving collaborative artwork, a filmic game of consequences made as it was screened.

In 1990 I was elected workshop organiser at the Co-op. My primary interest in this period at the LFMC, was that a substantial number of users of the workshop facilities were female and largely because of this I was inspired to develop my own relationship with technology. For most of its existence the LFMC made a concerted drive to have equal male/female representation across all departments of distribution, cinema and particularly the workshop. The rationale being that the presence of female technicians would make the workshop more approachable to other female users. A rich source for artists generally, female filmmakers in particular welcomed the creative freedom and the possibility of making film without reliance on laboratories or others, and without censorship or intervention. The Co-op offered women the means and support to produce work autonomously, and ironically it was, 'because of its marginalised status, [that] avant-garde film offered women access to production and a validation of personal filmmaking'.[2]

Female artists using film and video have since been enabled by the parallel movements of co-operatives and feminism to take control of the technologies of production, using complex equipment to explore subjectivity through their own visual language. To support its ethos of 'dry hire' (without technicians) the LFMC offered skill sharing (inexpensive technical instruction in-house). Combined with the strategies of hiring female technicians and gender equality, it proved a successful formula. Through most of the early 1990s the Co-op was full of women using technology. For example, Sandra Lahire's densely woven optical printer films explored the effects of technology on the body. *Plutonium Blonde* presented an ambiguous image of a female figure both controlling and controlled by technology. Tanya and Alia Syed, were operating the printer and processor for personal and professional work. Alia Syed's *Fatima's Letter*, is as much about the journey of the film as it is about the film of a journey. With its repeated looping and re-printing of sequences, frames and faces, the motion and processes of the contact printer are parallel with that of the train journey. Nina Danino described the approaches of women working in the avant-garde tradition, 'systematic procedural methods described by terms such as "pure" and "rigorous" as a mark of critical esteem used to different ends by women, all expanding or multiplying levels of meaning'.[3]

As the third 'Workshop Organiser' I was following on from Noski De Ville, Carole Enahro and Gina Czarnecki (my mentor and co-worker). Many of my skills were learnt on the job and are now largely redundant, but the experience of working with allen keys, nuts, screws, solder, sockets, shafts and all the other film apparatus, had a major impact on my art and life. Using this technology in reflective periods informed my being. The longer I communed with the film apparatus, the more confident I became with its operation and the desire to communicate that experience became articulated through my artwork.

The 1990s was the final decade of dry hire access to mechanical film production. Assembled in the workshop: the processor; contact printer; optical printer, the animation rostrum and the selsyn sound bay were the industrial giants of 16mm film special effects and post production.

My specialist practice being animation I quickly began to attribute life and personality to these inanimate machines. 16mm film equipment combines the visceral with the mechanical – well oiled bodies with protective shutters, motorised hearts, intestines, claws and a pulse – the film 'blood' coursing through the veins is as compelling in its kinetic materiality as the machine is in its solidity. A superficial relationship with these complex beings would not be satisfying. Operators are summonsed to explore deeper inside camera, printer, and projector components. The reward lies deep behind a series of doors or refracting prisms, shutters and lenses – like the female organ a secret cache – a delicate orifice just the size of a little finger.

It is not only the aperture of the machinery that makes me relate to the apparatus as female. The contact printer has classic female proportions – curvy symmetrical undulating outlines with generous feed and ample take up. Look into her light opening peep-hole as she is reproducing images in positive or negative. The unprocessed film must then be transported in lightproof magazines to the processor, which consumes the film into her mysterious dark liquid tanks. The film is immersed, travelling through the chemical vortex. After moments of nervous anticipation, the film is born into full daylight; a revelation as it enters the warm glass chamber with thousands of (hopefully) tiny perfectly formed frames. The newborn film is delivered, curled safely round a core, and the cord is cut.

I am drawn to one machine in particular – the animation rostrum camera. It is capable of shooting single frames, a mechanical being with a camera suspended upside down on a spine. Her face is a flat table equipped for minute incremental motion. The refurbished rostrum at the LUX was cobbled together combining mechanical and electronic components, sprawling and unwieldy but with a computer interface that relieved the human operator of repetitive mechanical tasks.

The animator Vanda Carter explained the attraction for women to this practice, stating that animation is relatively inexpensive, and crucially, can be made autonomously in a controlled environment. Female filmmakers, she speculated, may not feel enough confidence to work with a film crew preferring the privacy of solo practice. 'The relationship between film-maker and equipment and film itself is one of the foundations on which individual style is developed', and '... your intensity doesn't get broken down',[4] i.e. artists can work at their own pace.

For me, the animation rostrum is my crew and cast. The rostrum room becomes a private studio. The door is locked the lights are hot, the equipment hums with anticipation. It's just me in control of a complicated machine, but we know each other. Nina Danino described the sometimes uneasy relationship that women have with self-expression, '... the difficulty of saying or of finding the right language to say ...'.[5] It is not until I gaze into the depths of the empty table and consider the reflexive frame of chance and uncertainty that I find inspiration from what I can only describe as a mystical source. Stan Brakhage described the process of animator Larry Jordan's hermetic practice, '... drawn for reasons he could not understand ... having the (art) before him on the table, he felt moved to begin to cut them out and then to let them tell him where to move them ... there seems to be an area that's reached in the creative process for most makers where ... mysterious forces or persuasions come to bear on someone lending his or her most personal experiences and habits to the unknown ...'.[6]

The Rostrum allowed a great range of techniques. I set the table into a 360-degree rotation, and with every revolution the table spins faster as the camera simultaneously zooms in. I allow the technology to record its presence, balancing calculated methodology with spontaneity and an emphasis on the role of animator as witch, casting spells, selecting the ingredients, stirring her cauldron and remaking the world to correspond to her inner visions. 'The film-maker is no longer the apodictic source of ideas which are mechanically translated into film, but rather these arise out of an intuitive interaction between the machine process and the artistic mentality ...'.[7]

Technology marches on, a new century and new modes of production. Many female artists have found creative freedom using electronic imaging. Able to work inexpensively in the privacy and convenience of the home this autonomous practice brings those artists close to the experience of making animation, which is a solitary process. I have my own Bolex camera, tripod and lights. This is sufficient equipment to make stop frame film at home. But I chose to work in the public space (which could be made private) because of the benefits to practice of artists sharing equipment, physical space and ideas. I was motivated to write this retrospective of the Coop because I was able to locate a nurturing context there for my work and because of the many young film artists I meet today who are seeking a context for theirs.

Notes

1. Malcolm Le Grice, *Experimental Cinema in the Digital Age* (London: BFI, 2001).

2. Nina Danino, 'The Intense Subject', eds. Nina Danino, Michael Maziere, *The Undercut Reader: Critical Writings on Artists' Film and Video* (London: Wallflower Press, 2003), p. 9.

3. Ibid.

4. Vanda Carter, 'Not Only Animation', eds. Nina Danino and Michael Maziere, *The Undercut Reader: Critical Writings on Artists' Film and Video*, (London: Wallflower Press, 2003), p. 168.

5. Nina Danino, 'The Intense Subject', eds. Nina Danino and Michael Maziere, *The Undercut Reader: Critical Writings on Artists' Film and Video*, (London: Wallflower Press, 2003), p. 11.

6. Stan Brakhage, from Malcolm Le Grice, *Experimental Cinema in the Digital Age* (London: BFI, 2001), p. 92.

7. Peter Milner, 'The London Film-makers' Co-op: the Politics of License?' *The Undercut Reader: Critical Writings on Artists' Film and Video* (London: Wallflower Press London, 2003), p. 42.

Section III

Philosophies and Critical Histories of Video Art to Cinema

Karen Mirza and Brad Butler
Mutation on a Form

Stephen Partridge
Video: Incorporeal, Incorporated

Cate Elwes
Tamara Krikorian, Defending the Frontier

Jackie Hatfield
Another Place, David Hall

David Larcher
Interview with Stephen Littman, Alchemy and the Digital Imaginary

Malcolm Le Grice
Reflections on My Practice and Media Specificity

Jackie Hatfield
Expanded Cinema – Proto, Post-Photo

Mike Leggett
Image Con Text (1978–2003)
Film/Performance/Video/Digital

Chapter eighteen

Mutation on a Form

Karen Mirza and Brad Butler

In response to the need for a central space for artist led critical debate and practice around the moving image, in November 2004 the artist filmmakers Brad Butler and Karen Mirza set up a centre for artist film production in London called no.w.here. Their aim was to establish a cultural centre for the artist filmmaking community, and provide access to a unique set of facilities (optical printing, contact printers, rostrum camera, steenbecks, 16mm processing and telecine) alongside practical workshops aiming to educate a new generation of artist filmmakers. Through programmes screenings and exhibitions by international moving image artists they aim to trigger critical debates investigating experimental film and video makers' dialogues with contemporary culture. This opens a space for the meeting of practice and theory, expanding, extending and examining the place of film within contemporary artistic production. In dialogue with each other, they discuss their manifesto.

Is film still relevant as a contemporary artistic medium?

BB: Clearly artists are benefiting from access to digital cameras and computer editing at low cost. Digital media enables the possibility of new forms of imaging, experimentation, complex collage and accessibility. In contrast filmmakers approaching their material must now ask themselves 'what is the value of the film medium in a contemporary moving image context.' Film is at the threshold of technological displacement, but has yet to throw off its uncertain relationship to the gallery space. Awkward, fragile, elitist, nostalgic, expensive – all criticisms that have been levelled at 'film as film'.

In Nicky Hamlyn's book *Film Art Phenomena*[1] Guy Sherwin writes about film's ontological link to the objective image source. He suggests 'digital imagery always appears synthetic in comparison to film, even if the image itself has more detail'.[2] This is a powerful argument for media specificity (grain versus pixels) in the hands of

Guy Sherwin, but for many artists all of the abstracting devices of film (with the exception of hand colouring) are available with the digital.

However, as an artist, when I think my ideas I think them in film. It is my personal relationship with film that dominates the visual field of my thought process. My relationship with film can often be frustrating. Film is unforgiving. Each mistake or miscalculation is magnified exponentially in projection. The tools of production require precision and trial and error to close the gap between the act of perceiving through the camera and the final projection of the film. But this is also what is interesting. The perceptual stages of construction contain a visual transformation of the portrayed that is always surprising and (occasionally) sublime. This at least is one among many transformations that film makes possible during shooting, editing, printing and the projection event.

As Anthony McCall has said, movements are often cyclical, stamped out in one place only to return in a different context in another time and space. Mutations on a form. I recognise the context of multiple specialisms and blurred boundaries and seek to address these complexities with no.w.here. What we could be talking about is innovation: how we can invent new ways of using film. Why should a film projector present itself as if from a retrograde position, what about new ideas with old forms?

Exhibition space

KM: There are two points I'd like to discuss, a) about de-mediating the art process, and b) removing the barriers between the artist and the exhibition of their work, the impact of artist as curator.

I am an artist whose inclination is to primarily work things out, or work things through by making films. At the same time, my practice has involved a significant proportion of time spent on curating, programming and facilitating the screening and exhibition of other artist's films.[3] My first opportunity in programming came when the Robert Beck Memorial Cinema[4] asked me to screen work at 'Collective Unconscious' in New York June 2001. The RBMC was run by the artists Bradley Eros and Brian Frye and they presented me with a broad context in which to think about my work. Inspired by their philosophy I recorded a dialogue with Bradley in Sept 2001. He talked about the RBMC philosophy as follows:

> We have this possibility of encouraging film and video makers to show something a little unorthodox from their work. Or even to approach their own work in an unorthodox way, showing something out of the closet, something they have repressed, something that they never thought they would

want to expose publicly, some encouragement to get them to do a unique program never to be repeated again. Also the possibility of conferring with artists and makers of film and video to put their own work into a context people have never done before. The exciting ability to suddenly become artist and curator in one, to sort of integrate those roles. People then have the sense of thinking about the context both locally and globally of how their work fits in both the history of other art and maybe their own history, the history of their peers and their mentors. Sometimes not even things from the world of art, but other things from the world of science, the world of history, you know any other kind of image making that they see their work in the context of.[5]

From this opportunity I put together a programme of films called 'Rarely seen established and emerging British artists film and video'.[6] Looking back on that programme I see that all the thematics are still relevant to my current thinking about film art. This screening included Peter Gidal's structural materialist film *Hall* (1968/69), Nicky Hamlyn's *White Road* (2000) ordering and disordering features of the landscape. The form, content and structure of David Hall's *Phased Time* (1974) is resolutely 'time-based' where the passage of time is treated as a material component of the work (and is essential to the viewer's experience of it). Jayne Parker's poetics of montage in *Thinking twice* (1997) combines performance with a rigorous control of the film medium, an underlying sense of visual order, language and gesture. Alongside these artists were younger makers including an untitled super 8 psycho drama by Jake Astbury (2001) Simon Payne's interrogation of the digital aesthetic in *All that is* (2001) and *Non places* (1999) by myself and Brad Butler. At this time in 2001 these films were rarely seen so for me to screen them and programme them was a way of engaging with influences and trajectories of thought about contemporary practice.

The opportunity to become artist and curator, and to integrate these roles is very important as an extension of my studio practice, it's a form of communication and articulation through the dissemination of artists' films. Invariably ideas for screenings and exhibitions come out of an interest in something that I would be working on in my own work. For instance the *Sculpture of the Screen* programmes at the Tate[7] came out of the process of making my film *Where a Straight Line Meets a Curve*. With the 'Light Reading' series Brad and I have continued the idea of inviting other artists to curate programmes. This process of removing the barriers between the artist and the exhibition of their work has all sorts of benefits. Work is exhibited before others have validated it and

Actual Space,
16mm Black and
White film, 1997.

therefore there is the possibility of a newness, a fresh immediate response to culture. An opportunity for the artist to make connections to other work through the perspective of hands on knowledge of things fitting together, connections that curators might not have seen. This also empowers the artist.

Production and accessibility

BB: Making accessible film post production facilities (optical printing, contact printers, rostrum camera, developing, steenbecks and telecine) inevitably opens up the notion of material and also film craft. Firstly it seems important to clarify that no.w.here is set up to make available film technology, rather than filming. We do not intend to resource cameras so our concern with the cameras' methods; procedures of observation and perceptual transformations are mostly contained within our periodic workshops on cameraless films and introduction to Super 8. What no.w.here is able to facilitate is structuring at the printer/processor stage – film copying procedures which directly impact upon the artists potential for exploring their content (or material as content). Historically artists have used this in many ways from Le Grice's *Berlin Horse* (1970) to Nicholson's *Slides* (1970) Jacob's *Tom, Tom the Piper's*

(Both images):
Actual Space,
16mm Black and
White film, 1997.

son (1969) to more recent studies such as Chodorov's *Charlemagne 2: Piltzer* (2003) and Nicolas Rey's *Terminus for you* (1999). For some of these films the capabilities of the printing machinery was used to draw forward the physical aspects of the material of film. For others the printer allowed them to rework their material in retrospect. To introduce high contrast film stocks, freeze-frames, add filters and masks, long dissolves or repetition to accentuate their observations from the act of location filming.

The challenge facing artists using these facilities is determining their meaning during this complex ideological and technological moment. Fighting for the continuation of a chosen medium in a

Both images:
Where a Straight Line Meets a Curve,
16mm colour film,
2003.

conservative artworld is nothing new; David Hall's *TV Pieces* (1971) are a classic example of the nature of experiment in the face of a reluctant media. However with film as your chosen material, the hardest part is in finding where you are within the heritage of what has been, which remains a powerful force, as well as determining where you are in the present landscape. Accepting you are part of a heritage is also to accept that audiences will project the

past onto what you are doing which has implications for your work. My perception is that some artists work around this by choosing to ignore the context of experimental film history. Others act as if they have invented the artform. That this is even possible reflects the emphasis placed on the social, political and cultural context of film: academicised by the experimental film world but largely ignored by the artworld. Hence the need for no.w.here.

By making accessible film production, one must also face its increasing perception (or displacement) to the status of a 'craft'. This balance between craft and art also reflects the ease of digital editing which has made technological processing ubiquitous.[8] Of course owning the means of production and educating people in how to use film facilities has other useful by-products, it makes it more accessible, less precious, less expensive and more common. But no.w.here's real interest is in film 'as a way of thinking'. In an art world where there is a plethora of ways to build a time/space experience there is value in the forms of engagement between the psyche of the filmmaker, the film medium and the techniques and preconceptions of filmic construction; and the thought processes required of 'film' making in the digital age.

Old vs new

KM: Intense technological transformation leads to new situations and new conditions for making, exhibiting and distribution of artist's film and video. In the 1960s and 1970s you had the rise of new electronic media such as television and video, which had a freeing effect on artistic explorations and uses of film. Since the 1990s the new digital media has had a similar effect.

In the round table conversation 'The Projected Image in Contemporary Art' Hal Foster suggests that 'there are usually two dynamics at these new technological moments. There are artists who want to push the futuristic freedoms of new media, and others who want to look at what this apparent leap forward opens up in the past, the apparently obsolete.'[9]

I started making time based work in the early nineties and from the start I knew I wanted to deal with the spatial and temporal ambiguities of projection. This is what drew me towards film. It wasn't immediate but after a year or two I found myself becoming more and more interested in the idea of returning to older media and using it in new ways as a critique of newer media. This led to me making a film installation *Actual Space* in 1997 in my degree show at the Royal College of Art. The installation took the form of a 6ft by 10ft space constructed within the main gallery to enclose the 16mm film and sound. The installation was constructed to work on two levels: either to be viewed though the cell like window of the institutional door, or for the viewer to physically enter the space. One was to read the work as if it were a painting, the other was a more sculptural experience.

> *Actual Space* emphasises the central role of the human body in the perception of space and time. The film loop shows the view of – and out of – a window, shot at different times of day and night. The viewer is offered to consider the pictorial space of the projected image as dematerialised object or to contemplate its temporal aspect. The projection extends across three walls, making visible the conditional relationship between the pictorial plane of the projection and the physicality of the screen itself. The investigation of space and perception extends to the acoustic realm: four soundtracks collide and correspond within the physical dimensions of the exhibition space. The various perspectives and temporalities of architectural space, projected image and sound overlap to create a heterogeneous perceptual field. In order to locate the body in relation to it, the viewer re-combines the physical space of the gallery, the projected image and the aural space created by the sound installation.[10]

Whilst acknowledging the research being undertaken by artists using what has been termed 'new' media, I wanted to use film along similar lines, i.e. in an immersive way. One of the functions of this work was to critique the virtual reality installations of 'new' media where their most compelling characteristics were their point of newness. By working with film, by returning to the formalist black and white frame, by treating film reflexively, as a material; thinking about process; working with the apparatus; being concerned with the embodiment of the viewer and the parameters of the space, I desired a critical reaction to the illusionism that mimicked the mainstream cinema's dissemination of images. The sudden plethora of projection in galleries left me experiencing some work that didn't seem to care whether I (the viewer) was there or not. These thoughts were echoed by Hal Foster in 2003 'When you say that film now is related to painting, I wouldn't say painting so much as "pictorialism". There's a rampant pictorialism, which is also a rampant virtualism, that the sculptural and spatial interests of your generation, Anthony [McCall], wanted to challenge, or at least to probe. The pictorialism of projected images today often doesn't seem to care much about the *actual space*.'[11] This context inspired me to concentrate on space and time as opposed to virtualisation and as time has progressed so seemingly has the potential for new critical relationships to emerge between photography, film and moving image culture (digital/video). As Brad commented 'when I think my ideas I think them in film' and when I think in film I find myself naturally wanting to ask questions and interrogate rather than telling stories. This intuitive need leads me to ask questions about the medium and I think my focus on the physical 'here and now' is an attempt to continue my phenomenological interest in film.

Notes

1.   Nicky Hamlyn, *Film Art Phenomena* (London: BFI, 2003).

2.   Ibid., p. 9.

3.   Through the curatorial banner 'Light Reading' Karen Mirza and Brad Butler have now presented work by hundreds of established and emerging film and video artists. This has included site-specific installations, multi-projection work and single screen projections. Since 2001 'Light Reading' has collaborated with the LUX, the 291 gallery, The London Film Festival, Ikon Gallery, Tate Britain, Tate Modern, The Curzon Cinema and is responsible for the first ever experimental film festival in India (now in its third year).

4.   The RBMC ran once a week for four years at the 'Collective Unconscious' on Ludlow Street. Since December 2004 the RBMC has mutated into 'Roberta Beck' with monthly screenings at Cinema Zero in Brooklyn.

5.   Bradley Eros, interview recorded by Karen Mirza June 2001

6.   RBMC June 2001, NYC.

7.   'Sculpture of the Screen', July 2003 Tate Britain.

8.   There remain only a few material facets to film, which digital technologies do not replicate, the physicality of film travelling through an installation space for example.

9.   Hal Foster, *October* 104, Spring 2003, p. 73.

10.   Hannes Rox, unpublished text.

11.   Hal Foster, *October* 104, Spring 2003, p. 75.

Chapter nineteen

Video: Incorporeal, Incorporated

Stephen Partridge

'... video has only a conceptual, and not formal connection to any previous medium ... formalist research into magnetic videotape seems absurd, whereas the development of film's photographic essence was actually the foundation of experimental film'
Marc Mayer[1]

'... nothing with a history can be defined ...'
dictum by Nietzsche

In recent years, there has been a gradual re-awakening of interest in film and video artworks from the late sixties and early seventies, and I have found myself re-experiencing much of this work alongside young enthusiastic and knowledgeable audiences.[2] One of the interesting aspects of these events and many others like them all over Europe[3] is the absence of partisan distinctions between the mediums of film and video. The new generation viewing this now historical work inevitably has a different relationship with it to its contemporaries, and this is related to the convergence of mediums – where digital technologies are producing a confluence of all previous media: sound, text, image and their various forms and placing them within a new stage or setting, which is partially the library, the theatre, the cinema, or the home or personal (computer) space.

> **Convergence**: uniting, or merging tendencies that were originally opposed or very different.[4]

Continual and changing, convergence places us (artists and audience) in a post film and video era, where digital forms (mostly) replace, substitute, or simulate the previous media. This process of substitution and simulation explains the current lack of (perceived) distinctions between forms or media. For instance, it is common for us to say that we are going to watch a film on video or a DVD when what we actually mean is that we intend to watch a *recording* of a film or movie (without recourse to celluloid). It is possible that this lack of distinction is likely to erode even further with the advent of high definition television (HDTV) for broadcast and DVD with the improvement in picture quality and adoption of movie theatre aspect ratios. It may be worth asking whether this matters and why in the process of convergence, video has been substituted, while film has been simulated by digital technologies. To answer this question, there is a need to re-examine the development of video as a medium and its incorporation into digital form, while making some comparisons with film, and in turn, its simulation within the digital domain.

The convergence or incorporation of video with digital forms could be considered as almost complete. In any case, video as a term has had many definitions and uses, both culturally and technologically, and has become a generic word for a number of different things. As a specific term it refers, originally, to an electrical analogue waveform produced by scanning the light (the latent image) focused onto a photosensitive plate in the video camera which is then re-created into the pattern (or raster) of horizontal scanning lines made by an electron beam onto the photosensitive surface of a cathode-ray-tube that in turn creates the image that appears on a television. This waveform in the digital domain is now essentially bit-mapped or sampled to appear on a contemporary television, computer screen or flat display panel. This converged analogue/digital use of the word can be referred to as the video-plane and as such was and remains incorporeal like its cousin, the audio waveform or sound sample, with which it is usually incorporated. This distinguishes it from the photographic and material-based medium of film – even though both film and video strive to produce one similar effect – a moving image as perceived by the human brain.

Video was from the start a bastard medium – and inherited a collection of conventions and properties from earlier media including radio, theatre, and, to a lesser extent film. However, early proponents were at pains to discover and exploit its singularities and establish autonomy. The doyen and pioneer of New York video art, Korean born Nam June Paik revealed '... the relative nature of time as the malleable component of video art ...;[5] UK writer and video maker, Stuart Marshall: 'the video system is a very new and different mirror, not only presenting a non reversed image but also allowing for an observation of self which is not spatially or temporally fixed';[6] In Germany, Wolf Kahlen: 'Just as the mirror makes us forget it as a utensil, so the monitor obliterates the camera';[7] the British, sculptor, artist-filmmaker, video artist, David Hall pointed

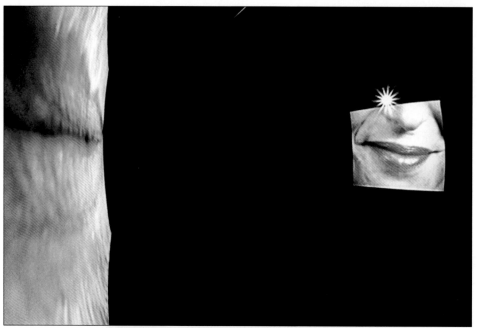

...For One of Your Smiles, Video 1998.

Installation No. 1, Video, 1976.

out the 'peculiar' characteristics of the medium, '... which some artists have realised are integral phenomena and consequently inevitable components of the videological syntax ...'.[8] In Vienna, the artist Peter Weibel reduced this videological syntax to '5 qualities of VT and VTR: synthetics, transformation, self-reference, instant time, box'.[9] These various statements led Sean Cubitt to write that 'the notion of medium specificity is a central one in

Monitor,
Video, 1975.

understanding the development of video as a cultural form.[10] It is certain that the investigation of specificity gave rise to many important and key works by these and other artists, but video, even practiced as a cultural form, did not achieve an established autonomy. Sean Cubitt has further argued that 'video is neither an autonomous medium, free of all links with other forms of commu-

183

nication, nor entirely dependent on any one of them',[11] and that video is not singular but a collection of 'video media'. Or as Marc Mayer would have it 'video is more an end than any one specific means'.[12]

The specificities and autonomy that were being sought by the early international proponents were apropos a medium that was transient. This transience is partly due to the fact that television (or video) has been part of a process of constant radical change since its invention. Television was designed in the early 20th century as *primarily* a system for transmission and reception. For the first thirty years it could be said that the language of television was illiterate. There was no form of 'writing' of the television signal or waveform until Alfred Dolby and his team at the Ampex Corporation produced the first commercially viable Quadruplex Video Tape Recorder (VTR) in 1957, which used 2-inch magnetic tape to record the television raster. It was not until the early sixties that broadcasters adopted the VTR as a means of recording productions for later transmission, and artists would not have access to the technology until the late sixties, after Japanese companies had developed various industrial and relatively low-quality smaller gauge formats (1/2-inch EIAJ).[13] Roy Armes said that: 'continual technological development makes it increasingly difficult to pin down a fixed identity'.[14] The VCR replaced the VTR, which in turn is likely to be replaced by disk systems and then by solid-state memory. The video monitor has mutated to the VDU display or LCD panel; black boxes or cards are now needed to display the TV raster upon them.

Most of the video specificity therefore being articulated in the late sixties and seventies was tied to the particular technologies of those years: the vidicon tube in early cameras, and open reel-to-reel video tape recorders, both long obsolete. Associated with this was the virtual impossibility of editing with the early VTR, which drove artistic interest and experiment away from filmic conventions such as montage, towards the performative and particularly the use of closed-circuit systems (installations) and instant playback. Central to this approach was the notion of intervention into a *process*, manipulation of the video plane in time or space. The intrinsic properties were emphasised: immediacy; transmission; the 'live'; the closed circuit; record-replay with time delay; feedback oddities; synthesizer manipulations; and synchronicity with sound.

Some of the properties, if not strictly the specificities, have transferred to the new digital domain but most notably, synchronicity with sound has not. Sound is now recorded as a separate data stream from the image stream, and in digital post-production and broadcasting, synchronicity (especially the crucial 'lip-synch' of speech and dialogue) can easily be lost or compromised, (a situation with which filmmakers have always been familiar.) Some specificities that have disappeared along with their associated words and acronyms include: electrovision,[15] videotaping, VT, VTR, video shooting, video editing, and video switching.

Convergence has meant that video has been both incorporated and subsumed, (in line with Marshall McLuhan's assertion that new media do not replace old, but almost always contain them).[16] Within the digital domain video is further merged with the adoption of the filmic conventions of picture origination, editing, aspect ratios and cinematic presentation, but remains incorporeal.

It is productive to examine the convergence between film and video by focussing on the video projector, which provides *prima facie* evidence of the progress of convergence in its technological form and functionality. No longer trapped within the tube, video can be viewed 'cinematically' on large screens or utilised in installation, either within the gallery or any suitable public space. It is worth emphasising however that by the time video projectors became of sufficient quality, reliable and relatively inexpensive, it was certainly not video*tape* that was being projected but the video-plane, derived from the stream of data coming from a disc read by laser light and interpolated by a computer chip, whether inside the computer or a specialist device such as laserdisc or DVD.[17] Foretold by Nam June Paik in 1968 when he declared 'TV without a box is no longer TV, but a video 'environment'.[18] Furthermore the optical device used for originating the images is just as likely to be a film camera as a video camera – be it digital or analogue.

The idea that the video projector has merged film and video into a new unified electronic cinema isn't totally exact. It is still relatively easy to distinguish film from video (and especially computer de-rived text and vector graphics) when they are projected. Some of the distinction can be attributed to the higher production values still prevailing within film production (for example, superior light-ing and art direction). Other distinctions lie within the cinema-tographic: the much higher contrast ratio of film stock, and the human perception of the grain of film emulsions and the film weave within the camera. However, the video projector throws light upon a screen, just as a film projector, and very unlike the television tube or LCD or plasma panel, all of which are a source of light. It does appear though that film has lost some of its fixed-ness – in a machine or technological sense and as material. Compared to video, film technology (referring to the camera and projector) has re-mained relatively stable for eighty years, despite continual small refinements and variations of aspect ratio and gauge. The basic material, which gives the medium its common name (film), has changed even less following the abandonment of the volatile acetate composition of early stock and adoption of celluloid safety film.

Another technological development which suggests a merger of media is the suite of boxes that include a wide-screen television or plasma display, surround sound amplifier and speakers, sat-box, and digi-box, which is marketed as 'home cinema' – although cineastes (i.e. those subscribing to the convention of the word cinema to be characterised by a *public* space, darkened for projection, experienced peripatetically as an event), might groan at the inherent oxymoron of the term.

To re-iterate then: in the case of video the convergence process within the digital domain can be characterised as mainly a *substitution* of incorporation; in the case of film the convergence is marked by the digital *simulation* of filmic characteristics. Early digital devices produced for the television visual effects industry such as Quantel's Harry (1986) incorporated effects that would simulate, and impose upon the video-plane; film grain and film weave to make the resultant product (usually a TV-ad or pop video) look as though it had been shot and produced on film. Software 'plug-ins' are now widely available even for pro-sumer packages such as Adobe After Effects, Final Cut Pro, desk-top-video editing and effects software applications, that will simulate the entire range of Ektachrome film stocks used in motion-picture making. Further plug-ins can simulate scratches to the film emulsion, dye-fading and ageing and so on. The 50-field per-second alternate odd-even cycle of the video-plane can be converted to 25 or even 24 full-frames per second to further emulate the frame rate of film, and smooth out motion artefacts to more closely resemble film's characteristic motion blur. Furthermore, many digital video cameras incorporate options for shooting in anamorphic 16:9 wide-screen ratio, and will also shoot in 25 or even 24 full-frames per second mode. These digital effects or sub-technologies were not designed to simulate the look and feel of video; the motivation was to simulate the idealised film paradigm and aesthetic.

This simulation is only possible because of film's inherent fixedness, its immutability. Perhaps simulation only works for something that we are very familiar with, not with something that has been constantly evolving. Moreover, from a commercial point of view, it is also only worth simulating something that has perceived value: film's material nature, its sheen and associated glamour of production and distribution infrastructures. Why would anyone want to spend time and money trying to simulate the look of early video? – It poses no 'aura', to use Walter Benjamin's famous term. Another contributory factor to film's fixed-ness lies in associated craft practices and the attitudes embedded within them. One distinctive aspect of craft is that the craftsperson has an affinity and relationship (not to mention vested interest) with a particular material, which might be characterised as inherently conservative or even nostalgic.

The concept of 'aura' could explain why some video material, which would not hold the attention of many people when displayed on a TV monitor, transforms to an artwork when projected, particularly in a gallery space. (The gallery or museum adding extra aura, validation and authority.) Compare this to a statement made in 1976 by David Ross, one of the first American museum video curators: 'Video works created with an understanding of the audience often seem out of place in the context of an art gallery – the works become filmic (in delivery) and their original intention is easily perverted'.[19] Ross was referring to monitor based works, whether single screen or installations. The works produced by the YBAs in the nineties and the explosion in video-based art-pieces since, also point to a lack of distinction of media. Setting aside these artists' market-led need for separation and distancing from an experimental film or video history, the works directly reflect the process of convergence.

The new approach is non-materialist – in the sense that there is little interest or even recognition in the video media or the digital media employed. It has a tendency towards commoditisation and a denial of the reproduction properties of media in favour of granting and pursuing uniqueness and the 'aura' of the art object. Similarities with 'expanded cinema' abound but the intent of the artists confounds this comparison or recognition. The approach is inherently post-film and post-video, and points towards a convergence within a digital time and space, without medium specificity or material condition.

Video was invented primarily as a means of communication and its development driven by military/industrial agency and imperatives. Film, or more correctly, cinema, originates as a medium of illusion, and its history can be traced particularly through the proto cinema devices created by the gentleman scientist, the amateur, magician or trickster of the nineteenth century.[20] This leads to the argument of film itself being only a constituent part of a continuing development that has been referred to as the 'cinema of attractions'. The total history of cinema suggests a much wider suite of technologies than the film camera and projector. The digital domain collects, incorporates and simulates whole suites of past and present technologies and is the contemporary expression of the development of cinema in its broadest sense.

In conclusion I would argue that digital technologies provide a flexible platform for cultural practice where hybridisation, and the lack of distinctions between historic media do not matter, but ignorance of the process might, at least for the scholar. Video continues as a proxy within the digital domain, while film is flattered by digital simulation of its material qualities.

> '… computers have gone way beyond the TV that they are about to subsume and are the first machines able to make use of all modes of language and expression, and to transform one into another and modulate them any way anyone wants.'
> Raymond Bellour[21]

> '… cinema so clearly traces a history from mechanical to digital time …'
> Sean Cubitt[22]

Notes

1. Marc Meyer, 'Digressions Toward an Art History of Video', *Being and Time: The Emergence of Video Projection* (New York: The Buffalo Fine Arts Academy, 1996), p. 8.

2. For example: A day devoted to Michael Snow's *Wavelength* at CCA in Glasgow; two days devoted to the prolific output of Woody and Steina Vasulka at the Candida Arts Centre, London, and the Old 'Lumiere' Cinema, University of Westminster; *Early British Video Works* at Tate Britain; *Shoot! Shoot! Shoot!* at Tate Modern and other venues; Wojciech Bruszewski performing with his film *Points* at the *Evolution Festival 2004* in Leeds; and Anthony McCall's *Line Describing a Cone* at Dundee Contemporary Arts in Dundee, 2004.

3. *X-screen*, Wein, Austria, 2004; *Future Cinema*, ZKM, Karlsruhe, Germany.

4. Oxford English Dictionary.

5. David A Ross, 'Nam June Paik's Videotapes', in *Nam June Paik*, ed. John Handhardt (New York: Whitney Museum of American Art in assoc. with Norton and Company, 1982).

6. Stuart Marshall, 'Video Art, The Imaginary and the Parole Vide', *Studio International* May/June, Vol. 191, No. 981, 1976, p. 245.

7. Wolf Kahlen, 'Video – El temps I L'espai, Series Informatives 2', *Collegi d'arquitectes de Cataluna y Institut Alemany* (Barcelona, 1980), pp. 148–150.

8. David Hall, 'Towards an Autonomous Practice', *Studio International* May/June, Vol. 191, No. 981, 1976, p. 249.

9. Peter Weibel, 'On the Philosophy of VT and VTR', *Heute Kunst, Internationale Kunstzeitschrift*, No. 4/5, December 1973 – February 1974, Milan. Reprinted in: *Video-Apparat/Medium, Kunst, Kultur. Ein Internationaler Reader*, ed. Siegfried Zielinski, (Frankfurt a. M/Bern/New York/Paris, 1992), p. 125.

10. Sean Cubitt, *Videography, Video Media as Art & Culture* (Macmillan, 1993), p. 32.

11. Ibid., 'Introduction'.

12. Marc Meyer, 'Digressions Toward an Art History of Video', *Being and Time: The Emergence of Video Projection* (New York: The Buffalo Fine Arts Academy, 1996), p. 17.

13. Nam June Paik is credited with being the first artist to buy and use the legendary Sony Video Rover in New York in 1965. The subsequent event at New York's Café Au Go Go, was well-documented but another forgotten half-inch format must have been used, as Siegfried Zielinski has proved that the Rover was not on sale in either Japan or the USA until 1967, see *Zur Geschichte des Videorecorders*, (Berlin, 1968), p. 155.

14. Roy Armes, *On Video* (London, Routledge, 1988), p. 1.

15. Paik in his proposal to the *New School for Social Research*, New York, Spring 1965, p. 1.

16. Marshall McLuhan, *Understanding Media: The Extensions of Man* (New York, McGraw-Hill, 1964).

17. The 'V' in DVD does not stand for video but versatile.

18. Nam June Paik, 'Aphorisms', catalogue for *The Machine as Seen at the End of the Mechanical Age* (New York, MOMA, 1968), Unpaginated.

19. David Ross, 'A Provisional Overview of Artists' Television in the US', *Studio International*, May/June, Vol. 191, No. 981, 1976, p. 265.

20. See eds. Laurent Mannoni, Werner Nekes, Marina Warner, *Eyes Lies and Illusions* (London: Hayward Gallery and Lund Humphries, 2004).

21. Raymond Bellour, 'La querelle des dispositifs/ Battle of the images', *Art Press*, No. 262, November 2000, pp. 48–52.

22. Sean Cubitt, *The Cinema Effect* (Massachusettes: MIT, 2004), p. 8.

Chapter twenty

Tamara Krikorian – Defending the Frontier

Cate Elwes

'It is through formal analysis that a real engagement with the institution must occur. Simply transmitting material transferred from one context to another is not sufficient'
Tamara Krikorian

Video was barely ten years old when, in the mid-1970s, the technology became available to artists in the UK. Tamara Krikorian was one of a small group who overcame the logistical difficulties and gained access to the expensive and cumbersome equipment whilst simultaneously combating the institutional discrimination that regarded video as a mildly diverting irrelevance.

Krikorian formed part of an interrogative movement, pioneered by Nam June Paik in the USA and David Hall in the UK, that took as its object of critique the medium of mainstream television, as well as its monolithic social and political institution. As Krikorian has written, 'it is not possible to consider television without taking into account its structures, not just in terms of technology but in terms of politics'.[1] The political strategy that Krikorian adopted took the form of an analysis of television conventions and a search for re-formulations that would destabilise the ideologies embedded in familiar broadcasting entertainment. As the video artist and writer Stuart Marshall put it, radical video practice is one that 'seeks to produce tension, insecurity and social unease'. If television soothes the viewer into a passive consumption of its products, video art, said Marshall, should seek to 'displease'.[2]

Many artists created that spectatorial irritant by investigating the electronic processes involved in the mimetic capabilities of the video image as well as the hardware it relied upon. Works by Paik, the Vasulkas and David Hall exploited the sound and visual disparities that occurred when misusing or misaligning the technology.

Others harnessed camera feedback and time-delay to achieve a materialist reference to the technology and undermine the realism of television imagery. Although Krikorian's work is marked by the culture of reflexivity that dominated the early years of video art, her first works already showed a lyricism that she developed in her later installations. *Disintegrating Forms* (1976) eschews all narrative content and instead presents the viewer with uninterrupted and unedited footage of clouds held within the frames of eight monitors. The monitors are placed at intervals in a darkened space giving the impression of being suspended without any visible means of support. The material base of the illusion is thus reduced, but returns like repressed knowledge when the clouds gradually disperse over the thirty-minute duration of the work. The audience is left with white light emanating from flat, square surfaces referencing the face of the 'box' to which audiences were increasingly enthralled in its mainstream entertainment mode at home. Unlike Yoko Ono's *Sky TV* (1966), a work that relayed live images of the sky to the gallery, Krikorian maintained a minimal element of narrative – the clearing of the sky – to subtly reinvest the monitor with its ontological object-ness. As Stuart Marshall observed, the image was left 'hovering or oscillating between image surface and image object'.[3]

The choice of the sky as an image of fascination and capture by the video camera was by no means arbitrary. Krikorian's work betrays a sensitivity to the natural world that links her practice to the landscape video work pioneered in the USA. Artists like Bill Viola and Mary Lucier were using the video camera to celebrate and mourn what other industrial technologies were destroying. Beyond the obvious environmental concerns, their work, like that of Krikorian, reversed the convention of nature forming the backdrop to film and television narratives, be it in Westerns, soap operas or re-enactments of the lives of great explorers. In *Breeze* (1975) Krikorian puts nature centre stage and brings to our attention the patina created by wind playing across the surface of water. The water is itself held in the glassy surfaces of eight monitors placed on the ground. As the wind shifts direction, patterns of lines appear and mutate echoing the then visible scan-lines of the television screens.

In *Breeze*, the flowing of the water and the flow of electronic pulses through the twin fields of the video image become conceptually enmeshed. Film consists of a succession of still frames whereas the video image is created by a flow of electronic information. As David Hall has remarked, 'one cannot consider tape as a series of separate instants, only as flow ... there is a continuous flow of light onto the photoconductive signal plate which is scanned and transposed to

Disintegrating Forms,
Video, 8 screen
installation, 1976.

the tape'.[4] Early video works were also predicated on the flow of real time, with unedited hour-long takes making the best travelling companion to our everyday lives before the perpetual wakefulness of contemporary surveillance technology offered us parallel lives in digital media. Deleuze has described how mainstream film extracts shots from their original time frame and inserts them into the fictional time line of a Hollywood narrative. In contrast, early video was built on a discrete continuum. With editing technology still unavailable, reel-to-reel video was dominated by the equation that the time it took to record was equal to the time needed to view the work. As David Hall put it, in video, 'time-span becomes an intrinsic 'substance'.[5]

Krikorian's *Breeze* and *Disintegrating Forms* work with blocks of temporal substance and maintain their elliptical critique of mainstream television. The artist refuses all narrative enticements and creates what Chris Darke calls an oasis of calm in the contemporary 'image storm.' That Elysian tranquility is not only an antidote to media overload, but also a personal reflection on landscape, a subject that has held particular significance for Krikorian over the years. She was born in the rolling landscape of Dorset surrounded by Bronze Age hill forts and the mechanical and animal paraphernalia of her grandmother's farm. As she says, landscape is embedded in her consciousness, but nowadays it is experienced like a video, forever bounded by the frame of a car or train window. Krikorian's early works contain a strain of melancholy, a yearning for the freedoms of a childhood enveloped in nature. As the artist remarks: 'Once you leave it, it is very difficult to be in that landscape again'.[6] The installations also point to the possibility of transcendence. The sky and the expanse of water escape into a space beyond the edges of the frames that constrain them and evoke the vastness of nature, unbounded space and infinity. The monitor frame that delineates the edges of the image also signifies 'the marking off of a system of coherent conventions'.[7] In the judicious use of expansive natural images Krikorian is able to suggest that televisual language and its ideologies can be transformed and re-invented – beyond the frame.

Although Tamara Krikorian's work was predicated on a counter-cultural, materialist stance, she shared much of Stuart Marshall's suspicion of modernist tendencies to fetishise the medium and so 'deny the facts of practice, social determination and history'.[8] More simply, Krikorian did not wish to emulate Nam June Paik's use of monitors, 'turning them into follies of piles of TV sets'. There now appeared in her work the first references to other signifying prac-tices, in the case of *In the mind's eye* (1977), to poetry in the form of a love poem by Rimbaud. The tape combines the text of *L'Hiver*, spoken in French, with grainy, black and white travelling shots of the English countryside taken from a train window. Those same sequences then re-appear in the reflection of a restless eye, suffi-ciently close-up to establish the source of the reflection as a televi-sion set. The train sequences are intercut with fragments of off-air material, invariably the news or children's programmes. The om-nipresence of media footage is a feature of much early video and in Krikorian's case anchors the work in its historical present while many of her other references evoke reflections of the past.

The role of television in the 1970s had not yet reached the point of sensory saturation that we witness today. In her writing, Krikorian quotes Georges Duhamel: 'I can no longer think what I want to think, my thoughts have been replaced by moving images'.[9] Tele-vision was viewed by Krikorian and her peers as not only a mental pollutant, but also inherently conservative and designed to promote the interests of the broadcasters who controlled it – mostly, as Krikorian remarked, 'Mandarins with English degrees'. In her video *Vanitas* (1977), Krikorian combined the image of the news-reader reflected in a mirror with that of her own head and shoulders surrounded by delicate personal objects, updates on the *Memento Mori* vanities that are depicted in still life paintings of the 17th century. Here, Krikorian is interested in demonstrating not only the transience of earthly goods and pleasures, but also the ephem-eral nature of the video image itself, a quality that, in fact, attracted many artists of her generation to the medium. The pioneering

Above: *Vanitas*, single screen, Video, Black & White, 1977.

Right: *Unassembled Information*, Video, Black & White, 1977.

194

German video artist, Gerry Schum applied a Marxist, anti-capitalist principle to the fact of video's physical fragility: 'There's no object that can be seen 'in reality' or sold as an object'.[10] Krikorian is less determined to avoid the art market and more concerned to address the ephemeral, indeed duplicitous nature of the televisual image and the highly mediated pronouncements that newsreaders in particular would have us accept as the truth. In *An Ephemeral Art* (1979) Krikorian went as far as filling several monitors with butterfly pupae interspersed with monitors tuned to the then four terrestrial television channels. This magical installation has been much copied and the image of butterflies hatching into emptied televisions has remained one of the most poetic in contemporary video. However, it also constitutes a trenchant critique of the deceptive illusions of broadcast media.

Beyond an interrogation of television realism, Krikorian constructs a darker vision of the artist, herself as transitory as those butterflies, portrayed in the now well-degenerated early video images. Death lurks in the hall of mirrors that Krikorian fashioned in her later works. Mirrors often appear as frames within frames with nothing but a dark void where we would expect to see a reflection of reality. The artist is no longer reflected in the mirror featured in *The Heart of the Illusion* (1981), nor, indeed, is the viewer. Krikorian gazes out at us with a direct address that would seem to confirm our presence, but she then denies our existence by failing to reflect us in the mirror. The work appears to be telling us that both artist and viewer have long passed into another realm, as is the way of all matter.

Looking back at her work today, Krikorian says that she was always a realist: 'People don't want to face up to the reality of living and dying. They think they are immortal and behave that way ... they also behave towards other people as though they were immortal Gods, arrogantly putting themselves about.' Art itself has always contained an acknowledgement of mortality even as it celebrates life. Krikorian reminds us that this intimation of death was at the centre of most medieval and Renaissance painting and it wasn't until the 18th century that painters 'became obsessed with portraits of pretty women and men in gaiters'. *Vanitas* and *The Heart of the Illusion* bring together an ephemeral medium of the 20th century with allegories of dissolution and death that hark back to earlier traditions of still life painting. Within the image of the newsreader Krikorian makes reference to the fragility of truth and reality as portrayed in the dominant ideologies of broadcasting.

Krikorian's choice of the Vanitas theme as a subject matter for her work raises the question of narcissism in early video. Rosalind Krauss famously levelled the accusation of narcissism at works in which artists used the instant feedback of video to create extended self-portraits. In Krauss' view, the artist becomes locked in a hermetically sealed video loop that divorces the individual from the social and historical context in which s/he exists. In live-relay installations, the audience members are offered a similar opportunity to view themselves narcissistically outside the messy business of real politics. And yet, Krikorian's careful, muted and elusive presence in her work would appear to resist such a reading in her case. In *Unassembled Information* (1977) the artist produces what she regards as the antithesis of the TV portrait. She presents to the camera the anonymous mass that is the back of her head. A small hand mirror periodically comes into view over her shoulder as fragments of radio programmes animate the soundtrack. German songs bleed into American commentaries only to be displaced by Middle-Eastern music reminiscent of Krikorian's family origins in Armenia. And yet, we learn little or nothing about the artist. Her nose, eye, ear and chin briefly appear in the hand mirror, but the fragments can never be assembled into a representational whole. Where artists like Cindy Sherman and Eleanor Antin would display themselves in a cast of flamboyant disguises, Krikorian revealed little other than our act of looking from somewhere behind her head. Opening up space on both sides of the monitor plane Krikorian creates deep tunnels of visions aided by the video technology and the mirrors with which she lengthens and darkens the space into which the eye travels.

This denial of the pleasures induced by the image of a woman was a strategy employed by many feminist artists of Krikorian's generation and, indeed, was adopted by some of those who followed, myself included. The emphasis on what a woman does or sees rather than what she looks like was an attempt to mitigate the over-eroticism of representations of femininity that reduced women to either positively or negatively charged erotic objects. Tamara Krikorian vehemently denies any intention to engage with feminist debates around representation in the l970s: 'As far as I was concerned I was working as an artist and the fact that I happened to be a woman was not of interest to me, in my work, at all. When it came to the Vanitas subject, obviously I would use myself ... the objects would be feminine objects, like my jewellery.' However, Krikorian admits to avoiding performance art because it might have raised issues such as gender and detracted from her main concerns: 'I was absolutely concentrating on the iconic image of the newsreader, for instance and my relationship with that image as an artist.' Tellingly, she concedes that she never used female newsreaders, but warns me not to read too much into that because 'there were very few women newsreaders at the time.' Clearly, Krikorian was not making conscious references to the problematics of female representations. However, her use of stillness and duration, her denial of eroticised representations and the various strategies of concealment and refraction that she employed, all imply an awareness of the pitfalls of representation that faced women artists as they began to make inroads into the art world in the 1970s.

Tamara Krikorian was primarily concerned with forging a language and theoretical position that bridged hard-line formalism and what Peter Wollen called 'content-ism'. Krikorian would never be satisfied with a simple appropriation of narrative structures treated as a transparent medium through which a secure reality could be transmitted. Instead, she was seeking an alternative strategy in what Wollen called the 'space opened up by the disjunction and dislocation of signifier and signified'.[11] Here was where Krikorian developed her own subtle synthesis of lyricism and conceptual rigour, development and stasis, modernity and historical allusion. She created what she called an 'impressionistic formalism' that, while reflecting intelligently on all aspects of art, nature and humanity, always included self-referential elements in order to 'underline the unreality of TV information'.

I would argue that *The Heart of the Illusion* (1981), Krikorian's most accomplished work, achieved that delicate balancing act between didacticism and poetry that this early video frontierswoman pioneered. The three-screen installation introduced colour and a painterly sensibility that was less evident in her earlier black and white works. Krikorian collaborated with the company Spafax Television to construct a triptych combining landscape, still life and self-portrait with a self-reflexivity that also maintained the aura of *tempus fugit* that was so critical in her earlier work. In *The Heart of the Illusion*, it is no longer the artist who turns away to reveal only the back of her head, it is the monitors that would appear to deny us their faces. However, closer inspection reveals three mirrors fixed to the wall facing the monitors and it is by twisting our necks that we are able to see the images that they reflect. The first one-take sequence features the characteristic still life, containing personal ephemera, flowers, fruit, shells and butterflies. As the camera slowly pans along the display, the image shifts from colour through to neutral tones and finally resolves to black and white as photographs and papers pile up before the image vanishes entirely into a white screen. The middle monitor is devoted to a slow, 360 degree pan of a winter landscape beginning with a rural idyll and slowly revealing a nuclear power station in the distance and indicating an industry that has 'eroded and despoiled' the landscape. The final image is of the artist herself looking directly out at the viewer with the empty, deathly mirror behind her and a gash of red velvet curtain framing the ensemble. Krikorian turns as slowly as the camera turned on the landscape and the still life. All the major themes of painting are represented and underscored by the specific gravity of video, which, in Krikorian's hands, returns us to the free-roaming spectatorship of painting in defiance of the directed viewing of television. Colour plays an important part in the work. Based on the theories of Godard, Krikorian uses pure colour to create visual interruptions to the images as well as comment on the relationship of colour to fiction where black and white might come closer to reality. Reality here is a reference to the ontological presence of the technology. As Krikorian observes, 'black and white is less obviously seductive and has a built-in, distantiating flaw – no colour'.

With the greater technical sophistication of this work, Tamara Krikorian might have been tempted to make works for television particularly when the 1980s saw the brief but significant sponsorship of experimental moving image work by Channel 4. However, Krikorian chose to maintain a hard-earned independence outside broadcasting. Although many artists like Stuart Marshall and Gerry Schum embraced the idea that, in the hands of artists, television could become a democratic medium reaching a wide and heterogeneous audience, Krikorian believed that broadcasters were happy to exploit the visual experimentation of artists but 'have shied off experimental ideas'. Although television appeared to offer an alternative to the vilification of video in the art world, Krikorian asked, 'why should I want to make work inside the very institution I critique?' In the end, it was not possible for Krikorian to achieve a deconstruction of television within television itself.

Tamara Krikorian was satisfied to have made a major contribution to the evolving discipline of video art in the 1970s and early 1980s. It was wholly consistent with her view of life, art and television as a triumvirate of ephemeral conceits that she should, in the early 1980s, turn her attention to other creative projects. As Krikorian tells us, 'an artist transfers ideas for a short time and then moves on. This goes beyond the sense of self-importance of the artist as an image of authority, with his or her iconic status ...'. However, it is reasonable to claim that Krikorian's enduring contribution was her ability to draw out a specific quality of video, which Stuart Marshall has described as its talent for 'sustaining a flickering, delicate image for immense durations – a fragility coupled with monumentality'.[12] To this, Tamara Krikorian's work added a painterly sensitivity, and an analytical perspicacity that demonstrated the possibility of maintaining a critical stance in art, holding the viewer's expectations under tension, while revealing to the eye, layers of subtle aesthetic and philosophical meaning.

Notes

1.   Tamara Krikorian, 'Some Notes on Ephemeral Art', *Eye to Eye* catalogue, Scottish Arts Council publication, 1979.

2.   Stuart Marshall, letter to Art Monthly, 1976.

3.   Ibid.

4.   David Hall, 'Video, towards defining an aesthetic', Scottish Arts Council publication, 1976, unpaginated.

5.   Ibid.

6.   Tamara Krikorian in conversation with the author. All other unattributed quotes are drawn from this interview.

7.   Stuart Marshall, op. cit.

8.   Stuart Marshall, op. cit.

9.   Georges Duhamel quoted by Tamara Krikorian in *Eye to Eye*, op. cit.

10. Gerry Schum quoted by Tamara Krikorian in 'Video, towards defining an aesthetic', op. cit.

11. Peter Wollen quoted by Tamara Krikorian in *Elusive Sign* catalogue, ACE, 1987.

12. Stuart Marshall, 'The Use of the Static', *Fuse* Magazine, March, 1980.

Chapter twenty-one

Another Place – David Hall

Jackie Hatfield

A riddle: imagine images that are not images or objects, that happen in a single moment never to be repeated. Imagine a place that isn't a place, and artworks, which in their complete forms resonate only through the memory of the audience that experience them; or changed from its moving original, a photo fixed in stasis. How would an historian write this art work into art history? How would they map its perceptual, intangible, ephemeral language? How would we know it were true to its form?

For conceptual art, the existential is central to its becoming; for the artist through process, and through the audience in its reception. With film, the viewing of its moving frames is fleeting, and with video the materialised latent image is transient, so that similar to a performance these are momentary presences etched in memory. David Hall's art has traversed a broad history of forms, sculpture, film, video, television, and installation. Despite subsequent interpretations of his polemics being late modernist in tone and fixated on form, Hall has embraced different mediums and varying contexts. His trajectory through the conservative academy must have propelled him to work towards a political art, and confront the conventions of the art establishment directly through his work. In fact material was a political issue in the 1960s, sculptors were moving away from traditional processes, and exploring non-traditional materials, e.g. sandbags, wood, felt, and in this cultural context, this successful young sculptor's forays into film must have been perceived as rule breaking. Not only was Hall pushing the boundaries of sculpture, extending it through time and space, but he was questioning the very place of art, and asking the audience to do so too. David Hall's work and the driving force of his practice is not the object, but the experience, and he believes still, in an art

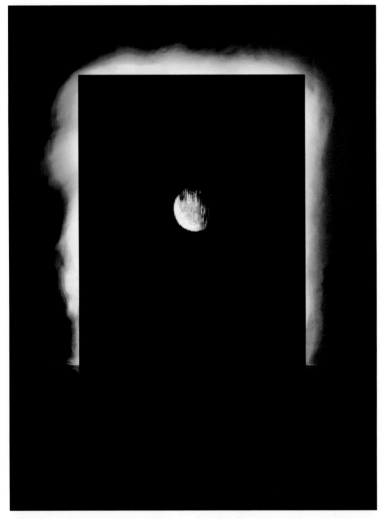

A Situation Envisaged, The Rite II (Cultural Eclipse), Video and live TV, 1989.

place accessible and not separated from society. 'My interest was at a point where I was having some frustrations about the context in which sculpture was seen, it was confined to a gallery; public art happened but it was a marginal element, primarily sculpture was made to be seen, was seen, from the nineteenth through the twentieth century in the "salon", a private elite context, where unless you were one of the initiated minority you wouldn't go to see it. That bothered me more and more.

That's why film (as cinema) and video (as television) became of interest, because they were the media of now; they were what most people were looking at, they weren't looking at art, art was in galleries'.[1]

Hall's contribution to the Artist Placement Group established by
John Latham and Barbara Steveni in 1965-'66 gave context to these
ideologies, and in many respects formed the foundation for Hall's
subsequent rigorous polemics. Latham was an advocate of the artist
as catalyst, or 'incidental person' acting as agent of change. APG
'took shape from artists who were already recognising that to work
in terms of event rather than of the art object was the main line of

Progressive Recession, multi-screen interactive video installation, 1974.

history'.[2] This analytical, process oriented art, was not driven by the marketplace, the gallery system or the establishment, and rather than the artist as guru, here was the artist as a member of society, a worker – interjecting with it and not remote from it. 'APG emerged from the idea that artists are a human resource underused by society. Artists are isolated from the public by the gallery system, and in the ghetto of the art world we are shielded from the mundane

Below left: *Vidicon Inscriptions*, Interactive video, 1974/75.

Below right: *Television Interruptions (7 TV Pieces)*, 16mm, Black and White, 1971.

realities of industry commerce and government. The idea was that artists ... would bring completely alternative ways of seeing and thinking to bear on the organisations they were placed in. APG would thus recognise the artist's outsider status and turn it into positive social advantage.'[3] This thinking has permeated Hall's working processes, and with his art 'work' he is consciously manipulating the physiognomy and psychology of the viewer and art as non-object.

With his seminal televisual art works broadcast between 1971 and 1993, Hall coalesced the ideas about context and concept, both, he argues, are inextricably linked. 'By context I mean the inevitable, unavoidable consciousness of physical environment through to perceived cultural framework – a phenomenological issue. A concept – once manifest externally in whatever form – can't be read in isolation as though in a void, but is necessarily read within its specific context and this context invariably influences, even shapes, that reading. With this recognition the choice of context must necessarily be given equal consideration from the outset, the two integrated are the condition of a perceived experience.' There were several series of commissioned TV interventions by Hall, *TV Interruptions* 1971, ten artworks broadcast on Scottish Television intermittently throughout the day over ten days, unannounced; *This is a Television Receiver* – featuring the newsreader Richard Baker, BBC 2 1976; *Stooky Bill TV* and a re-screening of four of his 1971 *Interruptions*, Channel 4 1990; and in 1993, also unannounced – *reacTV, contexTV, withouTV, exiTV* and *ecstaseeTV,* on MTV Networks.

Hall's broadcasts were radical for their time, uncompromising in their placement within the relentless media flow. Hall made tangible the intangible for those broadcast minutes; and extended the artwork into the place of the audience. This was not simply art *on* television, an artist having a stall in the midst of the marketplace – a place in an arts feature, but an obstruction, a political act, and provoked the viewer to ask questions about what they were seeing and perceiving. 'I had concern about art being confined, being compartmentalised within an elitist world, or seen as tangential to real life, I was interested in shifting ground, preferably into what I saw as the social context, into the broadest possible one across all boundaries, rather than specific to an elite. In that process there are political implications because it suggests that one is engaging in the broader world of being, of all social activity, and broadcasting work as intervention you're intervening in an establishment process, and that intervention, if not usurping, is raising questions by its very presence and interjection. If any action takes place that suggests a different kind of emphasis in behaviour on the part of an audience,

A Situation Envisaged, The Rite, Installation, diagram, 1980.

then in a way, one can argue there is in essence a political gesture there.' Similar to Hall's installations, the ephemeral lay at these works' conceptual and contextual core, the moment of exhibition *was* the artwork, and the context its conceptual material. There is no comprehensive anecdotal evidence, no empirical study of what affect these broadcasts had on the audiences, and perhaps, to write such works into history is to take out their soul, they were an art of now, not an art of the past.

For Hall's art, video must have been the perfect medium, and perhaps now we can say it was/is im-material, or the beginnings of post-materiality, and a precursor to computer augmented interactive art. In retrospect, it is clear to see that moment of shift in the electronic participatory video of the 1970s, where the radical art concerns of the twentieth century were made manifest: the sculptural, painterly, cinematic and interactive – i.e. gesamtkuntswerk. 'Video is incorporeal, it certainly doesn't have the tangibility even of cine-film – where you're dealing with frame for frame, where you can hold it to the light and see it – instead it is a stream of electronic information, blind, on a tape, and now in other formats. However, when manifest it has a time-life form; the time-life aspect of it is as concrete as film; but then extremely different in terms of its possibilities. One interest for me was the potential for live interactive work, where you were dealing with the here and now which you could never do with film; film is a 'past' medium in that the experiential event is one of viewing an idea manifest in the past and, in a sense, copied onto film. It's the copy you are seeing. With much early video work the element of excitement was that it wasn't a copy, it was an instant manifestation, and this continues as multiple digital forms develop.'

205

A Situation Envisaged, The Rite, multi-screen video and live TV installation, 1980.

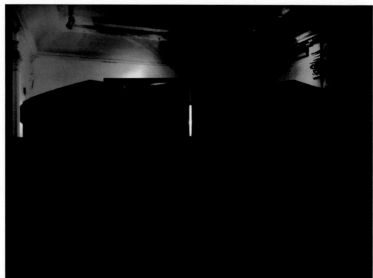

The Situation Envisaged, multi-screen video and live TV installation, 1976.

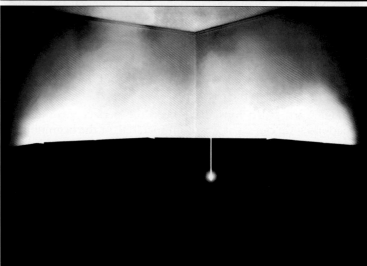

Hall's emphasis has not been surface, for film in a material sense this would be the emulsion, the indexical. At the centre of his artworks the conceptual and the contextual are intertwined, so that video's malleability and conceptual open-end-ness enabled many possibilities, and the use of video in itself was a political gesture. 'I think that because of the nature of the last sculpture I made, in a way I disowned the aesthetic. I am not too interested in aesthetics that have a seductive value or that are lyrical, I guess the progression from a minimalist thinking was into a conceptualist thing where I was using the means to impart some sense of an idea, rather than

Both images:
This is a Television Receiver,
Video, 1976.

offering an aesthetic experience.' Video was a form with no fixed history, attractive to artists such as Hall. However, there has been criticism that Hall's philosophies were of a fixed nature, arguing as he was for material autonomy. This has to be seen as a relative and not absolute position. 'The autonomy I was talking about in 'British Video Art, Towards an Autonomous Practice' in 1976[4] was an autonomy *from* film; a recognition for the concerns of the material and its languages. Initially we were dealing with a medium, which you couldn't edit, so it was all real time, in a way you were having to construct work in recognition of its context. When I was arguing for autonomy, it was for recognition that there were issues specific to it in terms of how you would relate to it. And there was potential there, like interactivity, which wasn't possible with film. So it already had the makings of a certain kind of autonomy, and I was arguing to give it breathing space so it wasn't confused with film in those earliest days'. The problem with these rigorous polemics, similar to the contemporaneous debates around film materiality by Le Grice and Gidal, is that they are often mis-construed when de-contextualised from the specific practice they are referring to, and have been taken as blueprints for the categorisation of sub-sequent works. Institutional canonising is inevitably a restriction on experiment and exploration. This has been a particular issue with the electronic, since its materiality is not static, and its languages are constantly evolving. The fact is, similar to Gidal and Le Grice, Hall never meant his arguments around autonomy to be written in stone but to be considered as debate and an integral part of the practical process. The difficulty lies in the interpretation and sub-sequent readings, particularly pertinent for art like Hall's which is ultimately ephemeral in its materiality: 'People write history in the context of the present, and in a very specific way it is shaped according to current interests which may cohere with the thinking of the time. It reshapes that history to accommodate the present and can lose sight of original objectives; you've got to be in a position to place yourself in the context that was, or at least try to imagine yourself there.'

I return to the questions posed by my riddle. How can an historian notate this transient art? How can we know whether their interpre-tation is faithful to an artwork that has existed for a single moment in time? Hall's television interventions cannot be re-staged; similar to a performance, the artwork has happened; and exists only in mind and memory for those who were there. Video has changed since Hall's first use of it, the cumbersome mechanical analogue apparatus has been replaced by the computer. Instead of the monitor, we now have projectors; and any projected image can be seductive, but this current moving-image context is fundamentally philosophically and conceptually different from that of Hall's early work and his principles for exhibition. 'There has been an ongoing synthesis of imagery since the middle of the 19th century, from when photography arrived and its various subsequent forms. Dis-play systems are moving along rapidly and what has happened since the advent of video projection is that because large scale imagery can easily be achieved there is a belief – certainly in the gallery world

TV Interruptions 93,
Context TV,
Video, 1993.

Stooky Bill TV,
commissioned for C4
19:4:90, Video, 1990.

– that because it is bigger it is in some way better.[5] Whereas large size set the scene as absolute necessity in much 1950s gestural Abstract Expressionism, the significance of the continued spectacle of 'big' as accepted status quo in all manner of later art is fundamentally questionable. Also, video projection has the look of cin-

209

ema, but the idea of working with cinema is one of confinement as well, you're inside this area, you're consumed by a screen bigger than you, anthropomorphically you're reduced, you're subservient to the image. In contrast the TV set at home is more intimate, it's not usually in a darkened space, and consequently there is an argument to suggest you're on equal terms. The reading is quite different. As an artist who was making work to be seen in that context as opposed to cinema, it necessarily had to be different.'

There could already be a problem of interpretation here, because Hall's statement could be taken to suggest that current work does not intentionally explore the 'social political' act of viewing, or that the monumental scale of projection and imagistic spectacle is somehow superficial relative to the 'pure' art of the video monitor. I can already feel it brewing, somewhere in that labyrinth of his language, a reductive reading of it, then an institutionalisation of form, and then categorisation for what art is or isn't. As artists, we know that Hall is referring to his *own* practice, his processes, the languages he has evolved; the paradigms revolving around his works and his ideas. More than that though, he is doing what the best artists have done throughout history, he is questioning the status quo; querying, and asking us to do the same. As he has said, good art poses questions. 'From birth we start open-ended to experience and accrue experience throughout life which we continually impose on any new experience. So, if I can somehow interject here and shake it a little, so that it challenges already established experience, it may stimulate alternative ways of thinking about the world. That seems to me the essence of what art should be about.'

A political art such as Hall's interventions grew out of a reaction to the cultural context of its making, in its concept eschewing the marketplace and gallery commodification – and selling is the raison d'etre behind curation in this era of capital. As Hall has said, in the 1970s there was no overt desire by video artists to show in private galleries, there was an inherent social political drive whereby artists were working within communities (London Video Arts – which he initiated, London Filmmakers Coop, Musicians Collective; Arts Lab; 2B Butlers Wharf, Acme etc) and the prime motivation behind the works was not the market place. But, how is it that Hall's work does not feature in the public art galleries of the UK? Why does the British gallery system ignore major film and video artists who have by and large continued to make extraordinary ground breaking works across a thirty or forty year period and who are recognised internationally as being some of the most significant practitioners of the late twentieth century? The apparent dismissal is puzzling, it surely cannot be because they are making art which

has at its roots an anti-object stance, since this would be similar to Dada or Fluxus artists who are feted by the gallery system (commercial and state). Is it because the state gallery curators reflect the marketplace and its gallery art critics, who either curiously have no knowledge of the provenance of these artworks, or actively avoid what they see as a commercially unappealing, distinctly separate, 'underground' activity? In time, with informed histories, this anomaly must surely resolve.

101 TV Sets, made in collaboration with Tony Sinden, multi screen video and live TV installation, 1972/75.

Notes

1. Unless stated otherwise, all subsequent quotes are from an interview with David Hall on 7 March 2005.

2. John Latham, *Report of a Surveyor* (Edition Hansjorg Mayer, Stuttgart, London, 1984), p. 40.

3. Extract from a Tate Gallery statement on purchasing the APG archive, 2004 APG staged a major exhibition at the Hayward Gallery, London in 1971. It continued until 1989 when it was reformed as O and I (Organisation and Imagination).

4. David Hall, 'British Video Art, Towards an Autonomous Practice', in the video art issue of *Studio International* magazine, May/June, Vol. 191, No. 981, 1976, p. 249.

5. 'Video has been around for thirty years but this generation has taken it off the television screen into a larger scale and given it a weight and an importance it has never previously had', Nicholas Serota, Director of the Tate Gallery on the occasion of Gillian Wearing winning the Turner prize, *The Guardian*, 3 December 1997.

Chapter twenty-two

Alchemy and the Digital Imaginary

David Larcher interviewed by Stephen Littman
January 2005

SL: In this interview I'd like to talk with you about the processes, methodologies and implementation of your work and how you manifest the imaginary through layering. The research laboratory at the Academy of Media Arts, Köln is a studio environment with high-end digital imaging technologies; comprised of digital tape environments, vision mixers, computers, all fed into a hub such as the Flame[1] compositing system, which enables you to work on eight levels of real time imaging. You've created set-ups, which collide image streams together; the images you are creating can only be realised within the technical environment that you and the school have constructed. This is not just about making pictorial images, but collage, and exploring the possibilities of imaging space and new structures, creating new pictorial environments within the screen. Originally, when you first started making work with film you were very interested in the optical printer.

DL: My first film was re-filmed off the wall or off a back projection screen. In *Monkey's Birthday* (1975) a lot of it was re-filmed but then I got access to an optical printer; and also I used a contact printer. So you could have six different loops running all together simultaneously; you could bi-pack or tri-pack many times. So if you are using an optical printer, which is slightly different, you are actually framing a frame and you're saying I want this once or twice or whatever. But if you are using a contact printer, you are actually using levels of different materials of films, as you get a thicker pack, it goes out of focus and stuff like that, eventually the printer rips into the film and you get all these bits falling apart, sprockets drifting across the screen and the screen looks great, if you like that sort of thing – it was more to do with the surface of filmic material. One got to know about stocks, various negative positive and high contrast ratios. They have a nice expression in French, which is travail sur le port, work on the support, which means when you get into the *matter* of that which is conveying the information. So it becomes almost an aesthetic exercise. An exercise in aesthetics rather than a narrative form like Hollywood.

SL: But that process of using a bi-pack, contact printer or optical printer is all about playing and having fun with the technology, to create images that are beyond the imagination but that exist within the material.

DL: You want to see what you haven't seen. If you want to work something out in layers, then it is a whole other process of compositing; if you throw things together which I tend to do; sometimes it works, sometimes it doesn't – and I'll say ooh I like that.

SL: You have had a long history of making layered work in filmic space, in a cinematic environment. Using the emulsion …

DL: Physically layered, and the thing is you would role the film back and then re-expose it either by matting or exposure of light.

SL: You could use a Bolex to wind the film back

DL: Not so much in the camera more in the printer. Let say in the case of *Monkeys Birthday*. With *Mare's Tail* (1969) most of it was on two projectors onto a screen, which was re-filmed. Like a VJ set now, several inputs coming into the screen, which is mixed live. A different kind of experience and process.

SL: It's like a painter deciding how to apply paint, isn't that what you are doing with your material; whether it's film, video or digital?

DL: Right now I have something rendering on the Flame, and I have not got a clue how it is going to come out; I chucked in some footage about six sequences of varying lengths and left it rendering for three days over the weekend and I'll look at it when I return to Germany.

SL: So you got bored with the optical printing or the bi packing.

DL: It was not so much that I got bored, it was the amount of work, and the money involved.

SL: So it was expensive then.

DL: Sure, unless you were developing it yourself, but you could only really develop black & white, for colour you'd have to go to the labs, then if you needed a print, it was outrageous prices. Now it's even more expensive. But that's when I switched to video; I got

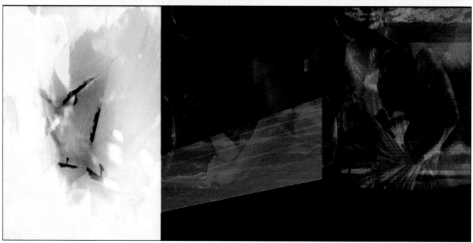

Both images: *Ich Tank,* Video, 1997.

The Gulbenkian Foundation Video Fellowship, that's where I met you in 1981, that's when I proposed it. I was awarded it in 1982, it was quite a mind-blowing experience.

Above:
Granny's Is,
Video, 1990.

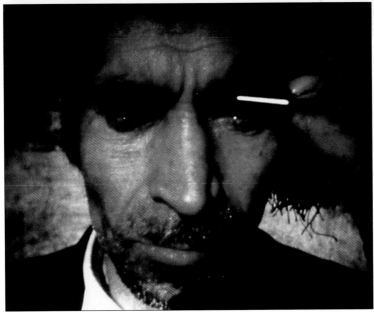

Left:
Monkey's Birthday,
16mm film, 1975.

SL: Was that your first use of video at that point?

DL: Well I had used black and white reel-to-reel Akai quarter inch. I did a performance with it. It was a crazy night at the London Filmmakers Coop in 1974, it must have been. Everyone came over from the Coop to the Fantasy Factory and we were recording everything on Akai quarter inch black and white and Hoppy (John 'Hoppy' Hopkins) was using Sony half-inch reel-to-reel video decks, he then moved up to the U-Matic[2] format. So I knew about video, but did not have it to hand, as such. Film was much more available.

SL: People like myself, started at the art school, playing with all sorts of mediums including film and video, and performance. We had access to U-Matic, then Betacam (mid 80s), I had a lot of contacts in industry which enabled me to use high end systems pushing the limits of video, then digital technologies.

DL: But you are talking about the beginning of the 1980s, that's when video really became possible. The point is, as soon as you started working on video everything was so immediate. I didn't have to send it off to the lab, there it was, the biggest shock was that it had audio on it as well.

SL: Was the image quality of U-matic video a compromise in relation to film?

DL: No, it was great. I loved it.

SL: Returning to the optical printer, do you consider the investigative processes of film and printing moved you easily into the U-matic environment and the video editing suites?

DL: U-matic was a bit of a shock. If you are working on film, and you know something about grain and something about processing, and a bit about different kinds of emulsions and stuff like that, suddenly when you have to think about and understand how an electronic signal works, field blanking, line blanking and colour burst. You just don't know. Blacking a tape is a mystery in itself. It took a long time to understand what was going on. Hence, miles and miles of drop out, but then you start to think that this is a significant part of the process. The trash that you get is as important as the picture that is in front of you or whatever you're trying to do or talk about.

With video, it was the first time I could achieve a mix. You can't really do a mix in film, well not live; I could do it in the printer or frame by frame in an optical printer, but that is a whole other thing. It is a whole other process in itself, but as soon as you're in a video suite, you just push a lever from one feed to another and it's done.

Either using a manual device or computer controlled, it's all done in real time. As soon as video came, video became like audio, visual audio, it's what you've got now, everybody is working on laptops, or working with pure data.

SL: Or they are doing VJ-ing or they are doing lightshows

DL: Absolutely, exactly, which was going on in the mid sixties, they were doing massive light shows.

SL: From using analogue videotape, such as U-matic, you were given funding by Channel 4 in the 1980s, which enabled you to exploit the emerging digital technologies (D1) can you talk about this?

DL: If you were working in the old days (seven to ten years ago) you would create multi-layered work by going over the same image again and again building up material on cut roles which would be added to over a period of time. The number of cut role tapes would be dependent on the type of editing system you had available. Typically, five video players or machines would be used as source material to one editing recorder through a vision mixer with digital effects channels – material from the recorder being placed in a source player after every pass. This process would then add an additional layer to the content manifested with every pass, adding and changing the visual space of the work/material, and bouncing back and forth to create images undiscovered before now. Using digital machines enabled the transparency of image layers to be achieved; with multiple image layers, there was no degradation of quality, no loss unlike the analogue environments of the 1980s and 1990s. The technique of multi-layered editing was still undertaken in these pre-digital environments; though quality limitations did not stop the aesthetical issues, however the images were plagued by technical standards problems which undermined the process of discovery.

SL: *Granny's Is* (1989–1990) can be cited as an example of the process of multi-layering.

DL: Yes, but a huge drop in quality. Which is quite funny if you look at *Granny Is*. Half way through when I was using the facility company SOHO 601 (which cost half the budget of the film) for two nights; I had twenty generations on D1 and then no more money, then I went to Component Video and negotiated another £3000, a thousand quid a night. The rest of the project was then put together using component analogue video, it just completely falls apart after five generations. You can see as the film falls apart in terms of quality it becomes total trash!! You get one sequence of digital, which looks clean and beautiful and then it goes back into analogue U-matic, and then it goes back into clean digital because I got some more time, and the rest suffers from quality loss.

SL: When you first started, did you have a general idea that you could layer with video?

DL: This was the point, not only was it live but you could actually remove one thing and put another one in its place at the same time, not only could you mix two pieces together but you could mix them into each other almost in an organic sense. The real shock comes ten years later when they brought in Flame, and then the image is no longer even mixable its just like another object inside another space. That's there and I'm going to walk around it and I'm going to look at it from down here, that was I think the biggest transformation, when what you're actually seeing becomes an object inside another context, you can talk about three things at the same time.

If you're dealing with cuts the way I ended up working for instance with *Granny's Is* which came after *EETC* which is when I was first learning video, so you would actually create the narrative as cuts, and go through and take all the bits you wanted off the original tape. I would take all the bits where she was speaking and I would just have a complete tape of her speaking, and I would take that and sample bits of the voice for the audio track, and then the actual image track, I would put that into different parts of the image. So that the cuts were inside the shots, but inside elements of the shots; you take reality and then compress it into significant moments. You don't have to think about cuts anymore because you let the whole thing do real time; that was the point of the digital aspect because then you can go into the suite and put all the compressed elements of the speech into each frame. Over the last few years, I've manly been working with audio, but it's mixed together with video, because it's all mixing. I've not edited for years, since about 1997, which is the last time I made a cut.

SL: You must compile things together?

DL: If you've got many inputs, it's a question of a mix rather than making hard cuts; continuous flows where you pick and choose.

SL: Is this process all intuitive?

DL: Well, it's what you can manage, there are so many things going on, various keyboards in the edit suite, three or four lap tops playing out, some playing video, others playing audio, it can be quite chaotic. Very few people are interested in the studio where I work;

usually only dealing with the straight image, which has nothing to do with the imaginary.

SL: would you call your work narrative?
DL: It narrates …

SL: But when it becomes multi-layered do you think it negates narrative?

DL: No because it becomes a question of the reading, you can read a piece of text in hundreds of different ways; but it makes it less rigid, less formal in the sense that if you stand in front of lets say an abstract expressionist painting different people will be subject to different emotions or interpretations; you are laying it open for those who might come later. When you do something like that, you don't realise how narrative it is … and a few years later you might think it so obvious.

SL: In your work, you make the linear space the construction, and you build up layer on layer on layer until there's a metaphysical space of light and image and sound, all happening at the same time. When you were working on Umatic, it was still relatively linear …

DL: … in Flame you can put it all in virtually, and not only that it keeps all your clip memory, so you have all the history of that clip … if you actually repeat a particular effect so many times it eventually comes back into phase and you find something else, it's a bit like harmonics on a guitar, you reach a harmonic point, its almost another planet of let's say visu-lisation, a bit like fractal stuff. It's not like performance, because it's more like repeating a mantra, it's almost like a literary process that you go through, or it's like a chemical experiment, you repeat a certain number of procedures that join together and alter somehow the parameters. The point is you alter the amount of whatever you put in.

SL: You cannot do this in film you cannot manipulate or wrap a surface around an object.

DL: That's right you can't do it. That's why I gave up on film years ago. I lost interest – really.

Notes

1. Flame is a visual effects and compositing system.
2. A videotape format introduced by Sony in 1971.

Chapter twenty-three

Reflections on My Practice and Media Specificity

Malcolm Le Grice

Reviewing my work since I began to make films, I think it has gone through a number of phases. I have often described the earliest phase of my work with film as 'primitive'.

I was well informed about mainstream cinema and the European 'art' cinema of Truffaut, Godard, Fellini or Bergman. But when I started making film I had already rejected all of these forms of cinema as a model – I sought a form that matched my understanding and experience of contemporary 'radical' art. My concepts came instead mainly from painting and what was known then as 'free-form' jazz. I described my early work as primitive because I had no technical knowledge of film, but more importantly at the time, I was uninformed about the early experimental films of Leger, Ruttmann, Richter etc., the American Underground of Brakhage; Warhol or Jack Smith films or their equivalent in Europe – Kren, Kubelka or for example my immediate contemporaries Birgit and Wilhelm Hein. This period lasted a short while as experimental film from abroad began to be seen in London and I also actively researched and sought out early avant-garde work.

The second phase emerged after I had built printing and processing equipment and later – with the help particularly of Fred Drummond – installed the first properly functioning filmmakers' workshop using ex-laboratory equipment. The opportunities offered by this equipment led me to explore the possibilities of film-printing, film image transformation and structures based often on loops and repeated sequences. Also, a major part of this second phase was experiment with multi-projection, installation and live performance with film. The two aspects of this phase of work raised different questions, but each was characterised by an exploration of the medium, its context of presentation and the encounter for the spectator.

The next phase began with a return to performance represented within the film – *After Lumiere* (1974) and *After Manet* (1975) – and proceeded to the three feature length single screen films that explored a minimal form of narrative. During this period I explored issues of the language of film, its semiology, the notion of its grammar and tense formation, identification with represented characters and with camera viewpoint.

The current phase, which began around 1984, took up some of the issues of my earlier films but through video and the digital rather than film.

Media Transitions – Film, Video and Digital Systems

My early work with film, concentrating particularly on the properties of film as medium, its materials and mechanical processes, has often been interpreted as giving some special priority to the intrinsic qualities of film – an essentialist attitude consistent with some aspects of modernism. Though much of my early theoretical work clearly stressed the medium and materials, I have never promoted the idea of 'pure film' or the clear delineation of film from other media. My earliest involvement with film, ran parallel to an interest in a wide range of media, including, even in the late 1960s, video and computers. It also involved: performances that stressed presence; cross media explorations; and from the start, a concern with the role and experience of the spectator. In one sense it had a modernist base, an awareness of those factors that were specific to a medium, but it also always challenged the limits of the medium, stretching these to a breaking point, as in *White Field Duration* (1973), or the conceptual performance *Pre-production* (1973) which involved only live readings and a blank white screen.

As in *Yes No Maybe Maybe Not* (1969) and *Berlin Horse* (1970), this early period was particularly characterised by an involvement in image transformation exploring the potential of film-printing and developing. It was also characterised by the development of temporal structures based on repetition and the film loop and by a concern with the role and conceptual experience of the spectator. This was explored in a number of ways but specifically through multi-projection with anything from two to six projectors, film-loop installations, projection performances where the projectors were moved during the performance, and shadow performances. My work of this period also explored minimal concepts of cinema with a focus on the screen – often blank – a focus on the film base

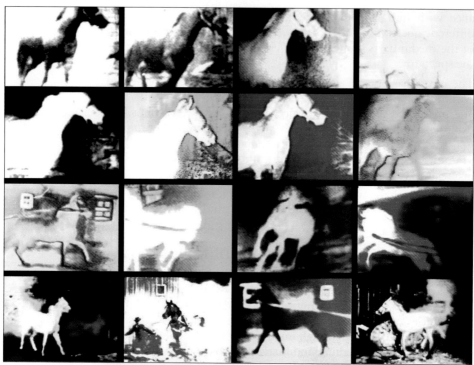

Above:
Berlin Horse,
16mm film, 1970,
composite.

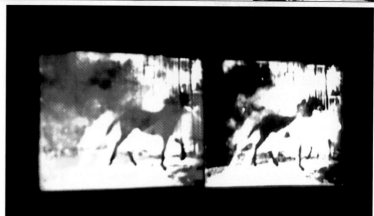

Right:
Berlin Horse,
16mm film, 1970.

(normally called celluloid but in fact acetate) and its aberrations of scratch and dirt particles and on re-filming from the screen. A example of this is the six-screen film and performance, *After Leonardo* (1973), which explores image deterioration beginning with a close-up detail, black and white reproduction of the crazed paint surface of the Mona Lisa. This deterioration – the trace of time on an object – is treated as a parallel for aberrations and loss in the filmed representation.

222

Both images:
Berlin Horse,
16mm film, 1970.

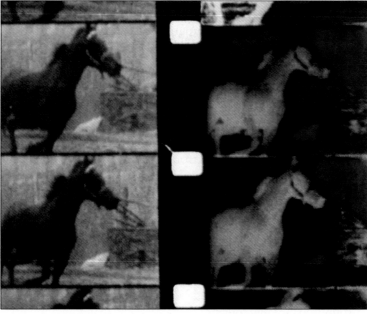

During the same period I published theoretical concepts about duration and the ways in which experience of present duration for the spectator might relate to represented times and spaces, for example 'Real time/space'.[1] The theory and my practice led me to a re-examination of representation, exploring the process of cine-

223

photography in the context of the indexical signifier and focussing on the notions of document and evidence.

The first works that pursued this direction were *After Lumiere – l'arroseur arrosé* (1974) and *After Manet – le dejuener sur l'herb* (1975) made with four cameras and shown on four screens. I then made three feature length films that explored aspects of narrative form and structure, *Blackbird Descending* (1977), *Emily* (1978) and *Finnegan's Chin* (1981), later shown on Channel Four. In particular these films focussed on the experience and construction of tense in cinematic language, the constraint of viewpoint and its 'fusion' with the spectator's psychological identification with represented screen characters. This was accompanied by a number of theoretical essays examining issues of semiology with reference to the work of Christian Metz but specifically discussing this in the context experimental rather than conventional mainstream cinema, for example, 'Problematising the Spectator Placement in Film'.[2]

This series of large scale and partly narrative films left me with a creative crisis and a sense that my earlier films, largely made outside narrative form, continued to represent a more 'radical' and challenging artistic framework. This conclusion coincided with the availability of the first high quality, small format video – Video 8mm – and with fast, flexible, programmable home computers with good facilities for image and sound. I began a number of short and exploratory works simultaneously using the new Video 8mm format and the computer. In the early 1980s a number of low cost computers with visual potential became available.

This started with the very primitive Sinclair Spectrum for which I wrote abstract image and sound programmes often in the most fundamental machine code form, for example creating the sound pitches by modulating the electronic signal frequency of the loudspeaker. The Sinclair was followed by the Amiga, and the computer that I chose to work with, the Atari. Though by present standards the Atari was slow and with very little memory, the image processor allowed programmes to be written that could modulate the image at rates beyond 1/25th second – the standard rate for film and video. At the same time the Atari had a direct output and input for MIDI (Musical Instrument Digital Interface) that allowed programmes to be written controlling music synthesizers. These synthesizers, widely used by musicians and composers, opened up a vast range of sound quality manipulation. I had largely abandoned my early involvement with computers after completing the very short film *Your Lips* in 1970. At that time even the largest computers available to industry, the military and university research establishments, had very little visual potential. They were difficult to programme and were largely inaccessible to artists. The Atari offered a level of sophistication of image and sound that matched my expectations of film or video.

I made a number of computer works based on programmes that I wrote to control the image and sound output simultaneously. First shown in 1984, projected directly from the computer, I continue to present two of these, *Arbitrary Logic* and *Digital Still Life*. These were later incorporated as sections in a long TV work, *Sketches for a Sensual Philosophy* (1990). These two computer pieces continued directions opened up in my early films. *Arbitrary Logic* explored non-figurative colour fields changing in time in a similar way to the installation and performance film *Matrix* (1973) that used coloured film loops accompanied by taped electronic sound. *Digital Still Life* explored the transformation of image colour and tonal distribution extending the work that originated for me with *Berlin Horse*. When I made *Berlin Horse*, I was unaware that this form of exploration had begun much earlier with Len Lye and is particularly evident in two of his films from the late 1930s, *Trade Tattoo* and *Rainbow Dance*.

Whilst my computer pieces of this period continued themes and ideas from my earlier work they also opened up new possibilities, and through my theoretical work attempting to define fundamentals of computer or digital art, they have led me to a major review of the concepts of medium, medium specificity and underlying assumptions of modernism. From this I think I have been able to define some of the creative opportunities and artistic issues opened up by the computer and more generally by digital systems.

The first of these was an expansion of the range of image transformation. Transforming the image in film relies on its mechanical and chemical processes. They are largely based on shifts between negative and positive or re-colouring fields through mattes made from monochrome versions of the image. Digital processes allow – indeed, require – a more fundamental level of image abstraction to the digital code underlying the characteristics of each pixel. Any of those characteristics that determine colour, brightness and position can be selected for manipulation depending on the depth of programming undertaken. The effects normally incorporated into commercial software packages, tend to mimic film and video, but in fact, digital manipulations are not constrained by cinematic processes and potentially extend the range available. However, as with film, the more important issues remain not the technical extension of a range of effects but the way these are used to create artistic meaning and experience.

The second major opportunity offered by the computer was the exploration of certain synaesthetic and rhythmic relationships between image and sound. By basing the work on a programme, the

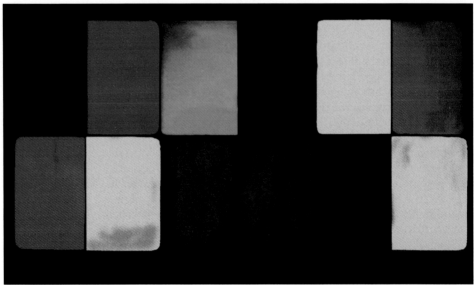

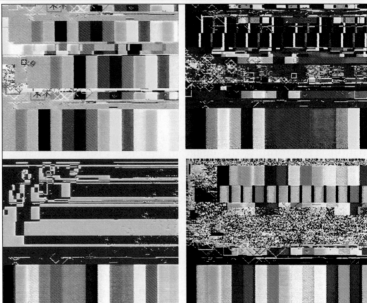

Above:
Matrix, 16mm film,
6 screen, 1973.

Right:
Arbitrary Logic.
Video, 1984.

sound and image control could be integrated. For example, in *Arbitrary Logic* certain pitches were attached to certain colours and were modified simultaneously. This linking of colour and sound has very early origins that even precede the 'Light Organ' experiments of Bainbridge Bishop and Wallace Rimmington of the 1880s and 1890s. Visual music has also been a recurring concept from the earliest period of abstract cinema and the synaesthetic relationship between colour and sound forms a major part of Kandinsky's theories. As it happens, I came to a conclusion that there was no intrinsic psychological link between a particular colour and a particular pitch – consequently the term 'arbitrary' in the title – but the construction of relationships between sound and colour within the abstract 'language' of a work remains valid.

The other features that emerge from the digital work – programmability and interactivity – are more fundamental and more challenging for our preconceptions of artistic practice. Creating a work from a programme has particular consequences. The first of these is that implicit or unconscious artistic processes need to be made explicit through the programme. In other words, in *Digital Still Life* for example, the programme is written and rewritten so that it 'makes the decisions' and produces the work. Of course it was my artistic desires and preconceptions that determined what kind of work, what kind of decisions the programme would make and so the programme modelled at least a part of my own 'sensibility'. And – the process of rewriting the programme was 'organic' and subjective – if the output did not satisfy my judgment I would rewrite sections of the programme. But – when written, the programme generated the work and small changes to values (variables) introduced to the programme would produce slightly different outcomes.

In one sense these programmes, as all computer programmes, are general models that can produce a variety of particular results. The way digital processes undermine the concept of the single definitive work of art is a challenge to our artistic preconceptions. The other major new opportunity made possible by computers and digital systems is that of interactivity. Though *Arbitrary Logic* is now shown in videotape form it began as an interactive work. The programme was written so that the progress of the work can be changed by interaction through the mouse. This interaction brings about immediate changes to the visual and musical output and to how it continues to develop in time. Despite a misleading mythology that interactivity brings the spectator 'democratically' into a work's creation, interactivity does have consequences for our understanding of the exclusivity of authorship – again a general challenge to our preconceptions about art.

Though in my practice I have not pursued this aspect of interactivity the inevitable separation of content from structure that it implies has formed part of my work with video. *Chronos Fragmented* (1995) a long work initially produced for television, brought together the two strands of my practice – video and computer – that have occupied me since the early 1980s. In truth, whilst most of my theoretical work in this period has been concerned with under-

Chronos Fragmented, Video, 1995.

standing the artistic consequences of digital systems, my practice has been dominated by video.

It was not an ideological but a practical and psychological decision to give up film as a medium in favour of video. However it has made a significant change to my practice. As a filmmaker I had rarely used the camera. Like others I had made occasional standard 8mm 'home-movies' but even in *Little Dog for Roger* (1967), based on resurrected 9.5mm shot by my father, the images of family have been distanced from any nostalgic function by the formal structure of the film.

Since I began shooting video, a little under twenty years ago, I have amassed well over one hundred hours of tape. In the twenty year period as a filmmaker before then, including the home-movies, I doubt if I had shot more than ten hours of film. Little of my work using film was concerned with events before the camera. Working with video I still tend to differentiate images that remain of private interest from those that may become incorporated into art works. However, this differentiation is blurred and may change as a personal image take its place in another metaphoric or symbolic context. This shift is unpredictable and is certainly not evident to me at the moment of shooting. Almost all the video work I have made – some thirty titles of varying lengths – have been the result of finding potential in sequences shot initially without any notion of their artistic use. In film I initially had a similar response to the found footage images that formed a library I plundered for particular expressive purposes, as in *Castle 1* (1966), *Castle Two* (1968), or *Reign of the Vampire* (1970) and much of my earliest work. Using images that I had shot and which carried some psychological and material connection to my own particular passage through life, represented a major change. I have tried to analyse aspects of this process in my description of what I have called rather too grandly *The Chronos Project*.[3]

I shoot video as and when I feel like it. No doubt my experience as an artist makes this act with the camera more than randomly spontaneous. I am sure I make continuous, if un-thought, decisions about subject, frame, pace or camera movement, and I am aware that these decisions include what I might choose not to shoot which becomes, by implication, part of content by absence.

Having shot the video it has normally 'rested' for some time on the shelf. I may half recall an image, I may look at tapes and from time to time I catalogue them, noting particular images. During this time the sequences seem to lose some of their association with the initial event they have recorded and become separated images – almost raw material that may have been shot by someone else.

In describing this process of shooting, collecting storing and re-viewing the material I have resisted calling it simply a video diary. It is a diary in one sense; though unmethodical, its chronology is recoverable as the shot sequences remain in date order and the tapes are numbered chronologically. However, little of the motivation for shooting the material is to do with preserving the moment recorded. For Jonas Mekas, the diary is a record – a form of 'nostalgic' access to the places, times and people he has filmed. My images only begin to interest me when they break with their origin and become 'latent', take on a mystery as something where the meaning has become unknown to me and is not contained within what I might recall of the moment of recording. The sequences become fragments. The term 'fragment' – as in *Chronos Fragmented* implies a view of the world and its experience where the connec-tions are fluid, shift and reform. Used as an analogy, the video sequences are thought of as fragments of memory. In a material sense they are documents, not memory, and they only document what is specifically visible or audible from the record. No inferences about the reality at the time of shooting can strictly be made beyond what is in the picture frame or time frame of the sequence. This returns to an interpretation of the representational limit of the cinematic image understood as an indexical signifier where mean-ings and connotation are isolated by the time and image frame.

In making a work – where I have selected sequences and have brought them together in a montage or superimposition with another sequence – I have recognised a clear desire to lose the personal and idiosyncratic meanings. Here I have taken up some of

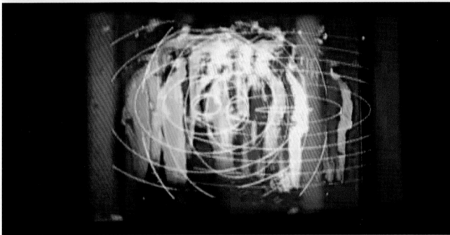

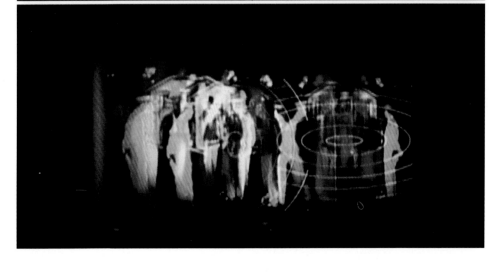

Facing page:
Threshold,
16mm film, 1972.

Left:
Digital Still Life,
Video, 1988.

the language of mythology, for example in the titles *Chronos Fragmented* or *Even a Cyclops Pays the Ferryman* (1998). I see this reference as 'poetic' rather than reflecting any system of belief. It frees-up allegorical connection and helps shift the specific image into the realm of archetype, and metaphor. These 'metaphors' however do not have any fixed and delineated meaning either for me as the maker or for the spectator. Their meaning remains latent and open to continuous review, in the way the dream works on the symbol, in the sense understood by psychoanalysis.

In works like *Even a Cyclops Pays the Ferryman*, I have continued the exploration of repetition – sequences repeated but superimposed or montaged in different relationships with other sequences. I have also continued to develop the 'language' of image transformation helping to separate a sequence from its initial connotations. However, something of a trace of this connotation remains. The sequences retain some signification that they have originated outside their allegorical 'purpose' so their duality draws attention to a process of transformation.

Within this project I have made a connection with my theoretical understanding of the digital, in this case drawing parallels between non-linearity or Random Access Memory and human memory or dream. Whilst working on *Chronos Fragmented*, treating the sequences as a database, I also wrote simple computer programmes to find, sort and assemble sequences according to 'subjective' characteristics selected from the database. This use of computers was different in character from my previous work in image synthe-

231

sis or transformation. It functioned as a practical aid to recalling and grouping sequences from, at that time, some sixty hours of material.

Using a computer programme was only a part, and probably a minor part, of the process of making *Chronos Fragmented* as, in the final stages of montage, I modified and frequently rejected decisions made by the programme. However, it helped me to bring forward certain concepts related to non-linearity and interactivity, that changed aspects of my video structure particularly as work developed after *Chronos Fragmented*. In particular, repetitions within the linear work came to 'stand' for non-linear flexibility between sequences. As well as the particular variations explored in the works, the form implied that this process of working and reworking the source material could be continued. The separation between sequences and their various combinations implied by the video form I adopted also implied that any combination selected had a provisional rather than a definitive quality and meaning. This implicit provisionality is in turn symbolic of the engagement of the spectator in making and remaking the meaning of the work – a symbolic interactivity.

During the same period I have also made a number of other video works using material from the 'diary'. In two series of videos, under the collective titles of *Sketches for a Sensual Philosophy* and *Trials and Tribulations*, instead of weaving a wide range of sequences into a large episodic or allegorical form, I have responded to qualities in certain short sequences. From this I have made works that might be only a minute or so in length, like *Seeing the Future* (1994), *For the Benefit of Mr K* (1995), or *Warsaw Window* (1994). I think of these, and more recent works like *Travelling with Mark* (2003), and the installation video *Unforgettable* (2002), as video poems or songs that are self-contained. Though different in form, like the larger work, I think they are consistent with the notion of fragment and disconnection.

There have also been some recent works, particularly *Joseph's New Coat* (1995), that have no representational source images but have been generated from colour fields and from various digital and analogue treatments of these fields. I would find it difficult to argue any direct connection between this non-figurative, abstract or synthetic work and the symbolic exploration of fragmentary documents. However, both strands have more in common with temporal structures that relate better to music than to narrative. At the same time both strands seem to encompass dramaturgy if not narrative. I understand dramaturgy, which is not the exclusive domain of narrative and has always been part of music, as characterised by the crucial importance of sequence. In other words, the order of unfolding – of revelation – is crucial to the understanding and experience of the work. The sequence in which the spectator interacts with the work, going from a stage of 'present' sensation through short or rhythmic memory to deliberate conceptualisation is special to time-based work. I have become aware of a consistent desire in almost all my work to make use of and enjoy a cinematic dramaturgy. It has led me increasingly to use the term cinema, rather than film. I use 'cinema' not to imply the culture of mainstream cinema but to distinguish between cinema as a discourse – a 'language of time' – and film as a specific medium or technology. In this respect film, video or digital forms may all be treated as cinematic.

Media Specificity

Increasingly as I worked with video and computers and as I grappled with theoretical ideas about digital systems, it became impossible to sustain the notion of a cinematic practice that was based specifically in the material conditions of the medium. Firstly, much of film technology, belonging to the nineteenth century machine age of wheels and cogs, has itself been increasingly eroded by incursion of electronics and digital control systems. It has been even more evident in the shorter history of video, that specificities of one period, such as the sculptural properties of the box-like monitor, have very quickly ceased to be seen as intrinsic to the medium. In the realm of the digital, the stability of a particular historical condition of the technology has been even shorter lived. But in the digital, the difficulties of defining it as a medium based on material properties are fundamental not just a matter of a developing technology.

At its base, the digital has no tactile form, it is merely transient pulses of minute electrical voltages working at a pace and at a scale beyond any human perception. It also has no fixed form of input or output. It is already hybrid beyond any predictable stability in its forms of interface with human perception. It can mimic or incorporate a wide range of media forms and absorb a range of discourses or language structures. I have attempted, theoretically, to define some characteristics of, so called, digital media, and, as long as I have been concerned with operations, or the behaviour of digital systems, this has been productive. But it remains difficult to link any theory of the digital to any based strictly on the notion that the language or practice of a medium grows out of intrinsic material properties. The boundaries of all art media have been challenged throughout the later part of the twentieth century, and with the predominance of the digital any notion of medium becomes a matter of choice and selection, not given a priori.

Both images:
Horror Film,
16mm, performance,
1971.

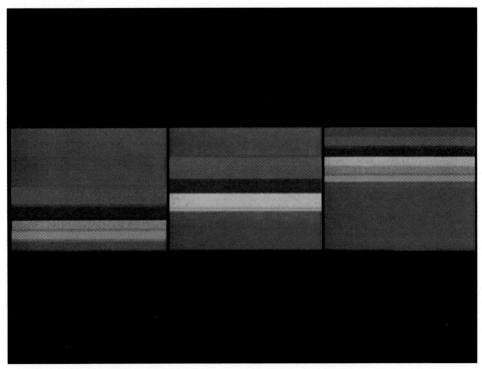

In one respect the notion of medium specificity can survive the digital. Whatever technology is used in recording, storing, restructuring or presenting sequential images and sound, there must be some interface with human perception – the eye, ear or other sense. This interface is both material, a perceptual encounter, and cultural, part of a discourse. Here the notion of specificity remains valid. In any encounter, the form of experience for the spectator depends on the output medium used in the final stage of a work. Certain artistic concepts can only be realised in certain forms of output medium. In my own work, I have always been fascinated by scale and immersive experiences of sound and image. And as part of this, with creating an encounter for the spectator incorporating a sense of presence and immanent surprise and drama. Though I was interested in video, until this could be projected with a visual power that matched film, I was not motivated by the medium. The notion of medium specificity therefore hinges on the choice of medium to suit the desired artistic experience – it is not an intrinsic constraint. At the same time, whatever combination of media, the form of this interface with the spectator also happens in a context of expectation. This is a condition of discourse and history not strictly bounded by medium. It results from the cultural as well as physical conditions in which a work is accessed and 'measures' the difference

Joseph's New Coat, 3 video channels, 3 screens, 1995.

between a work and assumptions about form, content and 'language' accompanying that context.

Some consistencies

In my own work I recognise a consistent desire for a large scale, spectacular encounter with the work and this links the abstract work based on colour and sound with the work based in representation and symbolic structure. There also remains a strong and general rejection of narrative as the main basis of cinematic practice in favour of what I might now describe as a quasi-musical form or a form of non-linear, allegorical, symbolic, 'multi-narrative'. An interest in the specific features of film as a medium, the acetate base, scratches and filmic processes, is no longer an active issue for me. I see this as having been the basis of a crucial and urgent encounter at a particular historical point. However, awareness of the material aspects of the physical and perceptual encounter with a work – the reality of its experience whatever its medium, remains crucial to any cinematic form I might explore, both in terms of image and sound.

Certain devices have also survived transition from film to video and digital forms, for example, use and re-use of the same source sequences has become part of my current concern with shifting structures of meaning and memory. Visual transformation of the image also survives. At least in part I see this as a way of counteracting the initial connotation of images and allowing them to have latency or multiplicity in their relationship to other images.

I have become increasingly aware that any work I make could be otherwise and could continue to be redeveloped in different versions. There is some consistency in this resistance to a 'definitive' form with the concepts I developed around digital systems – but think it has a more philosophical or psychological base linking ethics and aesthetics in the experience of work for the spectator. I continue to make cinematic works without any expectation or demand that they follow a consistent path.

Notes

1. *Art and Artists*, December 1972, pp. 39–43.

2. *Undercut* No. 1, March 1981, pp. 13–18; *Cinema and Language*, American Film Institute Monograph Series Vol. 1, 1983, pp. 50–62, published conference papers of March 1979, Milwaukee

3. Malcolm L Grice, 'The Chronos Project', Media Scape 3, Zagreb, June 1995; Vertigo No.5, 1966 re-printed in *Experimental Cinema in the Digital Age*, (London: BFI, 2001).

Chapter twenty-four

Expanded Cinema – Proto, Post-Photo

Jackie Hatfield

'One must free the cinema as an expressive medium in order to make it the ideal instrument of a new art, immensely faster and lighter than all the existing arts. We are convinced that only in this way can one reach that polyexpressiveness toward which all the most modern artistic researches are moving.'[1]

Not without ambiguities, expanded cinema[2] as a term generally describes synaesthetic cinematic spectacle (spectacle meaning exhibition, rather than simply an issue of projection or scale), whereby the notions of conventional filmic language (for example, dramaturgy, narrative, structure, technology) are either extended or interrogated outside the *single*-screen space. When in the 'Preface' to his book *Expanded Cinema* of 1970, Gene Youngblood stated 'expanded cinema isn't a movie at all' and 'when we say expanded cinema we actually mean expanded consciousness',[3] he was acknowledging that the term did not fully express the conceptual ambition and technological diversity of artists cinematic experiment practiced throughout the 20th century. In actuality expanded cinema stems from expanded histories, although the term a) implies a cinema (by implication narrower) than it has expanded *from*, and b) includes the word 'cinema', which is sometimes mis-understood to mean film. The terminology could insinuate a specific *form* or a material, and as a description for current digital practices, if taken at face value would appear to bypass huge chunks of its history, namely the electronic, the computer augmented, and equally, the *pre*-film or proto-cinema which included technological voyeuristic devices; and considerations about sites of exhibition outside the permanent location of the cinema theatre; also described as 'primitive' cinema or the 'cinema of attractions'.[4] The historical trajectory of expanded cinema in art includes the performative and synaesthetic spectacles of the Futurists; Bauhaus; the happenings of Fluxus; technological experiment (e.g. Experiments in Art and Technology[5] etc.,); expanded film of the 1960s and 1970s, and closed-circuit multi-channel participatory video of the 1970s and 1980s. Exploring interactivity; synaesthesia, semi-immersion; multiple screen configurations; and exhibition, these are an amalgam of Nineteenth, Twentieth and Twenty-first Century cinematic technologies and artistic ideas, the wider history including the technological innovations and public display of early cinema; and experiments with electronic systems display i.e. television. This current experimental moving image era physically and conceptually transcends traditional media boundaries and artists are evolving new cinematic concepts and intertextual languages, providing an imperative to reconsider and review the under-explored *practical* histories of the avant-garde.

At this point I must acknowledge the different historical positions on expanded cinema, i.e. American and European, and that experiments with expanded film (and proto-film) predated the electronic. It is not my intention to review the complex history in this short essay or to list the many artists who have pioneered expanded film, as I am simply making an argument here for participatory *video* and *digital* participatory cinema within the avant-garde tenets.

As with any academic language, terminologies are complex. I use 'cinema' not to describe film per se, but to signify a broad history, and to hint at the idiosyncratic discourses of practices that might also include spectacle. In this context, spectacle could allude to vaudeville, fairground, and public exhibition; the cinema theatre being a place of spectacle, whether the objective of the artist is to 'disengage' the audience or not. I like to imagine a philosophy of experimental cinema, which emanates from the cinema of attractions and expanded film, and includes the electronic, the computer, the active spectator, sculpture, collage, dramaturgy, narrativity, and representation. Importantly, the term cinema is not yoked to the material conditions of a medium and the cinematic experience can cross media boundaries or be achieved through a range of media combinations; 'old' media are *enhanced* by the 'new', not superseded. A cinematic configuration could involve intermedia, performance, spectacle, video, art and technology, and film, and could be located within the 'black space' of the cinema or 'white cube' of the gallery. But how is post-material digital cinema incorporated into a history of moving-image pre-occupied with materiality?

Digital forms can combine many materialities and languages; so tracing a critical history for current forms of participatory expanded cinema within the available tenets of experimental film and video is complex. Within the relatively short critical history, the debates have emphasised medium in the modernist sense; and the materiality and 'language' of specific technologies, film or video. Distinguishing film from video and emphasising ontological differences was particularly visible in the polemics of the 1970s, the then apparently polarised dialogue (in London institutionally bound through the London Filmmakers Coop and London Video Arts) overlooked the fact that artists were free-flowing individuals experimenting with different kinds of media, and more often than not were working with and expanding both technologies.[6] In point of fact the artists committed to video and its discourses were dealing with an imaging technology unlike any other, one that was continually evolving. And although the term 'video art' connotes an analogue era and an apparent fixed-ness, its material specificities are in flux. As such it necessitates continual theoretical or philosophical review; the polemics are open to change; so that video is and always has been a technology of combination, and in its current guise, a chameleon-like extant property in the continuing history of digital 'new' media. A philosophy based upon 'video' materiality per se would be built upon shifting-sands, but this has similar complexities to that of digital forms, whereby individual works and technological combinations might defy material classification. The practical history of experimental video typifies the formulation of post-material paradigms. While artists devoted purely to the conceptual material of video have been rare[7] and there could be many themes or categorisations for video art *works* from 1970 to date, similar to digital cinema, the technology itself resists definition on the basis of analysis of its material constituents. In the late 1960s to 70s, it was the *apparatus* of video*tape,* which was a definable object, i.e. a portapak, a monitor, the conduit of broadcast, but ultimately, *video* is a stuff of concept, and a challenge to medium specific rhetoric; a perceptual thing – post-material moving-image.

As yet moving image archaeologies have tended to underrate participatory video as a major component of the non-linear tradition in current cinematic discourse and 'new' media. However, since the technology became available in the 1960s artists working with video and the electronic have been extending the possibilities of moving-image interface research and cinematic spectacle. Exhibitions like *The Video Show* at the Serpentine Gallery 1975 with video installation and performances (amongst many genres) demonstrated to the public, the live and participatory quality of video art. Here were artworks that encouraged the audience to encounter the image, to intervene in the spectacle, the work, time, and environment. Experimenting with exhibition, interactivity and performance, they explored randomness, and audience participation with the art 'work'. The intervention of the audience or their complicity with the conceptual games of the artist has been a characteristic of many video artworks. The broadcast conundrums of David Hall's *TV Interruptions* (1971) may have tested and surprised Scottish Television audiences; but their reception relied on the budding media literacy of the non-passive viewer.[8] Gallery works such as Hall's *Progressive Recession* (1974), integrated the physical and existential presence of the audience, their live image fed back to them through monitors, but configured to reorder the real crowd in virtual space. Playing with the viewer's perception of time, their image was juxtaposed within the sculptural alignment of monitors in the space. When video was incorporated with trigger devices there was a technological means by which to control relatively basic audience interactive electronic closed-circuit events, and trigger based feedback. For example: Steve Partridge's *8x8x8* (1976), with its automatic video switcher, a programmable unit with a sixty four-way matrix of inputs and outputs,[9] or David Hall's *Vidicon Inscriptions the Installation* (1976).[10]

Though this is not to suggest that triggers were anywhere near as complex as computer based interfaces or matrices in current practice, but they enabled the audience to be an agent of change. The technical flexibility of video made possible the stage-management of time and space, pioneering the way for subsequent developments in interactive media and participatory cinema, it lent itself to delving inside its mechanisms, to looping and networking multiple channels, or to combining recording and playback technologies as gallery artefacts. It could be reviewed over and over, re-wound and fast-forwarded, and the recorded image could be interrogated by the artist and viewer from both sides of the camera, to evaluate the authentic relative to mirror-image or recording, and the direct address of self relative to total artwork and context of viewing. In this sense, if film was a technology of the indexical, video gave artists the means to articulate a time-based language of the un-seeable. Importantly, participatory CCTV work covered new ground in the relationships between context, spectator, screen, and artist. Play was incorporated as a dynamic aspect of the viewing experience, and the audience could inhabit the artwork and actively engage with the representation. Furthermore broadcast into the private space of the viewer, video artworks networked and streamed through the televisual conduit had ambitions to exist beyond the gallery space. Inherent in many of these works, was the interruption of the public broadcast; challenging the assumption of the televisual flow, and exposing the mechanism of the one way channelling of information. The purest of television interventions played knowingly with the assumptions of mass entertainment and the popular display of the 'telly'. The direct descendent of these works being interventionist internet art.

Monitor based works, which were more widespread until the late 1980s than projection,[11] resembled the characteristics of *optical* cinematic devices such as the kinetoscope, praxinoscope theatre or kinora, whereby the audience looked *in* on the image. The monitor and playback as an enclosed system, was akin to early cinematic devices, which similarly both generated (i.e. created the illusion from still to moving) and displayed the image. Key to this premise is also the monitor's location *outside* the cinema and temporary exhibition within the gallery space, where the audience walked around the work – i.e. the 'cinema of attractions'. Therefore, unlike 'front facing' configurations, in the closed-circuit environment or monitor based installation the audience's physical engagement could be actively orchestrated, and the act of viewing integrated as process, beyond the boundaries of the screen. For example, Ira Schneider's *Wipe Cycle* (1969) consisted of a camera, nine monitors with displays controlled by live and delayed feedback, which Schneider described 'was to integrate the audience into the information';[12] Dan Graham's *Opposing Mirrors and Video Monitors on time delay* (1974) involved two monitors, two mirrors, two video cameras and a time delay to switch the viewer's image unexpectedly from one monitor to the next – the monitors were placed at either end of the gallery space facing mirrored walls and the viewer would walk from one end of the gallery to the other to see their image finally appear on the monitors. Many artists were exploring video as a sculptural material at this time, expanding the artwork beyond the screen into the gallery, evident from the works in the exhibitions of expanded video, *Video Skulptur Retrospektiv und Aktuell*, 1963–1989[13] at Köln, Berlin and Zurich in 1989. When video projection was combined with time-delay devices to interrupt real time or pre-recorded images, or switchers to mix between channels it was *approaching* a technologically active and semi-immersive cinematic environment.

Lynn Hershman Leeson's *Lorna* (1984), was notably one of the earliest interactive video laser disc works by an artist, and enabled the audience to navigate multiple and non-linear strands of narrative via a remote control unit. With *America's Finest* (1992–1995), Hershman included an M16 rifle as a camera/trigger, triggering a projection of the audience holding the gun, fed-back into the gun-sight, and mixed with horrific situations where the rifle was used. Gary Hill's, *Tall Ships* (1992), used '16 channels of video, 16 monitors and projection lenses, sixteen laser disc players and a computer controlled interactive system' to create a projected environment whereby the audience's physical activity directly affected the images.[14] In a dark corridor the audience could move towards the projections of individually interactive characters, 'as the viewer walks through the space, electronic switches are triggered, and the figures walk forward until they are approximately life size'.[15] *Tall Ships* placed the audience in a central position both metaphorically and physically so that the image movement was related specifically to the audience movement. The audience were an inherent component of the work, as much a part of the visuals as the projected image, the projected subjects meeting with the real subjects, 'I wanted interactivity to be virtually transparent to the point that some people would not even figure it out'.[16]

Drawing from the practices of expanded film and video, current participatory and semi-immersive cinema, which the viewer can inhabit, is also the technological re-invention of pre film forms of cinematic display, i.e. panorama, camera obscura, phantasmagoria. Digital and computer based systems and interface evolution, have widened the sensory and tactile possibilities for audience participation with the moving-image artwork. The corporeal body can be central, and the subject as an active becoming rather than a passive given, can be both participant and accomplice in the composition of images. Having a tactile relationship with the images and physically intervening with the screen space, the structure of the montage is ultimately theirs. By their dynamic intervention the audience discontinue linear narration and extend the artwork beyond the boundaries of the screen, and as such these works continue the tradition of the avant-garde, which has *played* with, or intervened with narrativity, cause and effect and notions of dramaturgy.

In Grahame Weinbren's *Frames* (1999) a three-channel computer controlled interactive cinema installation, the audience effected a structural change in the montage sequences by their physical interaction with picture 'frames' suspended in front of each of the projections. By placing their hand through the frames and their invisible matrix, the audience triggered the layers in the projected sequences, with their own body central to the cinema mechanism. Tactility was crucial to Chris Hales' *The Twelve Loveliest Things I Know* (1991).[17] This interaction was oriented around the small screen and the projection, a frameless painting that the viewer could get close to and dip in and out of. The audience were required to touch things brightly coloured on the screen to navigate the structure and to traverse a series of stories. Masaki Fujihata's *Beyond Pages* (1995)[18] was a minimally beautiful sculptural installation, comprising a small table and chair and a projection of a door. The audience stroked the image of the book illuminated in the table, turning each page to reveal an animation and Japanese text with a voice speaking the word. Thecla Schiphorst's *BodyMaps:Artifacts of*

Touch (1996),[19] consisted of a life sized projection onto a velvet-covered table, of a woman curled up as if asleep, the audience stroking the image caused gradual and almost imperceptible changes in her movement. The work set up a quasi-intimate relationship between the physical intervening subjects and the projected body, and was sensual and intense, since the touch produced an apparent response. With each of these works the audience was absorbed into a synaesthetic and physical space and affected the montage or the structuring of the images – the collage – by intervention. The process was both in the making *and* reception; the technology and the existential were the essences of its staging.

I describe these works as cinematic, and locate them within the avant-garde film and video traditions, a trajectory centred on the established and unambiguous histories of artists experiment with spectacle, cinema and technology extending at least throughout the twentieth century (i.e. consider the cinematic spectacles of Caravaggio, the semi-immersive spaces of sculptor/architect Bernini). There are subtle specificities embodied by the term – expanded cinema – that distinguish digital (and usually computer augmented or switcher controlled) participatory *cinema* from what is often meant by the term 'new' media. Though too complex to deal with in this short essay (as distinctions are never clear cut) loosely speaking, experimental cinema in the digital domain centres on the *moving* image, and focuses attention away from the individual frame or the still image. It plays or intervenes with illusion transference, and the sensory, tactile, and experiential (often on both sides of the camera or in exhibition), often questioning the physicality of viewing; or the act of viewing. This is not necessarily a cinema of film (although could be), and it continues the tradition of experimental film and video; its critical context stemming specifically from a philosophy of the amalgam, *cinema*.

Artists' engagement with the practices and philosophies of cinema whether with film, video or digital media, exists beyond any prevailing material preoccupations. Contemporary innovators of expanded cinema are articulating the discourses and evolving 'languages' of the emergent moving image technologies, exploring their relative substances; processes of production and contexts of viewing. In 1970 Gene Youngblood alluded to the non-material cinematic: 'expanded cinema does not mean computer films, video phosphors, atomic light, or spherical projections. Expanded cinema isn't a movie at all: like life it's a process of becoming', i.e. a *concept* of presence more than it is a material of one kind or another. This does not negate the further study of materiality, and provides a dynamic philosophical context for re-assessment of previous de-

243

bates. Historical continuity should be acknowledged, but future experiment should be unfettered by historical rhetoric.

Notes

1.   Filippo Tommaso Marinetti, Bruno Corra, Emilio Settimelli, Arnaldo Ginna, Giacomo Bvalla, Remo Chiti, 'The Futurist Cinema' in *Lets Murder the Moonshine: Selected Writings by F.T. Marinetti*, ed. R.W. Flint (Los Angeles: Sun and Moon, 1991), p. 139.

2.   Expanded cinema here is a merger of Gene Youngblood's approach (including the virtual; electronic; computer augmented) with that of the European (space and spectatorship of the expanded event).

3.   Gene Youngblood, *Expanded Cinema* (London: Studio Vista, 1970), p. 41.

4.   See Tom Gunning, 'The Cinema of Attractions Early Film its Spectator and the Avant-Garde', in *Early Cinema, Space, Frame Narrative*, ed. Thomas Elasaesser, p. 56.

5.   E.A.T. was founded in 1966 by Billy Kluver, Robert Rauschenberg, Robert Whitman and Fred Waldhauer to encourage collaboration between engineers, scientists and artists.

6.   Testing paradigms of the then new media, many of these artists gravitated to video *from* film, i.e. David Larcher, Malcolm Le Grice, Tony Sinden, David Hall (who started with sculpture), etc. Institutional demarcation between mediums was particular to the British position.

7.   David Hall being case in point.

8.   'I viewed one piece in an old gents' club. The TV was permanently on but the occupants were oblivious to it, reading newspapers or dozing. When the TV began to fill with water newspapers dropped, the dozing stopped. When the piece finished normal activity was resumed. When announcing to shop assistants and engineers in a local TV shop that another was about to appear they welcomed me in. When it was finished I was obliged to leave by the back door. I took these as positive reactions …' David Hall, '19:4:90 Television Interventions' Catalogue, Third Eye Centre Glasgow and Ikon Gallery Birmingham, Fields and Frames 1990.

9.   Designed by Howard Vei a technical engineer at the Royal College of Art.

10.   'A camera registers the passage of time by continuously monitoring the observer through a Polaroid shutter. At intervals the shutter is momentarily released – triggered by the observer's movement across a photoelectric switch. The comparatively brightly lit images are burnt, or inscribed, on to the camera's vidicon signal plate. Both the time continuum reflex and the retained (subsequently fading) 'static punctuations' of that continuum are exhibited as one on a video monitor', description of *Vidicon Inscriptions – The Installation*, David Hall, *The Tate Gallery Video Show*, 18 May – 6 June (London: Tate Gallery, 1976).

11.   Peter Campus (i.e. *dor* (1975), *Mem* (1974), *Interface* (1972)) was one of the first artists to incorporate video projection with feedback in the early 1970s, confronting the viewer with his or her own image in the gallery space.

12.   Ira Schneider continued 'It was a live feedback system which enabled the viewer standing within its environment to see himself not only now in time and space, but also eight seconds ago and sixteen seconds ago. In addition he saw standard broadcast images alternating with his own delayed/live image. Also two collage-type programmed tapes, ranging from a shot of the earth, to outer space, to cows grazing, and a 'skin flick' bathtub scene' Gene Youngblood, *Expanded Cinema* (London: Studio Vista, 1970), p. 342.

13.   *Video Skulptur Retrospectiv und Actuell 1963–1989* (Koln, 18 May-23 April 1989; Berlin, 27 August – 24 September; Zurich 1989, 18 October – 12 November 1989).

14.   Hill has used computer controlled switchers in other works such as *Suspension of Disbelief (for Marine)* (1992).

15. Gary Hill, *In Light of the Other* (Oxford: MOMA, and Liverpool: Tate Gallery, 1993), p. 9.

16. Gary Hill, Regina Cornwell, 'Gary Hill Interview', *Art Monthly* 170,(October 1993), pp. 3–11.

17. European Media Art Festival, Osnabruck, 1995.

18. ISEA, Rotterdam, 1995.

19. Video Positive, 1996.

Chapter twenty-five

Image Con Text (1978-2003)
Film/Performance/Video/ Digital

Mike Leggett

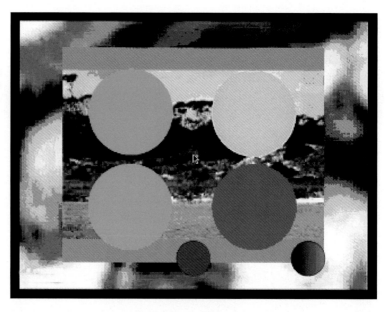

Frame grab from
PathScape prototype
interactive system,
2000.

R oy Ascott in the early 1990s described a culture developing in which its creators became part of a complex and widely distributed system. It involved both human and artificial cognition and perception and was 'an art that is emergent from a multiplicity of interactions in data space'.[1]

The data space in which we move daily and with which we are most familiar is the media flow within which we have been raised. It is an accumulation of signifiers – what Derrida termed the absent present:

> Signs represent the present in its absence; they take the place of the present ... when the present does not present itself, then we signify, we go through the detour of signs.[2]

When these words were first published in English, the computer was an expensive device limited to rich corporations and specialist university departments. Computer networks were the domain of the military. Computer-based information technology was emerging but still distant for most people. Artists working with analogue information technology, including photography, sound, film and video, were engaged in various investigations. These were not only about how the tools in the factories of dissemination and entertainment, the institutions of cinema and television, could be redeployed, but about the codes and languages, the signs and symbols that needed to be reassessed and overhauled. It was the cusp of a move away from the analogue and linear modes of mediated social relations, towards the binary and relational, relying on network and distribution building for circulating ideas, whether these were expressed as text or objects. As Daniel Palmer has recently observed:

Frame from *The Heart Cycle*, Video, 1972.

... video art is part of a broader shift from the representational tradition of visual art to one engaged in the more presentational modes of the 'theatrical', incorporating the sense of the here and now, of the viewer participating in the very space of the object, images and action.[3]

Reconsideration of the work of the 1970s, the methods and approaches used by artists, might reveal whether relational changes were anticipated and fulfilled, or whether the investigations, without an agreed program of work at the time, ('work on representation' would continue for ever), nonetheless encouraged a confidence amongst younger artists to embrace the 'multiplicity of interactions in data space' as the opportunity to do so emerged through the 1980s and 1990s.

This is not to say that some artists gained access to computer technology at an early stage. The Computer Arts Society was founded in London during 1968 and amongst the 'moving image' artists of the time, Malcolm Le Grice gained access to one of the largest computers in Europe in 1969. Grasping the basics of programming Pascal, over a period of nine months and after many bug fixes, he produced a graphical image, animated using a vector-based film plotter and incorporated as an 8-second loop into the film, *Your Lips* (1970). In an essay written in the same year, 'Outline for a Theory of the Development of Television'[4] he presciently anticipated the potential usage and affect of computers networked together to disseminate audio-visual material.

Apart from Le Grice's inspired diversions, the work by him and other artists to make and distribute programs based on the outcomes of film experiment, to greater or lesser degree took cognisance of approaches to theory. Though not entirely strange to those with an art training, to those such as myself coming from an industry background, understanding the context for activity was quite new. Industry demands competency, not thought. In 1969 when the LFMC Workshop opened in a temporary space just off the Euston Road in London's West End, it provided access for the membership to full production facilities for 16mm film-making, including the normally industry-centred procedures of duplication and processing. From that point onwards, for the next ten years at least, the LFMC was a focus point and generator for the production and dissemination of not only films, but also the discourse, between filmmaker artists and the audience of filmmakers, visual artists, performers, writers and critics. The pace was scorching at first, anticipation of new works palpable. It was not long before new audiences were left behind.

Film strip from *Film Lane*, 16mm film, 1973.

Image Con Text Project

The *Image Con Text* project when it commenced in 1978 was about interaction of the analogue kind, between the artist and an audience gathered for a screening. It presented a multiplicity of information, or contextualising material as it was called then, to provide for 'new' audiences a way into the artworks, but more particularly the practice-based research, as it is now called, being pursued or produced during that period.

The pro-active, interventionist strategy was partly in response to schemes that had been initiated by funders such as the Arts Council of Great Britain (ACGB)[5] to subsidise screening venues for the cost of transporting, accommodating and paying a screening fee to artists invited to show their work to a local audience. A condition for accepting the subsidy was that there would be no admission fee. This ruled out many commercial or semi-commercial venues with overhead costs to maintain. The majority of venues were those who already had these costs covered such as colleges of art, universities and public exhibition spaces and screens. Consequently, many of the audiences were younger people who had little knowledge of the work or its context.

The screenings I undertook in the mid-1970s followed a pattern adopted by many visiting artists – a few introductory words and then at the end of the screening, opening-up responses from the (usually) youthful audience. The *Image Con Text* project provided a context for viewing the film and video works I would often be invited to screen – it wasn't exactly a history lesson, or about philosophy, or politics, or a tenuously connected series of anecdotes, but something of a mix of all these. It employed a format that combined different media forms, described variously as expanded cinema, film performance or simply, performance work. It was part of a process of convergence of media that had been occurring amongst practitioners throughout the 1960s and 1970s. It was not until later that 'media art' became the generally accepted term for this activity.

The *Image Con Text* project comprised three parts. The first, described some of the conditions that had been involved in giving the films the form they adopted. This took two distinct approaches as presentational performances – from the artists' viewpoint in 1978, then later in 1981 from the audience viewpoint, (the filmmaker being a section of the audience too). The second aspect of the project was as on-going research, regular live presentations to audiences, the feedback from which could be fed into subsequent presentations. Thirdly, a videotape version not only archived the presentation performance but extended its meanings to later audiences. This process was later extended following transfer to DVD, introducing the possibility of interactive study utilising the dynamic linking of the format.

Image Con Text

Image Con Text (*Image Con Text: One*, as it was later known), set out to provide a context for the work from the point of view of the video or filmmaker.

> This live presentation, outlines rather than reports, material factors which affect many film-makers working independently of commercial film-making, at this point in time, Spring 1978.

> It is not only about the artifacts that have been produced – these are simply the residue of a range of activities – the presentation is more to do with the conditions that have been involved in giving them the form they adopt. So it is not

Frame from *Image Con Text: One*, Video, 1984.

concerned with examining their peculiarities, their style, their minimalism, the formalism, their whatever, or any of those things which could be used to describe their uniqueness or originality or any description which would seek to separate them, to distinguish them, to express an essential difference between them and another person's work.

The emphasis will be rather the opposite. To examine these various activities and the relationship they have to the formulative process of arriving at a completed artifact, as a means of establishing points of similarity in methods of production, connections with other people and the way they are working at present, or the way they have worked in the past. (Leggett, 1978)

Frame from *Image Con Text: One*, Video, 1984.

251

The form combines various mediums: projected slides; 8mm film with sound; 16mm film with and without sound; and sound played from a portable cassette recorder. The lecturer, besides addressing the audience directly, more often than not is also responsible for controlling these machines. This element of live performance will extend at the end into a discussion about the presentation and its contents. (Leggett, 1978, 1984)

Diagram from *Image Con Text: One*, 1978 (illustration courtesy *Screen*).

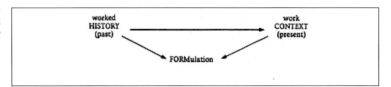

A diagram will be used as a guide for maintaining direction in the remaining 70 minutes and will propose a relationship between those who have worked in the past, History; and those of us who are working at present, Context; which determines more surely than a free-floating autonomous and 'creative' individual, what will be FORMulation in time, future. (Leggett, 1978, 1984)

The presentation began by proposing a triangle diagram linking these concepts. It reappeared as a titling or signposting device at the beginning of each section, seeking within the images and texts that followed, to provide a context for the range of activities and the resulting artefacts produced and the '... *conditions that have been involved in giving them the form they adopt*'. The title 'History' was followed by the sub-sections, 'Personal' and 'Social'. The title 'Context' with the sub-sections, 'Social', 'Economics', 'Political' and 'Discourse'. The title 'FORMulation by Discourse, Production and Personal'.

Diagram from *Image Con Text: One*, 1978 (illustration courtesy *Screen*).

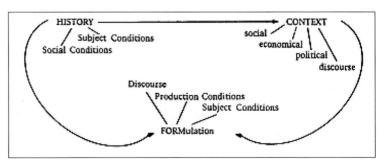

Within each section, the form of address was sometimes first person, sometimes third. Using a bricolage of narrative forms, throughout the whole presentation it was necessary for the audi-

ence member to be alert as to who (or what) might be 'speaking'.
Where the meaning lay in relation to preceding and following
sections, (the methods of dialectic and proposition), lay in contrast
to the abstract and material basis of the 'personal' sections, the two
spaces for screening a film or videotape art work in its entirety.

Later, Rod Stoneman in an article on film related practice and the
avant-garde paraphrased Foucault in relation to the *Image Con Text*
presentation:

> A whole web of relations is woven between the text and
> context – they support and contradict one another, modify
> each other … The presentation is a site for the intersection of
> discourses which differ in origin, form, organisation and
> function. In their variety and totality they do not constitute
> an exemplary text or a composite work but rather a truncated
> description of a contestation, a confrontation indicating a
> series of power relations that take place in and through
> discourse.[6]

The format proved to be a success. The first time it was presented,
there were so many issues and discussion flowing two hours after
the 70-minute presentation, that the same class all returned the
following week to continue for another 2 hours. I continued to use
the presentation for 'new' audiences, screening two or three short
films or videos at set points, varying the titles following discussion
with the venue organizer. It also had the advantages of a live
presentation, with the ability to vary and change the order or degree
of delivery, to respond to the indicators received from the audience,
and of course engage at a level of discourse appropriate to interaction with the audience, between one another and toward the
speaker.

> *Image Con Text* attempts to reintroduce elements of ideologi-
> cal and political discourse to articulate some of the structures
> which determine the placement and function of avant-garde
> audio-visual practices at this time, producing an under-
> standing of the processes by which films are financed and
> distributed. Posing a specific formulation of the present crisis
> in representation that attempts to break through the limits of
> contextual containment.[7]

The 'crisis in representation' identified by the writer for *Screen* had
developed from the vigorous debate between adherents and practitioners of several different, often competing, 'research' approaches, (though few amongst the artist film-makers would have
described their work in such academic terms). The core of the
differences were identified in two articles appearing in the mid-
1970s; 'The Two Avant Gardes' (Wollen c.1982) and 'Theory and
Definition of Structural/Materialist Film' (Gidal 1974). Gidal

maintained that the semiological project instituted by Wollen in his book *Signs and Meaning in the Cinema* (1972) was too narrowly focussed on recognising and analysing mediated images within the cinematic institution and that the debate should really be a holistic embracing of the entire phenomena of the viewed cinematic experience and its apparatus. Wollen and others critiqued such an approach as 'seeking an ontology based on the essence of cinema' and introduced into the debate further contributions by Derrida, on presence, which was regarded as central to Gidal's formulations on film's material substances and processes.[8]

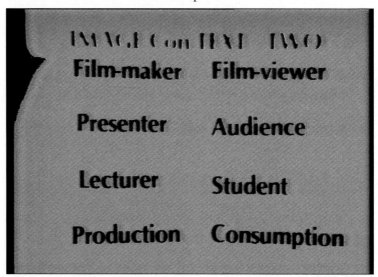

Title frame from *Image Con Text: Two* Video, 1985.

Image Con Text: Two

Arising from the discussions with audiences over a couple of years, in 1983, another approach was taken to *Image Con Text* using exactly the same presentational format, substituting texts, film and sound addressing issues affecting the presence and the formulation of the notion of Audience. The same triangle of related concepts was employed, the third part of the triangle being titled OBJEC-Tive, the sub-section 'Production' being replaced with 'Transformation'.

> This illustrated lecture presentation describes rather than reports a situation, which is common to the film-maker and the audience – the situation, the event, where the film or videotape is viewed, being the point at which meaning is made or where apparent meaning is interrogated.

> Such a critical approach to making meaning is consciously part of the process of production, the process which, for

Frame from *Image Con Text: Two*, Video, 1988.

Am I a spectator at a spectacle?

Or a consumer making a purchase?

Or the member of an audience?

Or a viewer making meaning?

instance, enabled the films and tapes you will watch shortly, to be finalized by the film-maker. A critical approach also occurs during the process of consumption by the audience, though the making of meaning is perhaps on a less conscious and demanding level. But the situation in which we as film-viewers encounter the world is only in relation to material factors which cause the world to be represented audio-visually together with the knowledge each one of us brings to the viewing space ... Some of the factors affecting that space is what will be described. (Leggett, 1985)

As in *One*, *Image Con Text : Two* examines a set of 14 photographs, (but a different set from One), most made in the early 1900s. The first time they were seen is silent, without comment. The three subsequent viewings were with a soundtrack commentary, read by different voices, each applying a different apparent interpretation. In contrast to *One*, the commentaries make extensive use of quotes in *Two*, from official reports, papers, journal articles, books and contemporary newspapers. It also introduced contemporary photographs to the 14 selected.

... a 35mm negative exposed some eighty years later in the St Pauls district of Bristol on the night of the 2nd April 1980 during some disturbances. A main road is blocked with burning vehicles. Flames burst from a nearby building, a white mass devoid of detail, the light emitted much greater to that reflected from the objects around. The shutter halts the movement of a figure in the background walking towards the camera but the large aperture restricts sharp focus to the

255

Frame from *Image Con Text: Two*, Video, 1985.

distant wall. Not included in the camera's field the old man in the foreground who gazes into the picture space into which we too are gazing. From behind, his hair and clothes, the shape of his head, resemble a portrait made some eighty years before ... (Leggett, 1985)

Frame from *Image Con Text: Two* Video, 1985.

... of another old man who by comparison bears an uncanny resemblance to the other. The two images could be referred to in motion picture editing terms as, 'matched images' making possible an action cut on the response of the subject to the scene he witnesses ... (Leggett, 1985)

Video

Later, in 1984/5, the contextual material used was transferred to U-matic videotape – *Image Con Text: One* and *Image Con Text: Two*, as two separate titles, made available for hire along with any of the film or video artworks.

> The playback of this videotape is another manifestation of a series of work projects drawn together originally as an illustrated lecture presentation. This video version of *Image Con Text* shifts these elements into another form of address that normally prevents on television an active response from the Audience towards the lecturer, the film-maker, the program-maker. It is assumed that the presentation of this videotape will provide a framework in which such a response can be accommodated. (Leggett, 1984, 1985)

As video the project is placed into the domain of the audience member, viewing as an individual, or as part of a group. The work becomes a hermeneutic medium, like a book, aiding debate though not always debate with the maker of the work. Whilst the 'text' cannot now be changed, because it is a source of represented knowledge rather than direct experience, (occurring with the live presenter or with the film and video framed by the presentation), its true relationship to the artwork referred is tangential, never causal. This relational link is echoed by the tenuous links set-up between the elements within the performance (or video), both the materials of sound and image, their technology format of delivery, and the alignment of spoken or quoted sources within the overall order of the sections within the presentation.

The videotape proved in practice to become an archiving stage of the *Image Con Text* project as few hiring's of the video/film combination were recorded. Perhaps by the mid-80s, the time for analysing the contextual issues for artists' film and video had passed, as attention was taken by the promises of new audiences on the developing television and cable channels across Britain and Europe. Or perhaps the presence of the artist together with the audience experiencing the work was the event which individuals were seeking. In the words of the final caption in *Two* – Personal OBJECTive: 'the interactive programme' – proximity, dialogue, a kind of inter-activity based on both familiar and unfamiliar encounters.

Fast Forward

Revisiting these debates, (these texts, as material, as presence in performance), whilst focussing on the possibilities of contemporary media and their intimate nature, (the book and the computer screen have a comparable presence and are seen at about the same physical distance), and potential responsiveness to the viewer's presence,

Frame from *Image Con Text: Two*, Video, 1985.

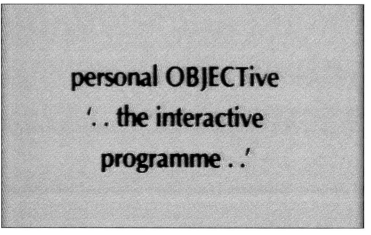

suggests some re-evaluation of the materiality of representation, some reconsideration of language, language forms and literacy.

Signs go back to an earlier data space. Plato, at the cusp of the wider adoption of the technology of literacy, was concerned to protect the oral tradition of the School of Athens and developed an argument questioning the real value of the new media of the time, reading and writing. As an 'early adopter' of the technology, in the *Phaedras* he lumps painting and the new technology of writing together, querying them with the observation:

> ... but if you question them, they maintain a solemn silence.
> Plato

Frame grab from *PathScape* prototype interactive system, 2000.

In an oral culture, the presence of the creator of the work is important, for presence allows the pursuit of verification, disputation and debate. In the *Phaedrus*, Plato used the new technology, writing, to preserve the old technology, oratory and ars memoria, by reproducing the dialogues of Socrates in a hybrid form, 'the book', a hermeneutic space where an interrogation of the text by the reader could occur. As with any new device, performing tests and trials, comparing the efficacy of its use with the familiarity and pervasiveness of the old methods was, as now, a part of a gradual adoption and continuing adaptation during the transition from the old to the new. The new method of literacy remained suspect, as the interpretive space opening between sender and receiver of the text diminished the authority of the speaker, less through the polemicists physical absence but more because of the sharing of the text with others, (fellow readers), who were inhabiting a shared data space.[9] Literacy, then as now, is as much about remote networking as about coding.

In the context of the data space of cyberculture, of telepresence, does the computer-mediated installation in the gallery space develop further opportunities for the expansion of dialogue between the artist/designer, the visitor and the artificial intelligence that lies potentially within the machine? Or is the form of the contemporary hybrid artefact, multivalent? That is, where it can be found, who makes it and how it is experienced?

The rapid deployment of global computer networks, in particular the World Wide Web for the general community, suddenly gave presence another meaning. Few of us will forget the first time we linked to a server on the other side of the world, receiving the image of a webpage a few seconds later – the finger tips tingled, the sensation was palpable.

Though ostensibly dealing with the human-machine linkage, many researchers consider psychological and social factors when advancing into defining 'interaction' and the 'interface', or the space, part physical, part virtual, which the subject's presence affects. It is a curious echo of the debates of the 70s, seeking to reveal the processes of representation, the linkages between machines, artists, audiences and consciousness.

Two research psychologists, Mantovani and Riva, building on the work of among others, Heidegger and J. Gibson, propose an 'ecological approach', establishing a relational presence based on resources not being the 'properties of either object or subject, but of their relation'. Gibson's image of a tree in the middle of a field on a summer's day being only an 'affordance' to those who seek its cool shade being an illustration of 'resources, which are only revealed to those who seek them'. Mantovani & Riva go on to amplify this distinction with the argument that presence is a social construction 'mediated by both physical and conceptual tools which belong to a given culture' in which there is 'the emphasis of ecological approach on the primacy of action on mere perception' and that 'action is not undertaken by isolated individuals but by members of a community... Ultimately, there are only two elements which guarantee presence: a cultural framework and the possibility of negotiation of both actions and their meaning'.[10]

A descriptive analysis of this kind enables empirical intervention and the measurement of response levels and they claim, the emotional component within presence perception. Interest in this area has initiated projects across a diversity of disciplines from psychology and physiology to ethology and ethnology. Much of the debate among interdisciplinary and associated research groups makes little reference 'across the fence' to parallel work that has been achieved in the humanities. But then, if the potential for developing machines – computer devices, rather than linear media – had not become as socially ubiquitous as today, would the enquiries by the artist, of the scientist, have ever advanced beyond the initial probing work of Le Grice?

Image With Text

The approach taken by the *Image Con Text* project in some ways foreshadowed aspects of science-based research into Human Computer Interaction (HCI). This sub-disciplinary area of information technology research recognised relatively late in the overall development of computer systems that computers could be more than substitute typewriters, adding machines and advanced calculators. Issues of functionality and usability become paramount as business began to fund the research. Sophisticated methodologies were invented to advance exhaustive evaluation with live subjects, so that painstaking and rigorous documentation and data gathering could prove some conclusions about interface design.

So now we confront the image of a printed page, the surface of a desktop, a piece of graph paper, a map, or specialist interfaces like that used for editing video and soundtrack. These two-dimensional spaces that have acquired the bevel edge, two, three and four pixels broad – embossed frames, windows, work areas, palettes, icons, trash cans and so on, remain in a pre-renaissance era of quality of experience if not functionality. These contextual devices are more about achieving 'the goals of performance' often associated with the interface and what can occur within the metaphor it sets out to establish. The interfaces that artists currently construct are about interventions, presences which are as tangible as that of the live performer and the live audience.

Later, in 2003, the archiving continued with the migration of *Image Con Text* from video to DVD, complete with the simple interactive components that the format offers, enabling the viewer to move from caption to caption at will. Like the video, but with greater speed and accuracy, interaction using a DVD moves the context of the presentation again. Instead of the presenter/performer being sensitive to the audience members indicators, (of confusion, of boredom, of comprehension), and responding accordingly, it becomes the receiving individual or group's responsibility to adjust the flow of information – stopping to discuss with others, skipping back to play again, moving to another section instead of playing through in the order determined by the linear video.

It remains to be seen whether it will migrate into the next format. More than likely, if this is to happen, it will be in the form of a distributed network resource, accessible by the individual, or the electronic seminar room, in which, it is assumed, 'a framework will be provided to accommodate an active response from an Audience towards the lecturer, the film-maker and the video artist'. (Leggett 1984, 1985)

Within a system of computer network distribution, the presence of the artist / presenter, becomes the presence of the audience. Indeed in a text-based environment of this kind, (a multi-user domain or chat room), any member of the group could assume the role of presenter or artist or author. Likewise, the primacy of the artwork as object is reduced. However, as with the films and videos of the 1970s, focus is upon the initiation of reflexive feedback loops and engagement with the cognitive and perceptual faculties of the (computer-based) viewer, emphasizing response and interaction within a dynamic representational system. The artwork made for the public and collective space of the cinema becomes an anachronism within a context where the viewing space, the space in which the presence of the artwork meets the presence of the singular online viewer, becomes another space entirely, a data space, where 'a multiplicity of interactions' make authorship uncertain of either an initiating proposal or responding rejoinder.

What remains to be understood better, is whether the location of data space can be developed to equal the dynamic space of live presentation and performance tested within the *Image Con Text* project.

Notes

1. Roy Ascott, *Telematic Embrace: Visionary Theories of Art, Technology, and Consciousness* (University of California Press, 2003), p. 261.

2. Jacques Derrida, *Difference, Speech and Phenomena* (NW University Press, 1973).

3. Daniel Palmer, 'Medium without Memory: Australian Video Art', *Broadsheet*, Vol 33, No. 3, pp. 20–21.

4. Malcolm Le Grice, *Experimental Cinema in the Digital Age* (London: BFI, 2001), p. 215.

5. In 1994, the Arts Council of Great Britain was abolished, and its functions transferred to three new bodies: the Arts Council of England, the Arts Council of Wales and the Scottish Arts Council under a new Royal Charter (Arts Council of England, 2004).

6. Rod Stoneman, 'Film Related Practice and the Avant Garde', *Screen*, 1979/80, Vol 20 No 3–4, pp. 40–57.

7. Ibid.

8. See Malcolm Le Grice, *Experimental Cinema in the Digital Age* (London: BFI, 2001).

9. See G.L. Ulmer, 'Reality Tables: Virtual Furniture' in ed D Tofts, *Pre-figuring Cyberculture* (Sydney, MIT Press/Power, 2002).

10. G.R. Mantovani, ' "Real" presence: how different ontologies generate different criteria for presence, telepresence and virtual presence', *Presence: Journal Teleoperators and Virtual Environments*, Vol. 8, No. 5, 1999, pp. 538–548.

Additional citations

Peter Gidal, 'Theory and Definition of Structural/ Materialist Film', *Structural Film Anthology* (London: BFI, 1974).

Malcolm Le Grice, *Experimental Cinema in the Digital Age* (London, BFI, 2001).

Mike Leggett, 'Image Con Text' (script for performance presentation, 1978).

Image Con Text : One 1984, Bristol Film Workshop, Bristol UK, produced by Leggett, M.

Image Con Text: Two 1985, Bristol Film Workshop, Bristol UK, produced by Leggett, M.

Leggett, M. 2000, *PathScape* (Prototype (2) interactive system), Sydney.

Plato, *Phaedras*, trans. W.C.R. Hembolt, (Indianapolis, W.G., Bobbs-Merril, 1956).

Peter Wollen, *Signs and Meaning in the Cinema* 3rd edn. (Bloomington, Indiana University Press, 1972).

Peter Wollen, *Readings and Writings: Semiotic Counter Strategies* (London, Verso, 1982).

Section IV

Images

Images

This section includes artists whose contribution to the Anthology is in the form of images

George Barber

Refusing Potatoes,
Video, 2004.

Shouting Match,
Video, 2004.

Jackie Hatfield

Little Dog Staccato,
Video, 2004.

*Walk in the Glens
Wearing a Camera
Suit and Tartan Boots,
Documentation
Version*, Video, 1994.

Distressing the Surface, Touch interactive cinema, 1998.

Inscription, Video installation, 2000.

267

Stephen Hawley

Above:
Bad Reasons,
Video, 1982.

Right:
Speech Marks,
Video, 2004.

Tina Keane

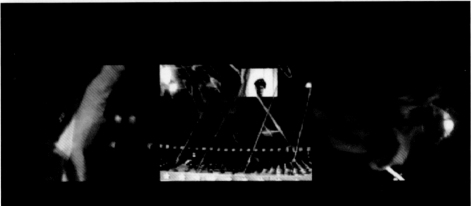

Above: *Circus*, Shot on Super 8 projected on video, 3 screens, 1990.

Below and top of facing page: *Transposition*, Shot on Super 8 projected on video, 3 screens, 1995.

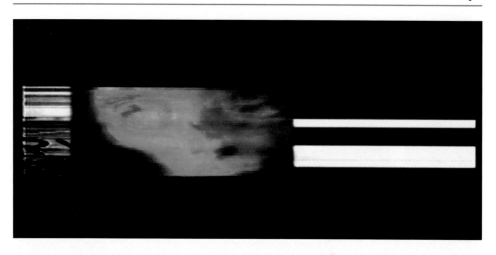

Below:
*The Heart of the
Illusion*,
Video installation,
1981.

Tamara Krikorian

Stephen Littman

I Want, Video 4
screen 5 playdecks 1
live camera, 1983.

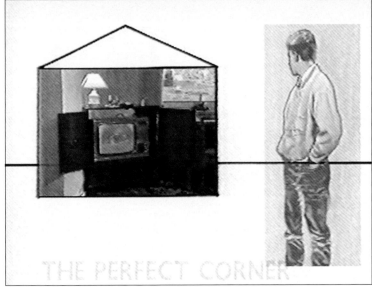

*Big Time - The House,
19:4:90,*
Video, 1990

271

Smile, Video 3 screen
4 playdecks 1 live
camera, 1984.

The Enlightenment,
Video installation or
single screen, 1993.

Surface Vale Boogie,
Video installation or
single screen, 1999.

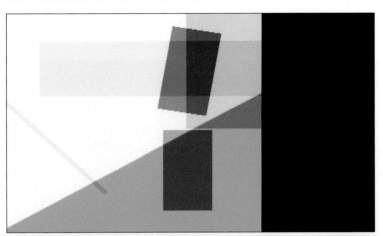

Digital Boogie
Woogie, Video, 1998.

*Predator Cat -
Selfish Diva*,
Video installation or
single screen, 1999.

273

25 of 85 Notes,
Sound/video
installation, 2001.

Jo Ann Millet

William Raban

Civil Disobedience,
35mm, 2004, sound,
David Cunningham.

Kayla Parker

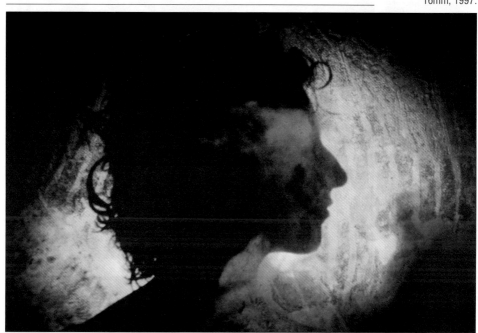

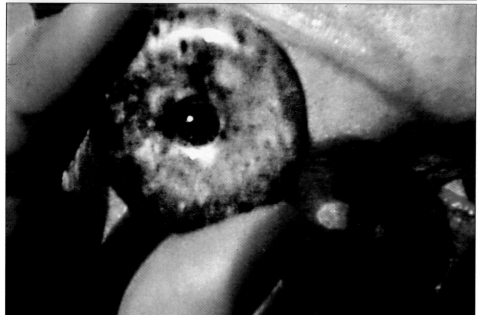

Guy Sherwin

Above left:
Musical Stairs,
16mm film, 1977.

Above centre:
Flight,
16mm film, 1998.

Above right:
Newsprint,
16mm film, 1972.

Right: *Animal Studies*,
Ongoing re-groupable
series of short 16mm
films, 1998–2004.

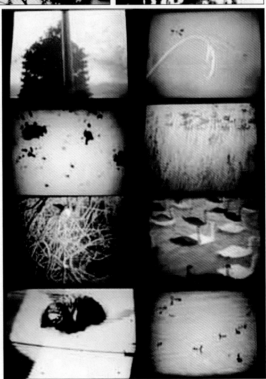

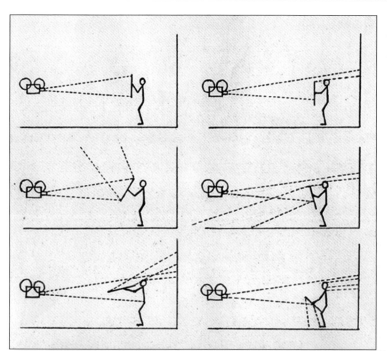

Both images:
Man With Mirror,
Super 8mm
film/performance,
1977.

Tony Sinden

Behold, Vertical Devices, Video/sculpture installation, 1974/76.

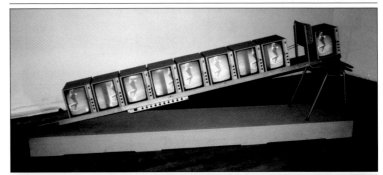

Cinema of Projection, 16mm projection, 1975.

Another Aspect/ Another Time, 16mm film, 35mm slide projection, 1986–89.

Images

Above: *Ancestral Voices*, Video installation 3 channels, 1994.

Below, left: *Pedestrian Colours*, 16mm film, 35mm slide projection, 1986–89.
Below right: *Everything Must Go*, Video installation/sculpture, 2002/03.

John Smith

Both images:
A Girl Chewing Gum,
16mm, 1976.

Both images:
Worst Case Scenario, Digital stills and video, 2001–2003.

281

Jeremy Welsh

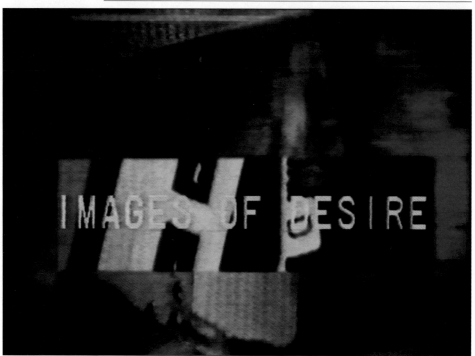

Above:
IOD, Video, 1984.

Below:
GREY, Video, 1995.

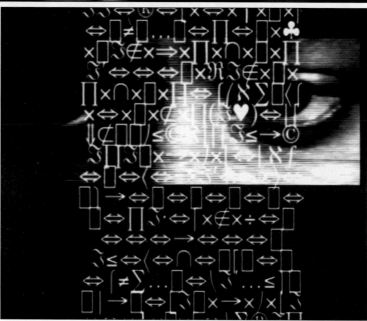

Above:
Come Together,
Video DVD, 2002.

Dialogue Transition,
Video installation,
2004.